RAINBOW
IN THE
DARK

THE AUTOBIOGRAPHY

RONNIE JAMES

WITH MICK WALL AND WENDY DIO

CONSTABLE

CONSTABLE

First published in the USA in 2021 by Permuted Press
This edition published in Great Britain in 2021 by Constable
This paperback edition published in 2022 by Constable

3 5 7 9 10 8 6 4

A CIP catalogue record for this book
is available from the British Library.

ISBN: 978-1-47213-514-8

Interior design and composition, Greg Johnson, Textbook Perfect
Printed and bound in Great Britain by Clays Ltd, Elcograf, S.p.A.

Papers used by Constable are from well-managed forests and other responsible sources.

Constable
An imprint of
Little, Brown Book Group
Carmelite House
50 Victoria Embankment
London EC4Y 0DZ

The authorised representative
in the EEA is
Hachette Ireland
8 Castlecourt Centre
Dublin 15, D15 XTP3, Ireland
(email: info@hbgi.ie)

An Hachette UK Company

www.hachette.co.uk

www.littlebrown.co.uk

For Wendy
and all my wonderful friends
and fans.

"Magic"
Ronnie James Dio

CONTENTS

PREFACE

BY WENDY DIO

When Ronnie first began writing this book his intention was that it would have no end. The cancer that would eventually overcome him had not yet struck, and as far as he was concerned, the future was still full of promise.

That was the Ronnie James Dio I first fell in love with and later married—an unstoppable force of nature for whom all things were possible, even when fate appeared to conspire against him. You might say, *especially* when fate appeared to conspire against him.

As you will discover from reading his extraordinary story, Ronnie was a born fighter. Tell him something could not be done; he would move heaven and earth to prove that it could. Once Ronnie set his sights on something, he rarely, if ever, missed the target. So it was with his autobiography. Even after he became ill in 2009, he was determined to leave behind a written record. As with his lyrics, everything was handwritten. He never used a computer. He had beautiful handwriting and would write out his memories, then pass me the pages, which I would have my assistant type up.

Ronnie was always a voracious reader and a born storyteller. He could make you laugh until tears ran down your face. And he could make you jump and cry with some of the stories of the desperately hard times he lived through to finally make his dream come true.

If Ronnie's rich and imaginative lyrics were his poetry, this book became his personal valediction, written from the heart, playing no favors, just telling it, because that was always Ronnie's way—his code.

Ronnie had gone deep as far as the Rainbow years before his encroaching illness forced him to slow the pace. At that point, he began writing notes and planning out how the rest of the book would go. I was able to help him sketch out his thoughts and memories almost up to the present. Whenever we discussed it, Ronnie was insistent that the story he ultimately wanted to tell was one of hope triumphing over despair, how joy and positivity, magic and light, will always overcome the dark. Never be afraid of the night—dawn is always on the horizon.

After Ronnie's death in 2010, the plan was to publish his memoirs as soon as possible. It didn't happen then because, at that moment, with my heart broken, I just couldn't face working on something so deeply personal to him. I always planned to help bring it to its rightful conclusion one day. It was the least Ronnie deserved. His story simply had to be heard.

Ronnie was a great believer that the right time for something will always make itself obvious if you can just be patient for the universe to reveal its truths to you.

Ronnie and I first met Mick Wall in 1980 when he was the UK publicist for Black Sabbath, working to promote the *Heaven and Hell* album, the one Ronnie considered his best with the band. Mick was only twenty, and he later laughingly told me how scared he was of Ronnie at the time, but it was the beginning of a lifelong friendship between the two. By the time Ronnie's post-Sabbath band Dio had exploded onto the scene, Mick was a familiar face. He'd gone on to become a legendary music writer and presenter of some great TV and radio shows, including a memorable at-home-with-the-stars-style TV documentary where he hung out at our house, playing pool with Ronnie, drinking beer with us at Ronnie's English-pub-style home bar, and wandering around looking at suits of armor and Ronnie's vast collection of antique and gothic artifacts.

In the mid-'90s, Mick returned to being Ronnie's PR in London. And in 1998 he became the creative editorial force behind the launch and subsequent huge success of *Classic Rock* magazine. It was while receiving the Metal Guru award at the 2006 *Classic Rock* awards in London that Ronnie renewed his friendship with Mick.

When a few years ago Mick inquired whether I was ready to start thinking about getting Ronnie's memoir off the ground, it was the beginning of a long conversation over many months and, eventually, years. Having had time since Ronnie's passing to finally put together a proper archive of his interviews over the course of his career, from thousands of newspapers, magazines, TV and radio appearances, and a ton of other stuff where he was being interviewed at length, first for videos we released, or later added as extras for various CDs and DVDs, sifting through and cataloguing a lifetime of incredible photos, stories and other personal mementoes, and, of course, his original notes and unfinished manuscript, we started our journey of finishing the book you now hold in your hands.

Holding the folders containing all the original handwritten pages, all the scrupulous notes and scattered thoughts, all the old computer printouts, was a powerful reminder of how important it was to make this book happen the way Ronnie had always planned it. I knew I would need help. Mick was the obvious choice. He had known Ronnie for thirty years and was clearly the best writer and editor I could get to work on the book. He didn't let us down, doing honor to Ronnie's incomparable story, first of all, then to the fans and me.

Mick was able to reconstruct the original draft of Ronnie's words and help flesh them out, where appropriate, by adding some of Ronnie's words from other sources, including his own cavernous archive, which holds many long and deep conversations with Ronnie over the many years they knew each other.

As anybody that ever spoke to him will testify, Ronnie liked to talk. Try shutting him up! Opinions on every subject under the sun! What didn't he know about? At the same time, Ronnie loved just hanging out with the fans, listening to what they had to say. From long before he became famous right up to his dying day, three legendary rock bands and over 150 million albums sold behind him, Ronnie would talk to people all day and all night, and still go out and sing better than any other rock singer you've ever heard.

Whenever Ronnie and I talked about where the book should end, he was adamant that this first memoir should end in 1986, on the very night Dio headlined Madison Square Garden. Ronnie was just a few weeks shy of his forty-fourth birthday that magical June night. He had headlined the Garden twice before with Sabbath, but this was his first headlining show there under his own name—a momentous occasion for the boy from Upstate New York who had dreamed of seeing his name in lights at the city's most famous arena since he was a teenager. It became the crowning glory of Ronnie's career. Literally and figuratively his dream come true. I was with him that night, as his wife, his manager, but most of all as his biggest fan. I knew what this show meant to him. He had finally climbed to the top of the highest mountain, against all odds, entirely on his own terms. As he put it that night, "If my life ended tomorrow, it wouldn't matter. This is as good as it gets for me."

Of course, Ronnie still had many years ahead of him in which he continued to make some of the greatest albums in the proud Dio catalogue. He also got back with the *Heaven and Hell* lineup of Sabbath, not once but twice, recording two more fantastic albums together, including the magnificent *The Devil You Know*, released just a year before Ronnie died, and his final Top 10 hit in America. After that, though, is another story.

He never stopped giving everything he had to his loyal and beloved fans, on stage and off. These were years of struggle sometimes, but as you'll see, Ronnie never shied away from hard work and always emerged victorious. In the end, the only thing he could not defeat was mortality.

There is clearly a book to be written one day about that final quarter-century of Ronnie's life. Certainly there is enough material in the bulging archive for us to one day shape into a superlative book along those lines, but this is not that book. This is a book about what Ronnie saw as "the first half of my life," in his own words, in his own inimitable style, and in keeping with the spirit of how he wanted to be remembered. Upbeat, never say die, absolutely undeniable.

That is the Ronnie James Dio you will get to know in ways not even I thought possible when he began writing it. Or, as he put it in one of his most memorable songs:

The world is full of Kings and Queens
Who blind your eyes and steal your dreams...
And they'll tell you black is really white
The moon is just the sun at night
And when you walk in golden halls
You get to keep the gold that falls
It's Heaven and Hell.

PRELUDE

riday, June 20, 1986.

Early evening, backstage in my dressing room, in that hallowed space between soundcheck and show time, where if you're lucky and no one bothers you, you can actually sit and think. An almost impossible thing to do at any other time on tour.

It's one of those melting city-summer evenings out there, the kind you only find in New York City. You can't slow down New York City, but this heat comes close. Even the cars seem to honk a little less noisily: all of Seventh Avenue sweating it out.

But it's Friday night and everybody wants some of whatever's going on this weekend. This particular evening, that includes my band, Dio, and me. We are headlining Madison Square Garden, and the show is a 20,000-capacity sellout.

There are people out there, made even more nuts by the heat, literally fighting to get in. This is some achievement for us. Dio has been a big arena band pretty much from the moment we released our first album, *Holy Diver*—but this is the Garden, and this is a whole new level of reality.

I'm a New York guy. Even after living and working in LA for so many years, which I love, I am and will always remain a New York guy. I have been dreaming of headlining Madison Square Garden for as long as I've known it existed.

Sitting here this fine Friday evening, shielded from the dust and heat by turbo-charged air-conditioning, contemplating how very far I have come in my musical journey, and yet how close to this place I have always been. Remembering with a shudder those chilly Monday mornings I would drive the 250 miles to the City, aiming to infiltrate the Brill Building on Broadway, where Carole King and Gerry Goffin wrote "Will You Love Me Tomorrow." Hoping for a break, any kind of a break. And where, somehow, in 1960, at the already-old-before-my-time age of seventeen, I was allowed to record a Tin Pan Alley ballad-by-numbers called "An Angel Is Missing." That was as Ronnie Dio and the Red Caps. It was not a hit. But it didn't stop me then, and it doesn't stop me now.

Call me an old romantic, but I have never sung for money. It's true I have always been happy, or merely relieved, to have been paid for my work. But that isn't what drives me, what got me through the times I thought I was done for, what inspired me to write my best songs, to always try to sing in my best voice, or to be a real friend to my fans, not just another picture in a magazine.

Sitting here now, looking back, reveling in the fact that it only took me a quarter of a century to finally get here, I can cheerfully tell you that whatever happens for the rest of my life, I will always be able to say I once headlined my own show at Madison Square Garden. That I did once, finally, achieve my goals, and give thanks to the gods for making the dreams more real than the nightmares.

To be in one world-famous band is a rare victory most musicians can't hope to achieve. To somehow find yourself in two world-famous bands is almost being greedy. But to find yourself being a success for a *third* time, especially when it's with your own band this time—well, I consider myself extremely fortunate.

Reading this book, I hope you will be able to find answers to all of the questions I know many have long wished to ask me. Whatever your judgement after reading it, I accept it. The Good. The Bad. The Beautiful. It was all me, everything.

But know this: If I die tomorrow, you will be my witness that I do so having lived my life to the full.

When I was a teenager, I used to walk by the Garden practically every week, looking up at whatever big name was on its billboard in lights, and making a pledge to myself.

"One day I'm going to play there."

Wendy told me we could have played the Meadowlands arena in New Jersey for twice as much money as we're getting tonight, because the Garden is a union hall. But I told her: "I have to have Madison. It's been my dream forever."

When Wendy and I stepped out of the limo today, we looked up and there it was: Dio in lights, Madison Square Garden, New York. We were so excited. I wanted Wendy to take a picture. But we had forgotten the camera. I didn't care. Nobody would ever have been able to take a picture that truly captured the significance of that moment for me. I still gave her shit for it, though. Obviously.

Right, I've got to go and get ready. I hear them calling my name.

Mom, Gramma, me, and Dad.

⊹ ONE ⊹

. . . .

ROCK 'N' ROLL CHILDREN

This was a special Saturday for me. The first day of summer vacation and a baseball game to play with the neighborhood kids. That would have been enough to keep me happy on its own, but it also transpired that this would be a special day for me in another, most unexpected way. This would be the day my lifelong journey in music began.

As I sat down with my mother and father to eat breakfast that morning, I sensed something in the air, some invisible tension tweaking my psychic antennae that usually signaled the arrival of some as-yet-unknown problem. Then my father laid it out for me. Which musical instrument would I choose to be taught to play so that I might become a better-rounded individual?

Huh?

I had not seen this coming. I was six years old. Up to that point, I had absolutely no musical aspirations at all. If you couldn't throw it, catch it, or hit it, then it had no use to me. Which musical instrument would I choose to learn to play? "None," I said. "Why would I want to do that?"

My father Pat—a tough no-nonsense Italian-American who brooked no argument, least of all from his only son—quickly and decisively reversed my veto and asked the question again. To which, of course, there was a different, more affirmative answer. Stalling for time, I asked which instruments I could choose from.

My mother Anna came to the rescue. Listening to the radio and deciding which sound I liked best would provide the answer to which instrument I should learn to play. The old Philco "Baby Grand" radio was revved up, and the golden tones of Harry James's trumpet filled the small kitchen. I'd like to say that at that moment my soul was uplifted, the windows of my mind raised to let the joyous sounds reverberate. I really would like to say that, but damn, I had a game to play.

"That's the one," I blurted out as I grabbed my baseball glove to go. To my horror, my father stood in my way and announced we would be going instead to McNeil Music, one of the two music stores in town, to obtain one Harry James-style trumpet for yours truly. How I hated that man at that moment.

My dad and I piled into the car—I guess this was a man thing—and as he backed out of the driveway, my heart was sinking lower with every turn of the wheels. *What about the game?* I thought. That was the day the games ended, and the real thing began.

I was overwhelmed by the music store. So many strange-looking shapes to see and sounds to hear. For some odd reason, I felt comfortable there. The McNeil brothers, Danny and John, who were a complete contrast to one another, greeted us. Danny, small and bald, and John, big, tall, and a sporting a well-thatched roof. Danny, the most effervescent and outspoken one, took control of the situation and led us to the brass section. There, he seemed to kneel behind the counter in short prayer, and then with a flourish, introduced me to what would be my closest companion for the next twelve years, an Olds Ambassador trumpet. It was beautiful, gleaming, brass and silver, lying on a bed of burgundy velvet. I would have bet that even old Harry James had never had anything like this.

Next we were taken to a basement area that seemed to have a medical feel to it and—bang!—back came the butterflies. No need to worry, though, for it turned out to be the practice rooms, where my indoctrination into the musical community would now commence.

My dad and I were introduced to a bookish-looking man with a friendly smile. This was Sam Signorelli, who became my first teacher. He took his job seriously and was very concerned that the trumpet might be wrong for me. He examined my mouth, my teeth, my embouchure (lips, to the non-horn-blowing). I half-expected him to tell me to "drop 'em" then turn my head and cough.

Apparently I passed the examination because Mr. Signorelli handed me the trumpet and showed me how to hold it. He then instructed me how to tighten my lips and exhale as a dry run without the trumpet, after which came the moment of truth. I blew into that thing and an astounding tone worked its way slowly through all the valves and out into the day. My father beamed; Mr. Signorelli's mouth fell open. And I put a period on the shortest career in baseball.

I progressed rapidly and became the target of quite a bit of attention.

"Where does all that power come from?"

"He's so tiny."

"Why, the trumpet is bigger than he is!"

Statements I learned to live with all through my days performing as a trumpeter.

My dad believed that practice makes perfect. In fact, I think he holds the patent on that phrase. So with that rule firmly in place and my father watching closely, I began doing four hours each day of practice on the trumpet. *Four* hours. *Every* day. A command never to be broken, not even on a Sunday, which, my father made clear, was not a day of rest.

I really hated that thing. The sounds of my horn became background music to the shouts and laughter of the neighborhood children playing outside. But slowly, as my abilities on the trumpet increased, so did my self-confidence, giving me a musical identity, like a superpower, that I began to enjoy. Although I couldn't have known it then, my increasing ability on, and knowledge of, the trumpet actually helped me a great deal later as a singer, partly to do with knowing how to breathe, partly to do with the fact that the trumpet has its own voice, its own way of phrasing. I realize now that if it hadn't been for all the years learning the trumpet, I would have been a different singer.

My father spent almost all of that daily practice time with me. He was so much more dedicated to this project than I was. I thought he knew and understood more about it than I would ever be able to learn. That went on for the first few years. But eventually his attendance dropped off as the music and technique required became more and more difficult. My father's early guidance was priceless, however, because as lazy as I was with anything I didn't like, his absolute insistence that I succeed set a course for all my future endeavors as a musician. Hard work, discipline, pride in being the best you can be, all these qualities were instilled in me by my father during those seemingly endless years practicing and learning and practicing some more that damn trumpet.

At least I didn't have to deal with this the way my dad had to when he was a kid. His father, not long off the boat from Italy, had one day brought home a banjo, a violin, and a clarinet. He called my father and his two brothers, John and Peter, into the front room, randomly handed them each an instrument, and ordered them to play it. My dad had the good grace to spring for lessons.

My paternal grandfather, Tony Padovano, was a hard, stubborn, and powerful little man. (I'm told the family name was changed to "Padavona" after his children began school and found the spelling somehow easier to deal with, but I've never really understood that.) My grandfather Tony's feats of strength were legendary. He ran a steel mill, which he and a whole generation of Italian immigrants labored at. Tony came wrapped in all the stereotypes of the transplanted Southern European of the time. He took no shit from anyone and parted with his affection only grudgingly, and my relationship with him was exactly like that. Pleasure not permitted, pain to be accepted.

8

Tony's wife was Erminia, my paternal grandmother. She was, by everyone's estimation a saint, but that estimation was too low. Erminia loved each of her children and their offspring equally. No one was slighted and everyone shared. English, both written and spoken, was a problem for her with others, but never for her and me. A piece of her amazing pizza and a "bella cup of coffee" (pronounced "coff-ay") were always enough to dry a tear and make a smile appear. How she coped with her marital relationship was always a wonder to me. But bless her, she did.

I walked everywhere with my "Gramma." Tony had a car but no driver's license and only had it to impress his friends. So Gramma and me would walk to the markets, to the steel mill to deliver lunch to my grandfather and his sons, to the church quite often, and to anywhere else that struck Gramma's fancy.

It was around this time that I first began to notice my grandmother making a strange hand gesture when strangers would come near or pass by too close. It was the raising of the index finger and little finger while folding the middle and ring finger into the palm where they were held in place by the thumb. I did not discover until years later that this was the Maloik, a.k.a. the Horns, a.k.a. the Devil Sign, a.k.a. the Mano Cornuto. Something my Gramma used for protection against the evil eye. Wait—protection against *what*? Hmmm. I'll come back to that later.

My first public performance as a trumpeter came at the New York State Music Festival, known to those of us who participated as simply a "contest." This was like the Olympics to our instructors, and so I was made to rehearse my solo piece over and over until it became so easy I could practically do it in my sleep. I was chosen to play "The Toy Trumpet," originally by Raymond Scott. A nice piece of music, but I'm sure to the audience it was me who looked like the toy, not the trumpet. The little sixth grader must have been on form that day, however, because I got a standing ovation and a speech of praise from the judges, at which point I burst into tears, drawing even more *oohs* and *ahs* from the mom-and-pop crowd.

The year following my first "contest," I entered Cortland Jr. High School. Grades seven through twelve were all housed in one giant red brick colonial style quadrangle of buildings. I was assigned my first seventh grade homeroom class and quickly became aware that our homeroom teacher was dating the school librarian. This enticing news set the tone for my first year of higher education. If the exalted teachers were fooling around, then this couldn't be all that serious a venture.

The school year began to pass quickly and predictably. Classes began at 9:00 a.m. and ended for me at 3:35 p.m. with the last class always being band rehearsal. This was my first competitive encounter on and off the baseball field, and here I thrived. With my practice regimen and natural ability, I was able to secure the position of first trumpet without too much bother.

My hero at this time was a neighbor of mine named Phil Natoli. Phil was a great trumpet player. Coupled with that talent were good looks, and with them came beautiful women. *Maybe there's something to this music stuff after all*, I thought. I idolized Phil to such an extent that I began stuffing wadded handkerchiefs in both my back pockets to emulate his broad behind. Hey, he got the girls—it must work!

The city of Cortland, New York hunches down between seven hills. The resulting seven valleys created by those hills must have reminded its Italian immigrants so much of Rome—also built amongst seven hills and valleys—that they were irresistibly drawn to it.

Our neighbors were the Pellicciottis, the Passalugos, the Morgias, the Tuccis, and the Fabrizios. We were at least a hundred pages torn out of an Italian phone book. This section of town was known as the "East End," where Italian markets dotted the quiet streets. Old men heatedly speaking in one dialect or another and weaving down the road were the only real danger here. We had our own parish church, St. Anthony's; our own grade school, Pomeroy School; our own bakery, our own restaurants. I realize now that we had all these things because it kept us at arm's length from everyone else in the city—and they gratefully kept away from us.

We were geographically located in an area called Central New York, which included the city of Syracuse, our largest neighbor, population 350,000, and Ithaca, whose citizens could boast of Cornell University and *Twilight Zone* creator Rod Serling. Scattered amongst Cortland's 20,000 residents were doctors, lawyers, shopkeepers, and factory owners. The rest labored on dairy farms or at the steel mills.

Both my father and grandfather worked at the Wickwire Brothers steel plant making nails and chicken wire. I can't tell you how happy I am that I didn't enter my family's business. On the few occasions that I visited the shop, it was like a scene in a Dickens novel. The light inside the massive brick structure was a harsh bluish hue that barely illuminated the sweaty men I remember seeing there. More than anything, I can still hear the incessant pounding of what must have been huge hammers, forging steel. You could always hear it in my part of town, and in some ways, it not only molded metal, but it somehow molded me too.

I ran from that sound until one day it caught me.

TWO

STAND UP AND SHOUT

y middle school, I started to secure friendships with kids who, like me, had entered the school from other parts of the city. First we defended our honor with brief skirmishes, then we became blood brothers ever after. One of my new buddies was Paul Consroe, dubbed with the not-so-flattering nickname of "Floyd Bum." Not because he was homeless or helpless, but because he embraced a totally different lifestyle than was considered "normal" in Cortland.

Floyd was a rock 'n' roll rebel. He introduced me to leather, revolution, and music that I'd never heard of before. And he had a *great* record collection. New stuff, old stuff, he had it all. First he played me some blues—B.B. King, Papa Charlie Jackson, Muddy Waters...*What was this, some kind of voodoo?* Pain, tears, laughter, joy...all contained in one round piece of black plastic. Next up, another breed of artist— Little Richard, Chuck Berry, the Everly Brothers, and Elvis. Pure rock 'n' roll. Elvis was already huge. I had seen him gyrating on TV, and I was familiar with the hits, but this other stuff Floyd played for me— suddenly I understood where Elvis had gotten it from. Incredible!

Then one day at Floyd's home, I actually met Elvis. Or at least someone who sure looked like him. He was holding a guitar, and that sure as hell looked like the King's pompadour on this guy's head. Enter Nicky Pantas. He played guitar. He looked cool. He was a rock 'n' roller. Nicky was who I wanted to be.

Nicky was a year older than me, and though we attended the same school, we had never met, as the different grades kept their distance from each other—except, of course, for the raids by upperclassmen on our womenfolk. Nicky was a left-handed pitcher on the baseball team. Elvis could throw a curve? Wow. What couldn't this guy do?

That day at Floyd's house, the three of us talked and dreamed and planned and raided Floyd's father's liquor cabinet and drank and passed out and got sick and swore we'd never do it again. We hadn't played a lick yet, but we were a band.

Floyd and I had another common interest: the Mafia. Maybe we needed some heroes whose names sounded like ours. Maybe we just liked the idea of tough guys with guns and no conscience, glorified on TV and in movies, vilified by authority figures, real and fictional. The Mafia were rebels with a cause that we didn't actually understand, but to young Italian-American kids in the '50s these glamorous gangsters seemed like our own family police force. So when Floyd said I needed to change my name—"You can't be a star with a name like Padavona!" he taunted me—I turned to the names of Mafia chiefs for inspiration. We wanted a name with few letters and one that was unmistakably Italian in origin. Then it hit me—Dio!

I still wasn't sold on it one hundred percent, but I did want to be a star and bring my friends on the wild ride with me, so I wrapped myself up in the new name and prepared to do battle. Ronnie Dio: Mafia Musician.

We were going to be a band, but there were still classes to attend, homework to submit, four hours of trumpet practice each day. Finding other musicians and rehearsing with them took a back seat to all this, and our plans became mainly talk. Talk and hope and dreams and wishes that we prayed might come true.

We turned the corner on Dream Street one night at a dance being held at the YMCA. A young band from neighboring Binghamton, who called themselves the Rickettes, were playing there. Nicky and I arrived early to check them out. We kept our distance, feigning indifference. But these guys had everything: guitars, an electric bass, amplifiers, and a PA system. When they fired up and launched themselves into the music, that was it. Our studied cool went out the window and we became two wide-eyed kids who desperately wanted to be just like the Rickettes.

We scoured the gyrating crowd for what we would need to make our own band a possibility. It wasn't difficult. Musicians are always to be found scoping out and admiring or hating others of their kind. There they were—a few drummers, a bass player, a piano player, and a sax man. The choice of a drummer was easy. One was a girl, and we all knew the rules. No chicks! So we talked to this guy Tommy Rogers and—luck!—discovered he had drums and a basement we could rehearse in.

Next we hit on John Alcorn, who played bass but only had access to one of those big upright acoustic basses jazz cats played. At least John could actually play bass, so we welcomed him into the fold. A young guy named John Kane filled the final spot. John, who also went by Jack, was a sax player with some experience playing live who could solo like madman. Suddenly, it wasn't talk anymore. We actually had a band. My only fear now was whether we'd be any good.

We realized the need for better guitar amplification after hearing the Rickettes and their high-powered offense, but with money being a problem, we settled for an ancient amp and set about repairing it. My uncle Johnny had some knowledge of television electronics and so he was drawn into the affair. He twiddled and fiddled inside that thing and then announced it was ready to be tested. The switch was lifted, and the first sign of success was signaled by a small red light that winked on and continued to burn brightly. A guitar cord was produced, and with a shaking hand, Nicky plugged into the beast. The sounds that were made that day certainly didn't show the promise to come, but oh, it was loud! We had contact. We had power!

My role was to be what else but trumpet player? We only had one guitar between us, and I couldn't have handled it at that point anyway. Our song list was comprised of instrumentals exclusively. We only began to think about vocals when we realized that we would never compete with all the other outfits on the scene until we had a singer.

Whenever I had any spare time, Nicky and I boarded his bicycle, and with guitar case wedged between us, we made our way to Tommy's house. There we pored over records to find the right chords to the songs we wanted to do. This proved to be invaluable training. Because we didn't really know what we were doing, we were forced to invent our own musical methods, which then became our own personalized sound. Tommy's parents were very supportive of us. They never complained about the noise, and noise it sometimes was.

This was the tipping point for me—the moment I became more passionate about music than sports. I could think of nothing else but making this new kind of music, free and unrestricting. So different from the rigid, technical disciplines I had been taught to respect as a student. I didn't reject that more formal approach, I just tried to incorporate the two. I was still awed by the classical works we performed with the Cortland High School Band. Our conductor was Burton Stanley, known to everyone as "Prof." He was a wonderful man: ethical, patient, stern when necessary, understanding, and a great teacher. But the closest his students got to "popular music" was the local dance band, known as the Stardusters.

Even the dance band had its upside though. When one of the Stardusters's trumpeters graduated, Prof nominated me to replace him. This was quite a feather in my cap. Better still, the leader of the band was an older former Cortland High grad named Phil Natoli, who was my trumpeting idol at that point. Phil had left in his senior year to join the US Army, where he quickly became a sergeant—and first trumpeter in the US Army Jazz band. Phil was so good he got plenty of offers to turn pro and tour the world. But he'd come home to marry the love of his life, Anita.

Now I got to watch him operate up close and personal. This was either going to be my downfall or the making of me, for a while I wasn't sure. I had never been "on the road" before, and most of the eleven other guys in the Stardusters were five or six years older than me and had cars. Not that we went far, mainly just one-nighters at local weddings and school dances. But because I didn't drive, I'd go along with whoever got stuck with me on the night.

Some of the guys brought their girlfriends, and the rides would be reserved and uncomfortable with me sitting in the backseat trying to be inconspicuous. It was never like that, though, when you rode with Joe Ferris. Joe had fast cars, which he drove like a road racer, and he had Connie, who was smoking hot. Our rides together were like fiestas. They played the radio with the volume turned up, smoked cigarettes, drank beer, made out all the time, and didn't seem to mind me being there. I loved it! The music was great, and you could always count on getting a glimpse of Connie's good bits.

Joe had road story after road story to tell, and I couldn't get enough. I wanted my own stories, my own road experiences, and all of Connie's good bits.

The only downside was that my new gig with the Stardusters cut into my as-yet-unnamed band's progress. But I couldn't turn down the nine dollars I got for three hours of blowing the horn and looking at Connie. So we practiced the band when we could and finally found time to write under the banner of our name.

We tossed around a few titles that didn't work. Then someone mentioned Las Vegas and someone else mentioned "Kings"—so we became the Vegas Kings! We hastily put a sign together, replete with stick-on gold stars, and swore our eternal allegiance to our new group identity.

Floyd and I were not letting our rebel roots wither and die at this point either. My boasts of all the drinking episodes with the Stardusters hadn't gone unnoticed, and Floyd now initiated a plan whereby we forged our own Sheriff's ID cards. The drinking age in New York at the time was eighteen, and we felt sure we could con some unsuspecting bartender into serving us a few brews. We had a friend whose father operated a print shop, and he knew how to use the printers. We copied the standard form, filled in our names and phony birthdates, forged the Sheriff's signature, and pressed the great seal onto the card, the great seal being a large aluminum coin with "Welcome to Atlantic City" carved on its rim.

When we were done, we studied our new ID cards with pride. We were men. Officially. Illegally. Finally. Now let's go get that drink....

My criminal career had actually begun prior to the big ID caper. I had found a key for a Buick in the street one day and unthinkingly stuffed it in my pocket. My mom always went shopping on Saturday afternoons, and my dad went fishing a few times a month with his brothers, so occasionally I was left alone. A ten-year-old boy with big ideas left alone to his own devices. What could possibly go wrong?

This day I happened to wander out to the garage where my dad had parked the family car. He'd gone fishing with his brothers in one of their cars, and he hadn't bothered to lock the doors. So I hopped in behind the enormous wheel and began my inspection.

I knew enough about cars to realize that without the key to the ignition, nothing was going to happen, and then I remembered the key I'd found in the street. I rushed up the stairs and fished it out of a junk box I had hidden under a loose board in the floor of my room, then hurried back down to the garage and the car.

I inserted the key into the ignition, breathed deep, and turned it. But it wouldn't budge! My exhilaration crashed to the ground. I pulled out the key and looked at it. Of course, this one must have the grooves cut differently than the real key. I rushed back into the kitchen where I knew my dad kept a spare key.

My dad had a full complement of tools in the basement, so down I went, the juvie-locksmith, where I grinded and filed and polished until both keys looked similar. Then I bolted back up the stairs to test my handiwork. In went the key. I turned the ignition and felt shock run up my arm and into my brain as the engine fired and started.

Scared to death, I leaped from the car and ran away from it, thinking that at any moment something disastrous was about to happen. Conquering my fear, I peered around the corner of the garage. The car engine was running smoothly and quietly and so, reassured, I eased myself back behind the wheel.

I reached for the accelerator and gave it a soft push. One small step for a boy, one giant leap for madness. The engine reacted with a moan. I pushed again, a little harder. It didn't moan this time, it growled. I experimented until I felt I had it under control. Next I switched on the radio. The radio was important when it came to driving a car. Everyone knew that.

Music filled the air as I worked up the nerve to move this beast. I stood on the brake and moved the gear lever to the letter *R*. The automobile shuddered slightly, and I could feel it wanting to move. I eased off the brake and the car began to lurch backward. I slammed my foot down on the brake and shoved the shifting lever back to *P*. That was enough for one day. My heart was racing as fast as the engine, but there was no key to turn mine off.

From then on, I sat behind the wheel whenever my folks were absent, getting a little more daring each time. I became skilled enough to eventually back the car out of the garage and onto the driveway. This was no easy task because reversing straight out of the garage meant hitting a major part of the side of our house, and aiming it too-tight at another angle placed our neighbors, the Pellicciottis' home, directly in the line of fire.

From watching my dad maneuver through the obstacles, I learned the little tricks to avoid an accident. I got good at backing the car out of the garage. I grew confident. Now, if all there was to driving was backing cars out of garages, I'd be all set.

My best friend in the neighborhood was Bobby "Rats Nest" Rightmire. (Don't let the name fool you. Bobby was a *paisan*, too.) Bobby earned his dubious nickname after discovering one of those rodent homes under the bank of the river Tioughnioga, where we fished, swam, and honed some of our bad habits. (We were in the heart of Iroquois Indian country, so names like Tioughnioga were liberally sprinkled throughout the territory.)

Nest and I kept no secrets from each other, so eventually he was informed of my adventures with the key and the car. When the next day of no adult supervision finally rolled around, I proudly demonstrated my ability to Nest by backing out of the garage and moving up and down the driveway, finishing with a flourish by replacing the car exactly in the spot where it had first been.

"Let me try it," said Nest, inevitably. "Okay," I replied, suddenly realizing the peril I had placed myself in. We switched places, as I cautioned him to do everything slowly. But Nest was a true adventurer, and I knew that wild look in his eye. I held my breath as he turned the key and the engine erupted into life. Next the radio—hey, my car, my rules!

The music seemed to soothe Nest, and he was as gentle as I had been that first time with the accelerator. He stepped on the brake and slowly moved the shifting lever into reverse while turning the wheel ever so slowly to the left. We were gonna make it, thank God....

Then, to my horror, Nest stomped down on the accelerator, and the car shot backward out of the garage like a rocket. The monster roared even louder as it ripped away one corner of the garage and slammed into the Pellicciottis' kitchen.

Mrs. Pellicciotti had just walked away from her sink and so avoided being crushed by two tons of flying metal. Water was pouring from broken pipes, debris was floating in the air, and when I dared to open my eyes, I could see the back of the car imbedded a few feet into the house behind me.

Nest turned his eyes to me and spoke four words I will never forget: "What have we done?" he cried with the emphasis firmly on *we*. There was no time for argument. A gathering crowd of neighbors had poured from the usually quiet block of houses to investigate the source of the almighty crash they had heard.

My father's sister, my Aunt Carm, was first on the scene, and as I reluctantly dragged myself from the car, she informed me of what I already knew: "Your father is going to kill you!" No trial. Straight to execution. It was what I deserved. I knew it.

Mrs. Pellicciotti, bless her, was more concerned about us than about herself. After confirming that Nest and I were uninjured, the crowd grudgingly dispersed, and we were left to confront our demons. To two uninformed ten-year-olds, the solution to our problems was simple: we would sell our bicycles and use the money to repair the car, the garage, and the house. All before my father returned the next day from another fishing excursion. We raced to the bicycle shop and offered up our precious wheels to the owner. Shrewdly bargaining, we were able to extricate from him the lordly sum of twenty-three dollars. Enough, we were sure, to afford the necessary repairs.

By the time I got home, my mom had returned from her afternoon of shopping and was standing in shock staring at the new addition to her neighbors' house. I hurried to her rescue, explaining that the problem was solved, that we had flogged our bikes. I handed her the twenty-three dollars.

I don't know if it was the state of my father's car or the neighbor's house—or my innocent attempt to solve the problem with twenty-three bucks—but she burst into tears. Composing herself, she confirmed my worst fears.

"Your father is going to kill you," she said. I was back on Death Row.

My mother and I cried through the long night for the condemned young lad scheduled to die at high noon. The fishermen would all be deposited the next morning across the street at my Aunt Carm's house. I had an unobstructed view of the drop-off point and spent the rapidly disappearing hours waiting for the first sight of my executioner.

When the station wagon finally pulled into the driveway and spilled out its passengers, their scaly trophies, and their glad-to-be-home smiles, I saw my aunt steer my father aside and, grasping his shoulders, engage him in earnest conversation. I later learned that

21

Aunt Carm broke the news to my dad then begged him for a stay of execution for me.

I didn't know that yet, though, and as I watched him turn his gaze toward our house, the Grim Reaper, Death by Fish, my heart nearly jumped out of my mouth.

My super-strict, old-school Italian father began the short walk to the house, and I ran to sit shaking at the kitchen table with my mom. The door opened. He walked into the kitchen and looked at me with unreadable eyes, then without a word he went out the backdoor to surveil the scene for himself.

After what seemed an eternity, he came back into the kitchen and closed the door behind him.

"It's not that bad," he shrugged.

The Governor must have called. I had been given an eleventh-hour reprieve! That's when I knew for sure that my father was a saint. He knew that no punishment (including death) could be as bad as the stress and outright fear I had experienced during the unending previous twenty-four hours. My prayers for mercy had been answered.

I never told anyone that Bobby had been behind the wheel that day. I knew that my dad would forbid me to hang around with him anymore, and I couldn't bear that. Anyone who would sell his bike for a friend wasn't all that bad. And anyway, I needed the Nest to help get me into more trouble.

Cut to a few years later and Floyd and I were now holding tickets to paradise in our hands in the form of forged IDs. We still weren't sure if they would pass a close inspection. We needed to field-test them first. We chose an out-of-the-way bar where we were sure no one knew us. Shrewdly, we picked a busy period when the bartender would be less likely to waste his time examining our shady credentials. It worked like a charm.

"Two beers, please," I told the guy as we reached for our cards. The barman simply turned around, filled two glasses from the tap, took our money and wandered off. We were thrilled—until we discovered he had accepted library cards as proof of age.

This wouldn't do. The beer was good and easy to get, but we needed our sense of victory to come with the assurance that we were bartender-proof everywhere. The decision was made to attack the problem head-on.

The Tavern was a college hangout populated by the students of Cortland State University, the local bastion of higher learning. We knew The Tavern didn't leave age identification to the bartenders and waiters and would be the true trial of our counterfeit paper. Stationed at the only entrance, perched on a barstool, sat the proprietor. He was well known to be as inquisitive as a gundog. St. Peter at the Gate, with the power of rejection or admittance to the heaven we knew waited behind the doors.

The line of applicants snaked around the corner on this busy Friday night, and as we joined them, I'm sure that Floyd wanted to abandon the venture as much as I did, but this was a man thing, and neither of us could lose face.

I was the first to present my ID, and after a brief examination, St. Peter said, "Padavona, huh? So how's your father, your mother, your grandfather, your third cousin twice removed?"

Jeez! He knew everyone in my family. What had I done now? Then to my surprise and no little relief, he handed back my card and waved me through. Floyd got the same treatment too, then, like me, was waved easily through the door. This was easy! But would we use our new superpowers for good or evil?

Shortly after we confirmed "Operation ID," the Stardusters were invited to perform at a small rural high school about forty-five miles from Cortland. I was chosen to perform a trumpet solo called "The Carnival of Venice," made famous by the late great Harry James.

Our two buses arrived at the host school at noon, which left us eight hours to kill, with *kill* becoming the operative word. While the greater part of the kids in the band rested or practiced their instruments before the show, a few of us (armed with our phony IDs) searched out one of the two bars in town and set about fortifying our constitutions with vast quantities of the amber liquid.

An hour before the concert, we staggered happily out of the pub only to be smacked in the face by the cold clean air of the early evening. The effect was devastating to the senses. I realized immediately that I was in trouble. I might be able to hide my condition among the entire band when we played, but the solo was going to be my undoing.

I struggled with the gag reflex throughout the concert and suppressed my desire to retch by digging deep inside to find a willpower I never knew I possessed. I was introduced and praised highly as an award winner of great promise, who will amaze and astound you with his prowess.

I didn't disappoint. I had barely begun the solo when my overextended stomach delivered an award-winning stream of Schaefer beer with the promise of more—much more—to come. I certainly amazed and astounded with the sheer volume of my prowess and was rewarded by *oohs* and *ahs* from the stunned audience—and sardonic cheering from the other equally tanked-up musicians.

Afterward I made an excuse, explaining I'd been suffering from the flu. Poor boy. Did his best. Such a pity.

Somehow I got away with it. But it was plain my days as the star trumpeter in the Stardusters were now numbered.

Suddenly it was goodbye Harry James, hello...what, exactly?

It wasn't long before I found out.

⊸ THREE ⊷

VEGAS KINGS

DANCE! FRIDAY NITE
8PM–11PM
WHERE? THE CORTLAND TEEN CENTER
MUSIC BY THE VEGAS KINGS!

This announcement heralded our first professional public appearance. All those painstaking spare moments used to hone our skills were finally paying off. I've often been asked to list my favorite shows, and the expected answer is a hundred thousand people at the LA Coliseum, or sell-out shows at Madison Square Garden, or the UK's Monsters of Rock festival. Or the first time I went to Japan and they treated us like The Beatles. But my reply always goes right back to that night at the Cortland Teen Center. After all these years I can still easily picture myself at that first "gig," as we'd learned to call our shows. We were the Vegas Kings, and we had come to steal your daughters' hearts! Me on trumpet, Nicky Pantas on guitar, some other guys from high school on bass, drums, and sax.

I can still see the faces of our classmates shining in the eerie illumination of our homemade garden lights. The gyrating dancers, the chaperones with fingers jammed in their ears to try and block out the assault on their senses, and the sidelong glances from the ladies in the audience. It was a truly momentous night. The first time I got the tiniest glimpse of what real stardom might actually be like. It wasn't fame I was dreaming of, though, more just recognition.

We were paid sixteen dollars for that first night's work. Three dollars and twenty cents each, or put another way, one dollar and six cents each an hour. Pretty good dough for a bunch of high school kids. For me, though, money wasn't the issue. From now on, music would always come first in my life. The joy of performing and the special sense of accomplishment were payment enough, which was lucky, as many times that would be all the compensation we got.

That first success opened the doors for us, and the bookings came pouring in. Playing to packed houses once or sometimes twice a week became commonplace. Musically, though, we knew something was missing. We brought a lot of people into the hall, but once we got going, they were starting to wander. We were becoming background music.

The answer came in the form of a slightly inebriated classmate. As all drunks do, he wanted to sing. We resisted until he grabbed the microphone, announced himself and his tune selection, and broke into song. We looked at each other. We could throw him out and disrupt the show, or we could join in. We decided to play along. The effect was instantaneous. Kids swarmed to the front of the stage, clapping in time with our guest vocalist. We looked at each other again. It was like magic.

The lesson for me was that instrumental pieces were satisfying as a musician, but give the people some words to shout and melody to sing, and we become one unit: players, chanters, and audience. We worked with our newfound frontman for a while, until we realized his limitations. As drunk-singers go, he was amazing. But he didn't move much.

Then a friend told us about this kid named Billy De Wolfe, who was said to be a great singer and an uninhibited performer. We auditioned him, and he was good. He had a passable voice, and he knew how to move. Better than that, he had also written two original songs. This was a big step forward for us. We covered every hit we heard on the radio and became the best jukebox in town. Now we had another string to our bows.

Things began to open up for us. Schools and other teen centers around the Cortland vicinity began booking the Vegas Kings on a regular basis. Towns with decidedly Roman and Greek names like Cincinnatus, Romulus, Virgil, Homer, Ithaca, Marathon, Pharsalia, and a few hybrid strains like Killawog and Apulia Station. We played in all of these places and countless others.

One of Billy's original songs called "Lover" always went over really well with our audiences, and that encouraged us to start thinking seriously about getting to the next level. We wanted to record our own material, be taken more seriously as an ambitious band. For that we needed a manager. We didn't have to look very far. Nicky's brother Jim owned a record store called the House of Wax, and he was seriously keen to expand his "empire" by moving into music management. We were his first signing.

Jim located the only recording studio in the area, forty miles away in Binghamton, New York. It was a two-track facility owned by a gentleman whose first profession was photography. As a sideline, he recorded radio jingles in the back room of his photo shop, and this is where we "cut" our first tracks. In retrospect, it was primitive and experimental, but we loved it.

Both sides of our soon-to-be 45 were finished in less than two hours, but we lingered there until we wore out our welcome. Nicky and I (especially Nicky) grilled our "producer" on every facet of his studio operation. We wanted to learn it all. We had already decided the next Vegas Kings session would be supervised by just the two of us.

We rushed home with the tape and an acetate recording. This was the music cut into a disc of acetate material that simulated a piece of vinyl and allowed listening on a record player, as tape recorders were rare at the time. Acetates were noisy and lost considerable quality with each ensuing play. But the record player was turned on, and with trembling hands, and warnings not to scratch it, the stylus arm was lowered and there we were, recording artists.

We repeated this process throughout the next day and the next day until the sounds on the acetate were impossible to recognize as music anymore. But it still sounded great to us.

Jim, who we always called Jones for some reason, sent the master tape off to be pressed into round flat seven-inch diameter pieces of black vinyl, to be played on an actual record player at 45 rpm—and we sat around for the next few weeks as nervous and jittery as kids on Christmas Eve, just dying to open their presents from Santa.

Then one day, after what seemed an eternity, they arrived. Five hundred copies of what we were sure was a number one record: Billy's song, "Lover," on the A-side and an instrumental, "Conquest," by the rest of us, on the flipside. My first writing credit! Hey, I'm a song-writer. This stuff's easy!

Jones suggested that we change the band's name for the record. The Vegas Kings sound a little too...well, *Vegas*, for a cool young rock 'n' roll group in the late '50s. In fact, Jones said, we might as well ditch it as a name completely. So first we became the Rumblers after the Duane Eddy hit, "Rumble." Then some promoter in Johnson City decided the word "Rumblers" was too violent and didn't want to encourage fighting, so with only a slight nod to Gene Vincent and the Blue Caps, who we loved, we became...Ronnie and the Red Caps! You can't fake genius.

Jack carved out a great solo on "Lover," and coupled with his enthusiasm, we couldn't have been more pleased by the change. The lineup shifted around me and Nicky and Billy. Guys came and went. I took over as the bass player.

Enter Sears Roebuck. Nicky and I would often drool over the guitar section of the Sears catalogue and decided to pool our funds and order a Silvertone electric bass. The arrival of my new instrument and the expulsion of the old stand-up acoustic bass signaled our entry into a more traditional rock 'n' roll format. Nicky and I were now able to communicate much better musically, guitar-to-guitar, and began to write songs at a rapid place. The material was awful, but we were slowly learning the formula.

My first real experience with artistic ego raised its ugly head at this point. Billy's increasing demands to dictate our direction and choice of music became a battle to survive as we now were. A meeting was called, which didn't include Billy, and suddenly we were without a vocalist. We weren't about to be held up by a big head that didn't even play an instrument! Who did he think he was? But we also understood the necessity of having a singer.

Nicky knew the words of every Elvis song ever recorded, so he was the obvious choice within the band. But Nicky didn't see himself in that role. His desire was simply to play guitar, and the rest of us respected that decision. So we tried to find a replacement for Billy from other sources. We tried everyone who applied, but with no luck. And so, with great reluctance, Nicky had to reluctantly face the microphone.

For the next few months we all, including Nicky, suffered through his attempts at singing live. He could sing and sound good on tape, but he just couldn't do it live. His voice and technique were too weak. Nicky was relieved when we decided we would have to look further afield.

Despite all my protests, it was me who was chosen next to step up front. I had zero experience as a singer. I had once appeared in a grade school play as a member of the choir, but I was pretty sure that alone did not qualify me to be the next in line to sing. However, as a team member, I had to comply with their wishes. To our collective surprise (mine most of all!), as soon as I opened my mouth and started to sing, you could hear it was something I could do—and quite easily.

I was astonished to learn that my singing voice was strong and responsive to the songs we performed in the show. Even though my preference, like Nicky's, was only to play my instrument, the die had been cast. My new identity was now to include the title of the singer. I found I could mimic almost any singer and was clever enough to retain and refine the best parts of each of them for myself. That was the easy part.

I was also now the frontman, a job I had to learn and fast. Once I realized my vocal capabilities though, I threw myself into the new role of frontman with complete abandon. Suddenly we were able to experiment with all kinds of material, and it proved to give us a much broader appeal, which was lucky, as things could have gone another way completely for me around that time. When I graduated from Cortland High in 1960, Paulie Consroe and I headed off to the University of Buffalo to study pharmacology. I saw myself keeping the band going while I did my degree. It was on one of our trips between Cortland and Buffalo in the fall of 1960 that Paulie came up with the idea for calling the group Ronnie Dio and the Prophets, which really stood out for the time, I thought. I dropped out of college a few months later, because I really wanted to make a go of it with the band. I persuaded my parents that I could always return to my studies if the band didn't work out.

Doing my best for the band didn't make me a saint away from the band. Even though most of our days were consumed by rehearsal and schoolwork, we still found time for mischief. Floyd lived near a car dealership, and its back alley was a convenient shortcut through to his home. There were always ten or twelve cars parked behind the main building in the alleyway, and our curiosity invariably led us to checking them out. We discovered that the keys to most of these cars were in the ignition, which switched light bulbs on in both our minds. We decided we needed to scope this out further.

The dealership premises closed at 5:00 p.m., and with our usual forethought, we waited an extra hour before entering the alley. Our initial thought was that the keys would be removed from all the cars and locked away inside, but there they were, still in place! We couldn't believe our luck!

While we thought we were being clever, we were too stupid to realize why all the automobiles clustered behind the dealership were of varied makes and models. This, after all, was a Chevrolet dealership, yet here were Fords, Dodges, Buicks—plenty of other cars totally unrelated to a Chevy. We didn't discover the answer to this riddle until it was almost too late.

We returned a few days later and took up our vigil again. Once more the lights were extinguished at 5:00 p.m., and the employees vacated the premises. The single overhead light affixed to the roof of the building was not considered a problem as we piled into the nearest car, a Ford. Given my past "driving" experience, I slid behind the wheel and fired up that baby. With a little prodding it turned over and began to cough itself into action. Floyd turned on the radio, and we were mobile.

We took the car for a spin around the empty early-evening streets—dinner hour in Cortland. Then we cruised it back to the car dealership, then ran to Floyd's house and up to his room to congratulate ourselves and bask in this incredible adventure that only we had shared.

It was time to formulate a plan. We had discovered that the Chevy garage reopened for half a day on Saturday mornings and then was permanently closed until 9:00 a.m. Monday. We decided that should we ever take advantage of this situation, we could have the use of the car all of Friday evening, but be forced to return it before they opened Saturday morning. Then when they closed at noon on Saturday, we could reclaim it and retain possession until Sunday evening. It seemed like the dream caper. But we would never actually do that, of course. Would we?

The following Friday found us cruising the back streets of Cortland, this time in a Dodge. The temptation was just too great. We began slowly and cautiously, and at first told no one, but this was simply one secret too juicy not to share.

A few months before this latest car episode, several of us organized a street gang formed in the image of a tenth-grade bunch of guys. They were bigger and older than we were, but our group was somehow magically smarter than everyone else. They carried switchblades, but we researched and were able to construct crude guns. These days we'd have gone online for that info. Back then we went to the local library. Looking back now I cannot believe how dangerous this was, but we thought we were tough guys.

So now that we had these crude guns, we needed a clubhouse of some kind. Instead of using someone's home or backyard, however, we built a large two-story structure on a small, isolated island in the rapids of the Tioughnioga River. We raised a sturdy, easily defended bridge across the rushing white-water and used the rapid river flow to power a generator. We had plenty of evil thoughts, but we called ourselves the Angels. Nothing to do with the Hell's Angels, I should add. We were more ironic.

So once we got into the whole car "borrowing" thing, Floyd and I couldn't wait to spread the news of our good fortune to the other guys in the Angels. Now we would take off in small groups and commandeer a ride together in one of the spare autos. We began expanding our driving, getting closer and closer to our neighbor, Ithaca, where we could confront other youth gangs and hear the music of the local bands playing at dances there.

One Sunday afternoon, Floyd, a fellow Angel Tony Minelli, and I decided to make it all the way to a daytime function at the Ithaca Teen Center to see our favorite band and biggest competition, Bobby Comstock and the Counts. We borrowed another vehicle from Angels Rent-A-Car and drove off into the sun. Halfway between Cortland and Ithaca lies the tiny town of Dryden, whose one impressive feature was a long, very steep, sharply curving hill that led to Dryden's only traffic light at the bottom of the incline. Floyd was driving, with Tony in the back and me riding shotgun.

We began our descent into the approaching town, and Floyd decided to accelerate into the curve. As we started to gain momentum, the car went out of control and inevitably headed toward the massive oak tree that guarded the greater part of the curve. I can still picture Floyd turning the wheel all the way to the left and seeing the car pitching far right. Floyd mistakenly stood on the brakes and our back end swung toward the tree. We slid into the loose stones of the road's shoulder, and with what seemed like pinpoint precision, cleared the mighty oak by a whisker.

Floyd managed to slow the car as the hill leveled out, and we limped to the curbside about ten yards from the traffic light. The rush of relief slammed to a halt when the rearview mirror showed a New York State Trooper's car gliding to a stop behind us. Our first impulse was to throw open the doors and run like hell, but the trauma of our near-death experience and the specter in the mirror kept us pressed into our seats.

The trooper slowly walked around the car while we sat there panic-stricken and immobile. He poked his head into the driver's side window and told us we had a flat. This, he surmised, was clearly the cause of our near miss. Did we have a spare, he asked? We had no idea what the trunk contained—probably a dead body. It couldn't get much worse.

We popped the trunk and discovered a tire (and no corpse), but it was flat too. I'll never know why that cop didn't ask for a license or registration from three such obvious minors, or why he called a service station for us and then drove away, but he did. At least we now knew why all the cars we had taken were so varied in make and model. They were there to be serviced. At any time, their problems could arise, and our narrow escape could easily have gotten us—or someone else—injured or killed.

The tire was repaired while we kept a sharp eye out for what we thought would be the sure return of the trooper to tell us he had checked the license plate number and was here to arrest us for auto theft. But as soon the job was done, we got in and drove the car home, freaked out. Ithaca would have to come to us. Floyd drove at a snail's pace all the way to Cortland while we slowly unwound from the drama of the day.

But the day's fun didn't end there. We were approaching the entrance to the alley parking lot when Floyd let out an "Oh shit!" and dropped to the floor of the car. We swerved toward an oncoming car, and as Tony managed to grab the wheel and straighten it out, from my own hiding place in the car I saw the faces of Floyd's mother, father, and little sister Jeannie intently peering into our windows. This was simply too much. Afterward, away from the others, Floyd and I swore an oath this would be the end. Every time we took another car, we retook that oath.

We were heading for a fall. It came soon after. Two of the more notorious members of the Angels had been secretly planning the robbery of a mom-and-pop grocery store. Just before closing, one of them diverted the attention of the attendant while the other quickly hid in a back room. After the owners had locked up and gone home, the one inside unfolded himself from his concealment and opened the door for the other. They found no money but removed a camera, some watches, and a few pieces of jewelry.

The following day they took a bus to Syracuse to pawn their swag. The theft had been reported immediately upon discovery, and armed with the serial number of the stolen camera, the pawnbroker called the police, and they were arrested. Each served a year at the reform school in Elmira, New York, and although there were many more incidents than what I've recounted here, this marked the end of our wicked, wicked ways.

Our extraordinary luck had held, but the conviction of the two now-ex-Angels was pushing it. It had all been a game to us. No harm, no foul, but two kids who had been laughing with us yesterday were suddenly gone, and I was determined not to follow them.

From then on it was only the band that mattered.

—+ FOUR +—
· · · · ·

UNCLE JOHNNY

*I*t was a time of change and we needed to join that parade. The beat we marched to was the one provided by what overnight became known as the "British Invasion." I was twenty-one when the Beatles went to Number One for the first time in America, with "I Want to Hold Your Hand." I was one of the seventy-three million Americans that watched them tear apart *The Ed Sullivan Show* one Sunday night in 1964. Afterward, just like every other young guy watching that night, including Bruce Springsteen, Billy Joel, Jimi Hendrix, Jim Morrison, and Steven Tyler from Aerosmith, to name just a small few who went on to become big stars—I didn't just want to get to know more about the Beatles, I wanted to *be* them. We imitated their accents, their attitudes, and their attire.

Even Bob Dylan, already being touted as a "spokesman of a generation," flipped out and wanted to be more like the Beatles. Within a year of their Ed Sullivan appearance he had left behind the protest folk songs of his earlier career and "gone electric," complete with surreal lyrics and sunglasses.

The Beatles were just the start of the British Invasion: longhaired groups that espoused a new musical formula that was a combination of vocal harmonies and instrumental music provided by the singers themselves. The songs and their arrangements were almost as refreshing as the brash and irreverent personalities that created them. They had strange and descriptive names. As well as the Fab Four—John, Paul, George, and Ringo—there were the Yardbirds, the Animals, the Rolling Stones, the Dave Clark Five, the Hollies, the Kinks...it really did feel like a music and culture revolution—a light bright enough to cut through what had become a mire of imitation R&B. This was music that white rural kids could connect with, and that certainly included Cortland. The chord changes were simple and attractive, and the songs dealt with juvenile love situations that we could all relate to. Help had arrived.

We had recently changed our name, again, to Ronnie Dio and the Prophets, after we lost our sax player. We replaced the saxophone with another guitarist, Dick Bottoff, who could also sing and would help give us The Look and The Sound, which, as we had already learned, were two of the three most important attributes in rock 'n' roll, the third being The Feel.

Dick was a few years older than the rest of us and had a real driver's license, and, for the first time, we didn't have to rely on parents or friends for transportation. As a result, we were now able to expand our touring itinerary to include the bigger cities around us. Most of them had colleges and universities with large non-resident populations and hundreds of sororities and fraternities on campus. Several weekends a year the brothers and sisters of these societies threw parties at their houses, and it became a kind of factory for bands in the area. Years later the National Lampoon film *Animal House* included an almost perfect portrayal of party night at what could have been any college in upstate New York in the early '60s.

From the band's perspective, it meant preparation, punishment, and payment.

For example, starting from our home base in Cortland, we'd load our car and set out in sometimes-blizzard conditions across the frozen countryside to Cornell University. On a bad night, we'd leave at least four hours before we were scheduled to start, thereby leaving ample time to travel the twenty-two miles to Ithaca and Cornell. The campus was a maze of rollercoaster roads, difficult enough to navigate on a sunny day, but almost impassable through snow, ice, and deep, thick mud. We rarely missed a booking, though. In fact, we had once driven through a road-closing snowstorm to a gig, and when we got there, feeling like heroes, we found that the town had closed down for the night!

Upon arrival at the fraternity, we would be shown to the usual unprotected corner of the library that had been made into a makeshift stage—or maybe the dining room, usually one that sported only a dual-plug AC outlet. If the brothers were cool, they'd show us to the bar first. Usually, though, we'd simply drag our instruments and gear into the building and through the already-drunken crowd to our appointed space while answering stupid questions from people who had no idea what we were all about. Rock 'n' roll as a career choice was still an oddity to most of the students, and we were viewed more as shiftless minstrels than equals.

We were usually booked to play four hour-long sessions, each set consisting of forty-five minutes of music and one fifteen-minute break. We were treated as hired help, which was fine by us. But as the level of the "Purple Jesus" (a homemade brew made-up most often of vodka and grape juice mixed in and consumed from a bathtub) got lower, the rowdy-o-meter would move ever upward, resulting in what we called the Attack of the Assholes! They were almost always burly men who insisted on shouting into the microphone, singing tunelessly while force-feeding you beer while you were singing, grabbing at the guitars, swatting at the drums, or the always popular "upending" of the full beer pitcher into the amplifier. This was Attack of the Assholes 101. I felt sure that if you could major in that subject in college it would be a wildly popular course. If you could handle all this with a certain tact and diplomacy and allow for slight levels of abuse and only minor damage to your equipment, the possibilities of a return engagement and additional payment increased exponentially.

We played all the popular songs of the day but learned early on that if you could perform the Isley Brothers' "Shout" and "Peanut Butter" by the Marathons, and any other tune that people could "bug" to, you were safe for the night—the Bug being a legitimate dance that involved spreading your arms and flapping your hands while buzzing around like a, uh, bug. In these circumstances, it became a great excuse for the brothers of the fraternity to throw themselves down and writhe around on the beer-soaked floor. (You will find a much prettier example in the classic John Waters movie *Hairspray*.)

This respectably lucrative and welcomingly steady employment offered by the huge fraternity market spurred the formation of hundreds of similar bands throughout Central New York, thereby raising the level of competition by leaps and bounds. Fortunately for us, the cream rose to the top. Our hard work and dedication placed us in the upper echelon of the local groups. We were in such demand that we would sometimes play at three houses on a Friday, three on a Saturday, and two more on a Sunday, earning sometimes as much as $10,000-plus for that weekend's work.

For some of the bands, this level of success spelled complacency. It was such an easy living, and of course they all thought it would last forever. Some of us could see past all that and had higher aspirations. Even though we could now dictate our own terms, we buried that idea of simply cashing in on our popularity with fraternity balls and began to play the club circuit, enabling us to spiral farther and farther out into the rest of our world.

One summer we decided to try for a steady engagement at a resort area called Lake George. It was a beautiful little village nestled in the mountains and curled around the body of water that the town was named after. Its amusement facilities attracted families, and the nightclubs were a magnet for high school grads and college students.

We didn't have a booking, but confidently set out to find some work there. Once they saw us play, how could they possibly refuse?

Someone spotted a large gift shop on the outskirts of town, and we stopped to browse amongst the rubber crocodiles, plastic tomahawks and long counters of turquoise jewelry that always seemed to be the bill of fare in these places. We noticed a car with a trailer attached pull into the store's parking lot and expel what was obviously another band. Striking up a conversation with them, they told us with pride that they had a two-month residency at a club called the Airport Inn, and that our chances of work here in Lake George were zero. Not the most encouraging sign, but nevertheless, we reasoned, we were here, and if you don't ask, you don't get, so we rolled into town and stopped at the first bar we saw, went inside and asked them if they could use a top group to help draw the customers in. They didn't have to think about it. They simply said no.

This was the answer we got at every other stop we made that day. No. No, no, and more no. Apparently the guys in the other band were right on the mark. To avoid letting the trip be a complete bust we decided to drive around the lake and found ourselves right outside the club where the other band had told us they had the two-month residency, the Airport Inn. We knew that but went in to ask anyway.

A band's instruments were set up on a stage in the backroom that we assumed correctly belonged to our friends from the gift shop, and another one stood empty behind the bar. The club got its name from the Piper Cub flying machine that hovered above the vacant stage. The bar was empty at this hour, and we easily located the owner, a man named Charlie Wade. We asked Charlie, a gruff-looking man, if he could give us any work, and to our surprise he said he would give us half an hour of his time to prepare our instruments and audition for him.

We ran outside and grabbed our gear, quickly set up, and played Charlie two songs. He loved us! Money was discussed, and we were offered $650 for working one fifty-minute set, seven nights a week, plus a three-hour matinee on Sunday afternoons, right under the belly of the airplane. Tiny log cabins were provided for accommodation, and we were given a choice of one peanut butter or baloney sandwich each following the end of our midnight set. Of course we accepted, but wondered what he would do with two bands. He simply told them to pack up and shove off. Wow! Sorry, guys! But hey! Charlie loved us, and we were probably the only people who could fit under the plane over the stage.

We played through that whole summer at the Airport and were asked to come back the following season. It had been a grueling schedule, but we learned so much and had such a great time doing it that we signed up for the next year on the spot.

We swaggered into Lake George at the beginning of the next summer season surer of ourselves than ever. Most of our fellow employees at the club had returned with the addition of a few new faces. One of them was a bartender who had recently relocated from Miami, and about halfway through the season he must have recognized the name Dio from his stay in Florida. That is, he was familiar with the name Johnny Dio, at the time a real-life mafia boss in Miami. One day the bartender asked me what my relation to the mafia was. I could have said that it wasn't my real name, but my old connection as a gangster buff forced out the words "Johnny's my uncle." Yeah, I actually said that. What was I thinking?

I didn't know the details at the time, which is just as well or I might have frightened myself to death, but the real Johnny Dio was not someone to be messed with. His real name was Giovanni Ignazio Dioguardi—Johnny Dio for short. He was a labor racketeer for the mob, who had done a lot to help Jimmy Hoffa become general president of the Teamsters Union. All that came out later, though. At the time, Johnny Dio was best known for being behind the acid attack that left the crusading newspaper journalist Victor Riesel blind in 1956. Johnny was arrested and charged—and later freed after key witnesses mysteriously withdrew evidence. Who woulda thunk it?

This was the "uncle" I now bragged about to my new pal the barman. This bit of stupidity opened up the floodgates of paranoia and stress for the remainder of our stay there. The bartender told me that the maître d' at the Fontainebleau Hotel on Miami Beach, a good friend of his named Mario, was an old associate of my "uncle." He suggested that he call Mario and have him notify Uncle Johnny of his talented young nephew's whereabouts. Maybe come down and see the show? I moved quickly to quash that idea by explaining that I was trying to succeed on my own and not use Uncle Johnny's influence. The bartender seemed to buy this line of reasoning, and left me to it, but I was suddenly icily aware that I had begun to build a web of deceit that could one day return to bite me in the ass.

A few weeks after our conversation about my ancestry, the barman sprung this news on me: Mario, his maître d' friend from Miami, was in town and planned to visit the club to see his old buddy—and to stop by and say hi to me, nephew of his good pal Johnny Dio. I could have stopped it all right then and there by simply admitting my initial lie, but I couldn't stand to lose face, and so the web got larger as I smiled and said I would look forward to that pleasure. When he arrived at the Inn, Mario the Miami maître d' lost no time in coming over to question me about my alleged lineage. Knowing that the Dio family was Sicilian, I cited the names of some of my friends who were tied to Sicily through their ancestry and claimed them as my own. For a kid, I was showing some balls, as they say. I shudder now, though, when I think just how badly that strategy could have gone for me.

The Sicilian connection seemed to placate Mario, at least momentarily, and he suggested that we contact my uncle, let him know how well his nephew in Cortland was doing. I repeated my heart-warming wish for success without any outside help, but my new pal Mario was having none of it. He promised to alert the "family" in Miami and assured me that someone would turn up in Lake George shortly after he returned home to Florida.

We only had a couple of weeks to go before we could return to Cortland, and I agonized every minute of those last few days. While we played, I constantly scoured the crowd for shady-looking characters;

in the sweltering heat of my room, I wouldn't allow the window to be raised or unlocked for fear of an attack in the middle of the night.

Finally our last day arrived. I only had to pass through one matinee (it was a Sunday), and the evening's final show to survive this nightmare. We were nearing the end of our last matinee set when I saw them. Leaning against a railing at the back of the barroom were three men whom I was sure were wise guys. They looked like prototypical made men, dressed like them, and seemed to conspire amongst themselves, with me clearly the object of their suspicious behavior and attention.

If only that plane hovering above the stage was in working order, I thought. *I'd hitch a ride right out of here, never to be seen again!* I thought about making a run for it out the back door, but I beat back that fearful urge and managed to stumble through the rest of the set. To my surprise and immense relief, they were nowhere to be seen when we finished, but we still had one last set to play later that night. The original plan had been for us to leave in the morning, but once I laid it out for the rest of the guys, those plans were quickly rearranged to allow us to get the hell out of Dodge right after the last set.

I worried my way through our break between performances and even refused my traditional peanut butter and jelly sandwich at midnight, expecting the doors to be flung open at any moment and the real Dio's captains to appear. But as the night wore on and no hoods actually appeared, my hopes of a last-minute reprieve began to rise.

"Thank you for a great summer, and we'll see you next year!" I shouted to the crowd. It was over. Had I created this whole scenario in my mind, I wondered as I walked off the stage, or did my future still include modeling a pair of concrete shoes? We loaded up our gear and suitcases and said our goodbyes to the people we had worked with at the club for the last two months.

Just before we were ready to leave, I searched out the bartender who had so helpfully set me up with the Miami mob, just to confirm or allay my suspicions. He said that he hadn't spoken to anyone from Miami that day or night with the exception of Mario, who had spoken to my Uncle Johnny—and that he had sent his regards and offer of help whenever I needed it.

Wait, what did he just say?

I could hardly believe what I was hearing. I was in the clear! Suffice to say that I never abused the relationship again. Nor did I ever make a return visit to Lake George.

That fall, back in Cortland, Nicky was really into recording after he had invested in some equipment, which allowed us to tape a night at Cortland's favorite rock club, Domino's. It turned into an album called *Dio At Domino's* which I'm sure only involved around 1,500 copies, but I've seen many more than that during all these years. Bloody bootleggers!

Ronnie Dio and the Prophets had lost Tommy, our original drummer, following the last Lake George residency. He had a steady girlfriend, a steady job, and had bought his first car. He decided his traveling days were over, though I always suspected that it was the Uncle Johnny Dio episode that made up his mind. We spread word of our need for a new drummer through the musical community and set about auditioning the ones who contacted us. A few were acceptable but lasted only a few months each, so the search continued. Then Nicky was told about a great young drummer from Ithaca and arranged for him to play a few songs with us at a fraternity party there. To my annoyance he turned up a few hours late—but that fault was immediately canceled by his date. He had an Asian girlfriend. Wow! This guy was already cool. He definitely had The Look. If he could play drums well, he was in.

He sat behind the drum kit and removed most of the tom-toms and the other flashy bits until just the most basic equipment remained. And then we played. Wow! He had an incredible sense of feel and played amazing fills. They didn't always come out right, but they were amazing.

Enter Gary Driscoll into my life. He was blond, baby-faced, and almost blissfully unaware. He once sent away for a pair of glasses that promised the buyer to turn any object upside down and was convinced that it would enable him to cause dresses to flip up over their occupant's heads and thereby allow him to see their exposed parts. The night before our first European tour he fell off the pair of clogs he had just bought and broke his ankle. He poked himself in the eye with a drumstick one night and played with a patch, until he put his medicine in the wrong eye and blinded himself for a week. The list goes on and on, but he brought a great attitude, and it seemed to pump new enthusiasm into us all.

Finally, we were on our way—again.

FIVE

SPIDER'S REVENGE

We were now being co-managed by Nicky's brother Jim and a booking agent from Ithaca named John Perialas. John was successful, aggressive, had connections, and, most impressive to me, he managed my hero at the time, a young singer named Bobby Comstock. Bobby was a local Ithaca boy about my age who'd had a big Top 40 record on the radio, "Tennessee Waltz," with his group Bobby Comstock and the Counts. There was no doubt in my mind: if John Perialas worked with Bobby Comstock, then he must be good.

He also believed in going straight to the source, which meant heading straight for New York City—and the sound of opportunity knocking, we hoped. John, Bobby, and I would drive the 250 miles to the City and haunt the publishing houses along Broadway, primarily the Brill Building at 1619 Broadway, corner of 48th Street, named after the men's haberdashery that originally occupied its ground floor.

This was where Neil Sedaka and Howard Greenfield wrote "Breaking Up Is Hard to Do;" where Carole King and Gerry Goffin wrote "Will You Still Love Me Tomorrow;" where Barry Mann and

Cynthia Weil wrote "On Broadway;" so many incredibly talented writers and singers and musicians making these and dozens of other timeless hits destined to be endlessly replayed on radio, recycled in TV commercials and movie soundtracks and rerecorded by younger generations of performers.

We had released a single in 1960, billed this time as Ronnie Dio and the Red Caps: a sappy ballad called "An Angel Is Missing," co-written by Clint Ballard Jr. and Fred Tobias, who'd just had a million-selling hit with "Good Timin'" by Jimmy Jones. Needless to say, our song didn't sell a million, but it did add to our growing feeling of confidence.

Now, as Ronnie Dio and the Prophets, and with John Perialas there to open doors, we would spend every Monday hustling in New York, searching for a song that might give us a hit. Then, exhausted, we would make the long drive home on Tuesday, sharing our thoughts, weighing it all up. We stayed at a predominantly black hotel next to busy Penn Station, all three of us stuffed into one musty room for six dollars a night. Nice it was not.

I hated the music publishing offices. Everyone knew Bobby from his Top 40 hit, and he and John would be hustled into someone's office, while I was left twiddling my thumbs in the waiting room. Occasionally I was introduced to someone, just to make nice, then immediately relegated to the sidelines while the grown-ups talked. I didn't even get to sit and listen while the publishers were playing their various demos. The few times I was played some demos in an office I soon realized that they were bottom-of-the-barrel tunes, the only ones someone of my status would ever hear. I knew better than to burn any bridges and to leave a door open rather than closed, but I would be back one day, I told myself. And then they would see.

Meanwhile, we released a string of singles on numerous long-forgotten record labels like Swan, Lawn, Derby, Stateside, Valex, Zapp, and Parkway, including such choice cuts as "The Ooh-Poo-Pah-Doo" (a No. 3 hit in 1960 for Jesse Hill, who wrote it, but a flop for us), "Will You Still Love Me Tomorrow" (a No. 1 hit in 1960 for the Shirelles, but a flop for us), "Say You're Mine Again" (a No. 3 hit for Perry Como in 1953, but a flop for us), and "Love Potion No. 9" (a No. 2 hit for The Searchers in 1964, but a flop for us). We were certainly consistent, if nothing else. I even had one of my own songs, "Mr. Misery," released in 1963, a syrupy pop ballad in the same mold as all the other Prophets releases, and true to form, that wasn't a hit either.

At the same time, the line-up of the Prophets was changing again. Our guitarist, Dick, had gotten married and started to look for security beyond the feast-or-famine existence that the band had to offer. The fact that he decided to leave a couple of days before the first show in a six-week residency in Miami meant we had to move fast to find a replacement.

We covered the 1,500 miles of highway from Cortland to south Florida in around thirty hours and checked into one room at a motel near the club we were due to appear at the next night, the Par-Tree Lounge. The trip had been cramped and uncomfortable, so we looked forward to a good night's sleep, excepting Gary, of course. He had a friend going to school in Miami and had planned a big night out with him.

The rest of us couldn't wait to hit the sack. Not having Gary around for a few hours would certainly make that sleep more peaceful. So after several reminders to Gary about locking the door when he got back, we sent him on his way into the night and fell into what must have been a very deep sleep because, upon waking, we discovered that we had been robbed. Wallets were missing, watches had been taken, and Gary was sleeping soundly with all of his belongings in place. We were pissed off but certainly not surprised. You had to make adjustments for Gary, and we had been too exhausted to remember to do so.

On our way to the club, we encountered the biggest spider that has ever existed on Earth, riding in the front seat next to the driver. There was a loud collective cry! Then we all (including the driver) hopped up on the seat backs and shrieked like little girls until we careened to a stop into the parking lot of the Par-Tree and spilled out onto the pavement.

Still in fear of this giant eight-legged freak of nature, we ran to the front of the club, hoping to get inside and slam the door behinds us, but it was locked. Now what? It sounds silly to you, maybe, but none of us had ever seen anything like it. We had no such animal in Cortland! So we waited outside the car, peering periodically into the lair of the monster.

John the manager finally turned up, and after listening to us rage about our latest adventure, he armed himself with a can of Raid, closed all of the vents and windows, and emptied the entire container into the car. When it was over and the beast had been slain, I remember thinking how cruel it had been. Looking down at the shriveled body of the spider lying as close as it could to a ventilation duct that offered at most only one final breath, I didn't like how I felt. We would pay for it later.

We were billed simply as the Prophets during our time in Miami to avoid any contact with the Dio family, and so managed to stay out of their reach and take $3,000 home with us stuffed into a suitcase. I was reminded of what could be when we observed the removal of some bodies out of the swamp located behind the club. The head of security at the Par-Tree, who had been a Miami homicide detective, told us that these episodes had all the hallmarks of gangland killings, and that it was not an uncommon occurrence in the area.

At the end of the six weeks, Dick had decided to fly home, so Nicky, Gary, our friend-cum-roadie Joe Smith, and I left Miami and made our way in the car northward up the East Coast. I was chosen to drive the first leg in our palatial Pontiac station wagon, which we had made even larger by bolting a big plywood box to its roof. Joe and I switched seats some hours later, and we carried on out of Florida into a small portion of Georgia before entering South Carolina. A superhighway didn't run up the coast back then, so the road was a conventional two-lane undivided thoroughfare bordered by dense, dark forest.

After confirming that Joe was awake and alert, I dozed off in the front passenger seat, only to be awakened by Joe's cry of "Look out!" I reflexively grabbed the pillow behind my head and shoved my face into it just as we struck a large object in the road. The windshield exploded into the car as we spun to a halt on the roadside. The hood had sprung open, and smoke or steam was pouring from the engine. The suitcases and instruments in the back of the wagon had surged forward into the back seat upon impact and buried Gary and Nicky from sight. A muffled voice from the back said, "Turn off the ignition before we blow up." I quickly did that then opened a back door and started pulling the pile in the backseat apart, and the other two scrambled out into the dark night.

Gary, Nicky, and I seemed to check out all right, but Joe was screaming that he was blind. We ran to him and saw that his eyes were covered with blood. Someone grabbed a towel from the car, and we gave it to Joe, afraid to get too close to the horror-show reality of what was happening. Joe might be blinded! He wiped at his eyes, blinked a few times, and broke into relieved laughter. The blood was coming from a gash in his forehead and had flowed into his eyes, making him go "blind."

Our first question to Joe was, "What did we hit?" We saw nothing in the road but our wrecked Pontiac, and when his answer was, "a horse," we were still mystified. If we'd hit a horse, where was it? We looked around us. No horse remains anywhere.

There wasn't time for more investigation because six or seven people now emerged from the forest and advanced toward the car and us. Nicky had the presence of mind to call out loudly that he was going to get "the gun" from the glove compartment, and either that dumb bluff or the headlights suddenly appearing on the road frightened them away.

We tried to flag down the approaching vehicles, but they whizzed right by us, and we were left alone again in the dark. Each car or truck that passed paid no attention to the wildly waving figures posted around the still-smoking wreck.

Suddenly out of the trees behind us appeared a man and a massive German shepherd dog. We didn't think "the gun in the glove compartment" trick would work on the dog, so we stood frozen while this huge menacing dog and this strange man silently inspected our car. He bent down to look at our license plate then asked, "Are y'all from New York?"

We reluctantly admitted that we were, nervous of what such news might do to the temper of a down-south hunter with a man-eating dog. Instead, much to our surprise and relief, he broke into a broad smile, announcing that he was from Brooklyn. Suddenly we're brothers. He promised to call the police for us and hustled off into the woods. None of us believed that he was going to send for the cavalry, so we continued signaling what little traffic was on the road at this hour.

It had turned midnight when a car finally pulled over and the driver leaned out of his window and asked if he could help. This man was taking his small daughter to the hospital in Florence. He probably shouldn't have stopped for hitchhikers, but when he learned of our dilemma, he offered to contact the police. Then he turned the car around back in the direction he had just come from. He stopped on his way back to reassure us he'd been to see the local police station and that help was on its way, and then he carried on to the hospital. I often wondered what his daughter's ailment was and hoped that he and she lived happy lives ever after. Thanks again, stranger.

We waited for the police to arrive and sighed with relief when we saw flashing lights approaching in the distance. Two patrol cars pulled up behind our vehicle, and I ran to them to tell the officers to call an ambulance for our bloodied friend Joe. The sheriff and his deputy ignored me and began talking to one another. We found what we had hit when I heard one laughingly say, "Looks like them n*****s'll be barbecuin' mule tonight."

They walked to some distant point behind the car. We followed, and sure enough, a big horse-like animal lay there off the side of the road. I repeated my plea to summon an ambulance, and this time was told to "shut up." This was the Deep South, and we Yankees had been regaled with enough tales of horror about these rednecks to know to do what they said and "hush up real quick."

We answered their questions and produced all the correct documents to satisfy these surly, suspicious men. They finally called a tow truck and herded us into one of the police cars that would drive us to the hospital in Florence. The deputy jammed the accelerator to the floor, and we squealed onto the pavement, eventually cruising at over a hundred miles an hour. I was scared to death by this high-speed idiocy, especially so soon after our recent crash, but I remembered the sheriff's caution and "kept my fuckin' mouth shut."

To make matters worse, he insisted on talking to us and turning his head into the back seat as we hurtled down the highway like a bullet. At one point he jokingly asked if we were "the boys who robbed the bank" in Manning (a nearby town) of $3,000; coincidentally, the same amount we were carrying. Visions of chain gangs danced in our heads, then vanished as the cop's thoughts accelerated into some other world he was living in.

They gave us tetanus shots and removed the larger shards of glass from different parts of our bodies. The windscreen had disintegrated into tiny pieces and showered us with such force that we kept finding tiny pieces of it in our clothes for months to come. We were told that the mule had been struck by our car and thrown into the windshield and then tossed into the air behind us, where it landed out of our sight. That explained that, then.

The deputy drove us from the hospital to rendezvous with our misshapen car at the junkyard it had been towed to, and we watched with deep admiration as the guard dog chased the cop around the lot and treed him up a pile of old tires. Good little doggie.

We sold our wreck for a couple of hundred dollars and had our gear taken to the train station for transport to Cortland the next morning. The freight train left hours before we were scheduled to go, so we had some time to kill. There was an old movie house opposite the train station, and that seemed a good way to pass the afternoon until our transportation departed.

The film had started by the time we entered the already-darkened theater and took seats in the back. It was advertised as a western, and we looked forward to John Wayne or Roy Rogers beating up on the bad guys. Instead it was Sidney Poitier mowing down white cowboys with reckless abandon, accompanied by wild cheers from the audience as each opponent clutched his chest and fell to the ground. Segregation was still the code in this rural section of the South, and we had chosen a black movie theater. I don't remember feeling threatened at all, but oh, how we cheered when Sidney "offed" another paleface.

The train stopped everywhere on our way to Washington, DC, where we could catch an express to NYC and then on to Cortland. Thirty-six hours later we were home, saddle-sore, disappointed, disillusioned, and disbanded—at least until we could find another guitar player to take Dick's place. Revenge of the Miami Spider Monster!

Our luck was in, though, when it came to finding a new guitarist. We didn't have to look beyond my own family. My cousin, a drummer, had his own band but wanted to play guitar instead. He was actually a great drummer but wanted to express himself in another musical way. As a guitar player he had plenty of rough edges but learned quickly and helped bring to us the aggression we needed. His real name was David Feinstein, but we changed that to "Rock" because the two together seemed so strange in combination, and it stuck. Under Rock's influence we edged closer to a darker and stronger style, but still carried on with our cover material to earn our living.

Our manager John's New York connections had gotten us a tour as a backing band for a few acts, including the headliner, Gene Pitney, who was doing a farewell swing around the East. We added two saxophones, a keyboard, and two trumpets to our line-up for the Pitney tour, with one of the trumpets being yours truly. I hated it, but we got paid and were allowed to play a few songs with our normal setup. That made it acceptable. You had to follow your dream, but you had to pay the bills to help get you there.

Nicky had been having stomach pains for about a year, and a physical examination revealed an ulcer. He was in great pain most of the time due to our lifestyle of too much partying and almost constant travel. Nicky was advised by his doctor to definitely not accompany us on our next journey. I was devastated. This was our dream together, and it seemed it was finally taking some shape, and not to have Nicky there to share it was unthinkable, but he convinced me to carry on. He promised to be there when we returned, healthy and ready for the next onslaught.

Now we needed a substitute for Nicky, and the easiest way to find one was to raid one of the many bands that Cortland now had circulating. We could almost have our pick. Our choice was a free spirit named Doug Thaler. Doug came to Cortland as a college student and promptly made it his permanent home. He formed a band with fellow students and then joined a local group called Brian's Idles. We had seen them play many times and felt that Doug would be perfect for the job. We asked him about it and got a positive on all counts. Doug was in.

The first few gigs were confusing to the bulk of the club audiences who had come to expect more pop-oriented show tunes, not Doug dressed as Punchinello and poured into bell bottoms the size of pup tents, shouting at them for being the fools he claimed they were. Doug had a musical vision and did not suffer what he saw as incompetence easily. We, on the other hand, barely said anything to the crowd, preferring to hide behind our wall of sound. But oddly enough we made contact. Kids were sick of syrupy, rubber balls that posed as exciting youth music.

The tour traveled in two buses, one for Gene Pitney and one for all the rest of the acts on the bill. They were nothing like the elegant vehicles used by the traveling entertainers of today. No beds, no bars, no televisions, just backbreaking vinyl seats and bad roads. This was the mid-'60s and national touring rock 'n' roll shows like ours traveled light.

We struck up a friendship on our bus with an Australian band. They were called the Easybeats and they were having a big chart hit with their record, "Friday on My Mind," and we thought they were the best things we had ever seen or heard. They were confident, professional, and experienced from years of playing rock 'n' roll in Australia's rough and tumble bars and clubs. Their guitarists, Harry Vanda and George Young, wrote almost all of their songs. Some years later, when I shared a stage with AC/DC, you could see the resemblance and influence that George had passed onto his younger brother, Angus Young.

We watched them jealously every night from the side of the stage. They didn't just suffer in front of an old crowd who had come only to see Gene. They never let up, no matter what the conditions, and we absorbed their every movement and attitude. By the time we returned to Cortland, we *were* them.

Doug's previous band, the Idles, had replaced him while he toured with us and wouldn't take him back. We felt guilty about him losing his job, but secretly thanked our lucky stars that they had set him free to officially join us. Doug dropped the guitar and became our new keyboard player. He had been writing songs prior to our meeting with the Easybeats, but under their spell he started to reach out further, find a new level to his writing, and we began to integrate our sets with the increasingly interesting songs that he wrote.

Venues with capacities of a thousand-plus began to spring up near the heavily populated universities throughout central and southern New York State. They were economically built warehouse-like structures with concrete floors and corrugated siding. The stage and the bar dominated the interior. A perfect combination: drunks and rock 'n' roll.

One of these places was built in the deepest darkest parts of the state: Specifically, Wellsville, New York. The venue was called The Heater. It would bulge with 1,500 people on a good night, and most nights were good ones. Alfred University was close at hand, but it was the local kids who really filled the place and knew how to party.

Girls from around the area would book rooms at the motel we stayed at, to attend the gig and the all-night bashes in our rooms to follow. They were down-home ladies, with a yearning for excitement and no time for inhibitions. They had nicknames like the Amazon, the Viking, and Axe Face (I'll never tell). The gig was great, but the parties were legendary.

Some of our clientele were from a biker club, the Coven. It was only a few at first, but eventually they all started to come, and they got crazier and crazier with each succeeding appearance. They began to good-naturedly threaten us with abduction to their clubhouse in the hills, but we always laughed it off with them. Then, one Saturday night after our last set, the Coven struck the Prophets. They grabbed us, and we were each put on the back of a bike. Then we all roared away into the night.

There were motorcycles everywhere around the house they took us to, and we were introduced to their scary-looking leaders and "old ladies" inside. They demanded that we share in the consumption of a clear liquid in a jug that was being passed around, as we fended off the advances of some of the girls, in fear of retribution from one of the boys. After we had all taken a large portion of this overpowering drink, they told us that it was pure grain alcohol. The last thing I remember from that night, before I passed out, was the sight of ten or twelve of the bikers ripping up the lawn in a wild free-for-all of Harleys.

I woke up with a massive hangover and somebody's "old lady" in my bed. *No! What have I done now?* You think Uncle Johnny's boys sound frightening? Try waking up with the hangover to end all hangovers in a houseful of Hell's Angels realizing you've just slept with one of their girlfriends.

"What have we done?" I inquired gently. Fortunately, this young woman seemed completely untroubled. She assured me that all was well, that the club members had chosen her for me. Oh. Right. Okay. Maybe.

I recovered just in time to dash for the toilet and puke up the contents of my stomach and a few more dead brain cells as well.

Are we having fun yet?

61

Nicky Pantas, me, and my cousin, David "Rock" Feinstein, recording at Nicky's little studio.

—+ SIX +—

ELECTRIC ELVES

*A*s Ronnie Dio and the Prophets, we released ten singles between 1962 and '65. Although none of them was a chart hit, the radio play we got from the local East Coast stations enabled us to keep widening the circle of places we were able to get bookings to play. One of those places was Waterbury, Connecticut, and going there would change the course of my life forever.

Waterbury—nicknamed the Brass City, after its history as being the center in the US for manufacturing brass—was an affluent city of approximately a hundred thousand people, situated in the southwestern segment of the state, about 75 miles from New York City and 240 miles from Cortland. When we first played there, we were booked into a club called the Sugar Shack, and during every break some guy named Bruce, who claimed he could get us big money at other venues in the area, kept pestering us. We gave him the brush-off, but he gave us his card anyway, and when we returned to play there again a few weeks later, so did Bruce.

Bruce Payne was a natural for the business side of music. He had knowledge and balls, and he believed in us. The more he talked, the more we decided that maybe we should listen to him. We had remained loyal to our first managers, Jones and John, but it had become clear to us that they were never gonna be the right guys to get the band to the next level. By 1967 it had become obvious that our dreams and dedication now surpassed theirs, so we threw our lot in with Bruce.

The countercultural revolution was in full swing, exploding into politics, fashion, science, and, most of all, the music that spoke for them all—King Crimson, Pink Floyd, Deep Purple, Jimi Hendrix, Black Sabbath, and, of course, Led Zeppelin. It was the beginning of the great guitar hero period. Players like Ritchie Blackmore, Jimmy Page, Jeff Beck, and Eric Clapton brought a studied yet instinctive musicality to the songs they wrote. They were all English and obsessed with American blues, but also very familiar with classical and folk themes. The singers were all different too—Steve Marriott, Paul Rodgers, Ian Gillan, Rod Stewart, and Robert Plant—vocalists with tremendous power and maximum expression. It was heaven for me. I could finally use my voice my way.

It was the era of albums overtaking singles as the prime source of interest for record buyers, the first time in rock 'n' roll when it became of paramount importance for bands to come up with their own original material, to experiment and really show what they could do, other than chasing hits. To underline how serious we were about evolving the band, we changed our name yet again, this time to the Electric Elves. Doug always referred to Rock and me as the "elves," so we became high voltage leprechauns.

Nicky had also built a small recording studio with plans to expand when we had finally "made it," and we could see how good he would become as an engineer. All we needed now was someone who understood where we were coming from and where we needed to go.

We decided that guy was Bruce. As well as encouraging our plans to grow into a more album-oriented band, he promised to double our earnings from our live shows. True to his word, with Bruce leading the way, we began to make some serious money in Connecticut. One of our steady gigs was at Guggie's, a club owned by a wonderful big Italian American guy named Frank Guglielmo. Bruce would book us in there for a week at a time and we always loved it. Frank's brother Angelo, or Augie, as we knew him, was a bartender there but had once been a National League umpire who was now slightly burned out on too many foul balls and would randomly leap in the air and shout "Safe!" or "Out!" He was heaven to Nicky and me, both devout baseball fans, and we would sit around between shows listening to his fascinating stories for hours.

It was eight o'clock on a Sunday when we finished our latest week's stay at Guggie's. The Connecticut liquor laws didn't allow the sale of alcohol after eight on the Christian Sabbath, so we usually drove straight home to Cortland. We had purchased a new extra-long van a few months earlier that afforded us more comfort, so the trip wouldn't be too bad. Nicky's ulcer still prevented him from alcoholic consumption, and even though the rest of us didn't drink much that day, he was our logical choice as a driver. Gary and Rock settled into the backseat, I took the front passenger side, and Doug sat on the compartment covering the engine that was located inside the truck between Nicky and me. We drove north on the two-lane Route 8 out of Waterbury, on our way to connect with the nearest superhighway.

We hardly saw another vehicle on the road that night, until we spotted headlights coming our way in the distance. As they drew closer, we realized that the car rushing toward us was in our lane, and we shouted panicked warnings to Nicky. He had slowed to about twenty-five miles an hour, but we still seemed to be drawn toward the oncoming lights as though we were both attracted to opposite ends of a giant magnet. Nicky swerved into the other lane to try and avoid a collision, but the other car followed us over there. Nicky then tried swerving to the right side, but it was the same result; the other car swerved, too, and then there was nothing.

I heard distant voices and felt something shaking me. I opened my eyes and saw a man trying to pull me from the van. Doug was hurt bad and screaming next to me, and Nicky was slumped lifelessly over the wheel. I put my hand to my forehead, and when I drew it away for examination, it was pooled with blood. Rock had been thrown forward at impact and smashed his face on a corner of the inside engine compartment. His ankle was broken, and he was unconscious on the floor. Gary was shaken but physically all right.

I wanted to help Doug, who was obviously in a great deal of pain, but Gary and the unidentified man removed me from the van and put me into the stranger's car. Out of the smoke and weirdly aimed headlights I saw a figure staggering toward us—the driver of the other car. He jammed his head into the car window where I sat, still in shock, and said with a big grin, "What's happening, man?" You could smell the alcohol on his breath. I lost it. Somewhere inside I knew that Nicky was dead, that I couldn't stop Doug's screams, and that this drunken asshole had caused all this and didn't even care. I went after him, but it must have been in slow motion, because before I could swing, I found myself back being pulled back into the car and then we were hurrying off somewhere.

Rock, Gary, and I were taken to a hospital across the border in Sandisfield, Massachusetts. When the two vehicles collided, I had been pitched forward and had broken through the windshield. The action-reaction principle invoked itself, however, and I was pulled back through the broken glass to my seat. At the hospital, the doctors told me that my scalp had been torn open and that I had sustained a concussion. A fractured ankle was also discovered at the hospital, and both Rock and I had cuts around the eyes.

We were rushed into the emergency room, where they chopped off all my long hair and tried to comfort me. I lay there moaning in discomfort and worrying about Nicky and Doug. A Massachusetts state policeman came in with another stretcher carrying the operator of the car that had hit us, and I went crazy again. They calmed me down by agreeing to my demands for an alcohol blood level test on this bastard. I knew that somehow the blame would shift to the longhairs, unless we had some proof of his guilt, even though his slurred speech made it obvious to everyone in the room that he was completely drunk.

They worked on me for a few hours then wheeled me into a room that I was to share with Rock. He was out like a light when I arrived. His leg was in a cast and hoisted in the air, while his face bore stitches around the eyes and was swollen and bruised. They gave me something for the pain, and I quickly joined Rock in fitful slumber.

I awoke in the morning and instinctively reached up to touch my injured head. My God! It was huge. My head seemed to have inflated into the size of a beach ball while I'd slept. I buzzed for a nurse and saw her cheery smile disappear as she entered the room and focused her gaze on my bulbous dome. She scurried out the door and returned in seconds, accompanied by a team of white-clad medical technicians, who surrounded my bed and filled the air with *ooh* and *ah* sounds. Apparently, a nurse had spilled hydrogen peroxide onto my scalp just before the stitches were installed, and as a result during the night it had expanded. The doctors had two options to consider. They could remove the fifty-three stitches that were now holding my scalp together and start again, or administer salt tablets to try and reduce the swelling. My vote was for the salt pills, and the doctor must have agreed. The tablets were administered, and within a few hours my hat size was almost back to normal.

So far though, no one had volunteered any information about Nicky or Doug, so later in the evening I asked our nurse if she could tell us anything. The pain that flashed across her face was all the answer we needed as she gently informed us of our friends' fates. Nicky, we were told, had died instantly, crushed by the steering wheel. Doug's legs, which were dangling over the engine compartment, had been pinned between the engine and the unprotected front of the van. Two tow trucks had to be used to pry him from the wreck, and by that time his legs had turned black from the lack of blood circulation. She said that amputation was a strong possibility, and that Doug had been moved to a better-equipped hospital in Hartford, Connecticut. Rock and I turned our heads away from each other and cried ourselves to sleep. Maybe we would wake up to find this nightmare was just that—a very bad dream. But no, the next day came and with it the enormity of what had happened. The feeling just got worse.

We received treatment for a week and were released for the dreary ride home from the hospital with Rock's father, who had stayed with us throughout our recovery there. I had decided this would be my last road trip. I had lost my best friend, and whatever dreams we had together, on a lonely road in a tangle of twisted metal, and I didn't want to look back. I couldn't bear to.

Over the next few days, I retreated into myself, surfacing only to receive the wonderful news that Doug had not lost his legs. The initial prognosis was for amputation, but a brilliant bone specialist had been in residence at the Hartford hospital when Doug had arrived, and he insisted that the legs could be saved. Hours of surgery and three months in Hartford proved him right. Months more in a body cast and therapy put Doug on his feet again. But that was only the physical side. What mental torments he must have endured were impossible for anyone else to gauge.

Meanwhile, I looked like Frankenstein's monster, with my bald, stubby head, crisscrossed with dozens of stitches, and the blackened eyes and bruises that accentuated the Halloween mask staring back at me whenever I summoned up the courage to look in a mirror. I couldn't go anywhere for fear of being seen like that.

My first public appearance was sadly at a special commemorative funeral service held for Nicky. His brother Jim had kindly organized the belated ceremony for Rock and I, who had obviously been unable to attend the first one. This was the first time that the surviving members of the band (Doug was still recovering) were together since the accident. Even in passing, Nicky had somehow managed to rekindle some of the dream. Rock, Gary, and I decided then and there to carry on, if not for us, then for our fallen comrade.

We began to rehearse as a trio but knew that we would eventually need another musician. Doug was going to be unavailable for at least six more months, and we didn't know if he would want to be involved at all, but we kept a place open for him.

Once again, we looked at the pool of musicians in Cortland and set our sights on a piano player-cum-singer who fronted his own band called Mickey Lee and the Persians. He was a throwback to the honkytonk players that he patterned himself after, especially his hero Jerry Lee Lewis. We weren't sure how well a piano would work inside our music, but at least it was a radical idea, and we liked that. When we did our first shows together and it worked, we knew we were up and running again.

His full name was Mickey Lee Soule, and he was perfect for us. He and Gary were instinctively drawn together by their party attitudes. Life and women were to be enjoyed, and that enjoyment could have no limit placed upon it. Thanks to them, none ever was. Mickey Lee looked like a young Paul Newman, and his seemingly shy manner and blue eyes proved irresistible to almost every woman he met. We would look on with envy as every time we played Mickey Lee walked away with the best-looking woman in the place.

There were a few instances, however, when we most definitely did not want to be in his shoes. One such occasion was in the Olympic village of Lake Placid, New York. We were playing a club called Freddie's, the only real rock club in the little resort town whose population rose each winter as the snow fell. Groups of girls would take one- or two-week ski holidays to spend their days roaming the plentiful slopes of the Adirondack Mountains and their nights searching out the plentiful entertainment on offer. This was nirvana for Mickey Lee, as he scored night after night with one knockout snow bunny after another.

Freddie's provided us with an old two-story shack to sleep in that was right next to the club—and that always turned into party central when the gig was over. The club was usually filled to capacity by the time we started, so we'd have a full set to check out that night's talent. On this occasion, Mickey Lee spotted a table of average lookers with one standout sandwiched in the middle, and he was there in a flash when we finished our first collection of songs. She was beautiful, and we had never seen Mickey Lee work so hard to get a woman's attention before. He bought her and her friends drinks throughout the night and spent all his free time chatting her up. When at the end of the night he announced that he was "in," we were anything but surprised.

The lights always remained dim for about half an hour after our final set, and when they were turned on, it was a signal to collect our conquests and retire to the house next door. The girls at Mickey Lee's table all stood up with the exception of his "date." He patiently waited for her to rise and when she didn't, he said, "Well, I'm going next door now. Are you coming?" She said that of course she was, and it was then that we noticed she had actually been standing the whole time. Famed ladies' man Mickey Lee had pulled a dwarf!

Being the uncaring fools that we were then, we fell down with laughter as she waddled quickly on her little legs to catch Mickey Lee, who by this time was moving as fast as he could to escape the beautiful gnome. She broke into a distorted run and caught him as he fumbled for the key to the front door, and he was doomed, or so we thought. But Mickey Lee truly loved the opposite sex, and she certainly did qualify. They parted in the morning with contented smiles and promises of reuniting that night, but by then of course he had eyes for someone else.

We continued to move up the pay scale with our new lineup while we waited for Doug to recover. The area was still ripe with places to play, and all the work we threw ourselves into helped to slowly dull some of the pain we could never wholly forget. This took precedence over stubbornness and pride, and we gladly played sets of covers at any venue that would pay us, slipping in an original here and there. You could go under the radar like that in those days. Polish your act by drastically cutting the songs you discovered were crap and ramping up the stuff that really worked.

Doug eventually limped back into the band, picking up guitar again as Mickey now handled all the keyboards. He also brought with him some songs he had written while he had been laid up. His injuries had left him stiff in one leg and had made him even more eccentric than before.

On the road, we now stayed at hotels like Marriott, Holiday Inn, and Howard Johnson's. Along the way, we started to collect an odd assortment of road crew and technicians. At first, they traveled with us to share the nightlife, the spotlight, and the driving. It wasn't considered a career opportunity at the time. Traveling with a working band was just a good hang. Most of our budding crew were barely capable of doing more than drinking beer and rolling joints and had to be replaced as we went along.

Igor was typical of our fledging roadies. Igor wasn't his real name; we never found that out. Igor was just what everyone called him, due to his large hulking presence, with a flattened nose and twisted mouth and a voice that was like Lurch from *The Addams Family*. But a sweeter guy you could not find. Igor was cool. Unfortunately, being cool doesn't always equate with an ability to do one thing right. Gary— of course it was Gary—had befriended Igor in a bar one night and had such a good time he told him that he could have the pleasure of hanging out with us in exchange for the loading and setting up of our gear. Igor didn't have to be told twice and suddenly we had another employee on the road with us.

Igor had been working for us (we found it cheaper to pay him than feed him) for about a year when we were able to buy a new truck. Our prior vehicles had always been old second-hand jalopies, expensive to maintain and unreliable, so you can imagine our excitement and joy at owning this sparkling new beauty. Igor would drive the truck with all the equipment early to the gigs so that we could follow much later in the car. Then we'd reverse the process at the end of the night; car with band in it first, truck with all the gear second.

It was one such special day (and night and early morning) that finally spelled the end of Igor's time with us.

We were booked at the Heater in Wellsville on Saturday, but couldn't spend the night and had to drive home following the gig. We left Igor to pack up our stuff and bring it back with the truck that night.

While loading the truck, Igor became deeply smitten with one of the many girls who had crowded around the stage door. They began talking, Igor fell in love, and when she said she wanted to go back to Cortland—she wanted to meet Gary—but had no ride, Igor had a great idea. He would give her a lift back in the truck. The girl was only too delighted.

Returning home to Cortland in the early hours, Igor and his new girlfriend scoured the neighborhood in search of Gary. As usual, the rest of us were tucked into our beds, with visions of major record deals dancing in our new heads. And just as usual, Gary was out somewhere, with Igor trying to find him for his newfound fixation. The two of them searched for hours. No dice.

Finally, at around six in the morning, Igor admitted defeat and gallantly offered to drive the disappointed girl back to Wellsville in our still-instrument-filled truck. He dropped her off and then, coincidentally near the Heater, where all of this began, he claimed that a deer ran in front of him, and in an effort to avoid it, he swerved off the road and landed on a concrete abutment. The truck's undersides were ripped apart as it skidded loudly onto the concrete piling, and just before it crashed into a telephone pole, the twelve-foot aluminum box carrying our precious gear was slashed open by trees and torn partly off the truck bed.

My phone rang at around ten that bright Sunday morning. It was Igor. He asked if we planned to rehearse on Monday, and when I said that we did, he informed with a maniacal grunt that actually we would not be rehearsing on Monday after all. Because, he explained in his deep, graveyard voice, he had just smashed the truck and destroyed all its contents. Another band-related road crash. How many times can lightning strike you? I asked Igor if he was all right. It was hard to tell from his voice, which sounded as low and doomy as ever. He assured me that he was, having come away with only a few scrapes and bruises.

When he told me that it had happened in Wellsville, I asked why he hadn't called last night. "I didn't want to worry you," said Igor. Sweet guy.

I was desperate to know the condition of our gear, but he wasn't sure. I called Doug and we rented a truck to bring Igor and our equipment back to Cortland. He had called a tow truck, and we were to meet him at the junkyard to view what remained of our means of livelihood. When we arrived, a partially banged-up Igor took us to our totally banged-up truck, where he used his big hands to pry open the back doors so we could see what damage we had to deal with. As we looked, my heart sank. Everything was in bits, as though there had been an explosion inside the box. We were ruined again. No truck, no instruments, and now no work.

On the extra-long ride back to Cortland, Igor owned up to the truth. Doug and I remained silent but became increasingly pissed off. I drove Doug to his door, and after promising to call him, headed in Igor's direction. I pulled up in front of his house and silently waited for him to open his door and leave—never to return. Unwelcome. Dismissed. Excused. Forever. As he got out, he turned to me and said, "Does this mean my job is in danger?" Very sweet guy.

Of the guys that worked on the road with me and the Prophets back then and that did make the grade as professional roadies, the best was Raymond D'Darrio. Raymond became our soundman and jack-of-all-trades and eventually stayed with me throughout the years of my next two bands. He was serious about his work and was a musician as well. Raymond's reliability became unquestioned when he was busted for a tiny bit of pot on the way to a gig, and still made the performance after spending hours under arrest at a police station. Being busted for pot—even such a small amount—was a much more serious crime at this point in time. The fact that he walked from that straight to the gig and got everything right on the night, without making a big deal of it, said all you need to know about the kind of guy you really need on the road, where everything that can go wrong absolutely will, and more than once.

Raymond was so good we let him hire and fire his on-tour helpers as became necessary, until he found a returning Vietnam veteran named David Needle, who became a permanent part of our family.

David was a former frontline medic who occasionally had battle flashbacks when he drank too much. But after all the "bar wars" we'd been through as a band, David seemed quite normal to us, and another great guy to have on your side in a tight spot.

Still there was trouble brewing in paradise. With my usual "How could anyone not want to do this forever?" attitude firmly to the fore, I hadn't noticed the musical problems now occurring between Gary and Rock—and Doug. Doug had continued to be the one reliable source of original music within the band and had presented us with several well-structured songs he'd already worked out arrangements for.

Our first single as the Electric Elves had set the bar high; an anthemic number Doug wrote and arranged called "Hey, Look Me Over." It was inspired by "Substitute" by the Who, which had been a hit in the UK and several other countries—but not the US. Maybe if it had been a hit for us, the Who would have been tagged as "inspired" by the Electric Elves when they came to America for the first time that same year. Except it wasn't a hit. Nor was the next single, another Doug original called "She's Not the Same." It was more of an orchestrated pop ballad, more Walker Brothers than the Who, but still not a hit. Undeterred, we recorded another Doug original as our next single, another upbeat orchestral pop song, leaning more towards the Monkees at this point, called "Amber Velvet"—"A beautiful name for a beautiful girl...." Again, not a hit.

Meanwhile, we had shortened our name to simply the Elves. Doug took charge of the live show, too, which featured originals but still relied mainly on crowd-pleasing covers. He'd have the set lists laid out for us. All we had to do was learn them and rehearse them, then straight out that night to perform them. Our few days off were not meant to be spent *writing* and *arranging* or even thinking too much about music. Doug was into it, and we were grateful for that. But we weren't going to stay indoors all day *writing* or choosing *set lists*. Not when we could be partying our brains out somewhere! What were we in a band for if it wasn't for that?

What I didn't know was that Rock, the most dissatisfied of the lot, had been noodling around for a while with some ideas for songs but had not told us about it, and so we had carried on with Doug's material and whatever covers he chose for us to play. Under Doug's musical tutelage, we had reached a pretty advanced stage where we would cover entire albums instead of the few hits that came from those records. We could perform the Who's *Tommy* from beginning to end. The Beatles' *Abbey Road* was done in the same manner. Doug combined different themes into one-hour sets. Audiences were stunned at the ambitiousness of our shows. We were stunned by it too, and as always, we were really good at it.

But dark clouds were rolling in.

Our policy was to bring whatever cover or original song any of us wanted to submit for consideration to the first rehearsal of the week. At one particular practice, Rock had brought in a Humble Pie album, featuring the brilliant former Small Faces frontman Steve Marriott and hot new guitarist Peter Frampton (recently voted "Most Handsome Man" in England). Rock played us a track from it he thought we might want to do called "Stone Cold Fever," a swaggeringly juicy and full-on rocker from one of the funkiest rock bands ever—and Doug went ballistic. Completely lost it. Doug suggested that Rock invest in a jackhammer to dislodge the concrete that had blocked up his ears and caused him to suggest that we waste our time learning this enormous pile of excrement. Doug ranted and raved for a few more minutes, glared menacingly at Rock, who had been stunned into silence like the rest of us, then limped up the stairs and out the door, having left us with an ultimatum. It was either Doug's way or the highway.

The door slammed as we turned to each other in astonishment.

Gary was the first to speak, saying out loud what we were all thinking. "What have we done?" Gary the party animal, so surprisingly articulate at this crisis moment, even sensitive. "Fuck him," he said. And so we did.

Elves: Me, Rock, Gary, Mickey Lee, and Doug Thaler.

SEVEN

PURPLE DAZE

*I*f there was one defining moment that became the gateway to my musical future, it was when Doug Thaler left the Electric Elves and I was forced into helping the band come up with some original material. This was not easy. Doug had been so in charge of that role we had become dependent on him. Now we were left to fend for ourselves.

Musically, we were pared down to what proved to be our best working order: a power trio with honky-tonk piano. It was 1971 and the fashion was for hard-edged rock bands that could deliver good times, good musicianship, and—hopefully—good songs. We knew Rock had been onto something by playing us that Humble Pie album. We also looked at where bands like Led Zeppelin, Deep Purple, and the Faces were now heading, musically. Even groups that had made it as singles bands in the '60s like the Stones and the Who were now flexing their muscles musically. The whole scene had gotten *heavier*, bluesier, more freewheeling.

Our first step in our new direction was, as usual, to change the name of the band—from the Elves to simply Elf. Somehow, to our ears anyway, Elf sounded heavier, more gang-like and self-assured than the Elves. Like: What's that you're listening to, man? Elf? Far out. Yeah, everyone digs Elf, man.

We had everything we needed to forge this new, more ballsy musical path. Everything, that is, except songs. Rock told us he had a few things he'd worked on but had been afraid to show us previously for fear of a sarcastic ear-bashing from Doug. "Don't be crazy," we told him, "let's hear 'em." When he played the first one for us, we all gave silent thanks that Rock had kept it from Doug's ears. The title alone would have triggered a Doug-sized meltdown. It was called "Sit Down Honey (Everything Will Be Alright)." But that didn't matter to us then. It was the simplicity of the melody and chord changes and the way we played it that opened the door to a freedom of personal and group expression that none of us had ever experienced before. If it had happened five years earlier we wouldn't have been good enough to pull off the sudden shift in direction that Rock's song led us to.

We must have banged on that first tune for hours, shaping it, refining it, and loving it. Like Rod and the Faces meets Humble Pie, our grins just got bigger every time we played it. Rock had another great one as well, "Dixie Lee Junction," which again was very much in the early Faces and Humble Pie mode—blues, but with a lot of hard-rocking soul. Rock got the title by blindly stabbing at a map of the US and landing on the small Tennessee town of the same name. Again, we played it over and over, wringing as much pleasure out of it as we could before it was time to stop for the day. We spent the rest of the night excitedly talking and planning for our next assault at a local bar. We decided we would never again play anyone's material but our own. This put a severe dent in our ability to play for any length of time without repeating ourselves, but it demonstrated our new, punchier attitude.

I now felt much more comfortable as a collaborator when it came to writing. Rock had his thing going, so Mickey Lee and I became song-writing partners. We wrote quite a few pieces on a Wurlitzer electric piano, in an out-of-the-way motel room that Mickey Lee was living in at the time. The instrument's warm, milder sound made it harder to write big block-chord guitar-based tunes, but it helped me immeasurably in learning how to substitute any sounds for its intended instrument in my head, especially guitar, a handy skill to have in the coming years when I would work with some of the best guitarists in the world.

We loved what Mickey Lee played, but an electric piano was lost and out of place alongside Rock's guitar, my bass, and Gary's drums. We were told about some pickups that were used to amplify an acoustic piano, and so, not to put the cart before the horse, we bought a baby grand piano whose legs were removable and that could be loaded on its side into a truck (provided you had the inevitable hydraulic tailgate). We located the pickup, bought it, and—wonder of wonders—it worked. Now we had the weight of the piano sound being blasted through onstage amplification.

My voice also changed around this time, becoming a little more gravelly and more like the real me. It suited our new music, and the more I went in that direction the more natural and right it felt. It was as though I'd been doing it the way I *thought* a singer should sound back then. As Elf began to take off in the '70s, my real voice finally came to the fore. Suddenly I was far less self-conscious about how it *should* sound and just allowed my real voice to express itself without boundaries. For the first time, I was singing from the heart.

By now we had enough material and room to jam for another sixty minutes at least, but we needed to test ourselves by playing the new original material live for the first time. With the safety-catch off: no covers.

We accepted a booking at a club outside of Binghamton called The Inferno. We had played there a few years before and remembered it as a place where dance was still king. We also recalled that the club owner had very sensitive ears. Armed with three-quarters of a set and a possibly hostile environment, we took to the stage not knowing what to expect. It was amazing from the get-go. The tables had been pushed aside and the audience was seated cross-legged on the floor.

They were there to listen. Serious heads. *Wow*, I remember thinking. *What have we done?*

We turned on our amps, checked to see if Mickey Lee and Gary were turned on, and jumped straight into the deep end. The reaction was instant, magic, unbelievable, and above all, heavy. It was an overused word at the time, but this really was—heavy as in a defining moment of my life: the first honest contract with an audience, take us or leave us, no more hiding behind covers, all our own stink—and the first acceptance of our own creation. Incredible!

But we had only gotten started. One of Rock's favorite bands of the time was Blue Cheer, whose Hendrix-style "Summertime Blues" was now an established rock anthem. Live, they had so much amplification and were so unbelievably loud that when they played in New York you heard them as far away as London. Unfortunately for Blue Cheer it didn't work out for them much beyond that, but it will give you an idea of the excruciating volume Rock liked to play at.

I had no problem with playing at maximum volume, but I wanted the sound to be balanced so that people could still hear us clearly. So we invested in eight 200-watt Marshall lead amps and four 200-watt Marshall Major bass amplifiers with two dozen 4x12 cabinets to match them. When this still wasn't good enough, we went to consult the master, John Stillwell.

Dawk, as he insisted on being called, was the guru of instrument and amplification modification. He worshiped at the altar of insane volume. Anyone who came to Dawk for advice on their gear had to first pass his stringent tests. If you played loud and wanted to be louder, you were probably all right, but beware the gentle musician. He would be berated for being "corn" (one of Dawk's most insulting words for weak levels of sound and attitude) and sent unceremoniously on his way. You can imagine the love affair he had with us.

Dawk immediately took it upon himself to boost all our amps from 200 watts to 375 watts. They generated so much heat that each amp had to have two fans specially installed to prevent them shutting down. He built us a PA system to handle the enormous sound avalanching from the stage and modified a power booster he called "The Hog" to help Rock achieve his goal of death by volume.

Wherever Elf played (barring absolute size restriction) we would set up our twenty-four cabinets. In smaller, more intimate spaces, the sound of twenty-four fans powering up simultaneously was loud on its own, but only a whisper compared to what would shortly come pounding from them. The mini-people with the sound of giants.

Along with the change in musical direction—and name—came a change in our look. We had moved pretty far away from the clean-cut image we'd had in the first half of the '60s, as had everybody else in America under the age of thirty. Even so, the four of us were a rough-looking bunch at this time. Gary, Rock, and I had full beards that matched our extremely long hair, and we dressed in our street gear (torn jeans and T-shirts). In the UK, glam rock and glitter was now holding sway, but it hadn't quite reached our corner of the world yet, thank god. It took a long time to grow all that hair. We were in no special hurry to chop it all off and start applying eyeliner, lipstick, and rouge.

We continued to play college fraternity parties, but soon moved up to concerts at these same universities. We were booked at a Connecticut college to open for the fast-rising Elton John and his band, and it was unforgettable. Guitarist Davey Johnstone, bassist Dee Murray, drummer Nigel Olsson, and Elton were at the top of their form and amazed everyone with their great harmonies, wonderful feel, and brilliant songs. If this was on-the-job training, I concluded, then the job must really be sweet.

Our manager, Bruce, had taken a position in New York City as an agent for the powerful rock agency ATI (American Talent International), which gave him ample opportunity to book Elf, but we all felt that recording all this great new original material we had written should be our next step, so Bruce set about securing a deal. He arranged an audition with then-Columbia president Clive Davis.

At the time, Clive was the hippest record label exec in the business. Since attending the Monterey Pop Festival in the summer of

1967, Clive had personally signed Janis Joplin, Laura Nyro, Electric Flag, Santana, and around the same time he was talking to Bruce about Elf, he was in the process of signing an unknown new band out of Boston called Aerosmith, and an even-less-well-known scruffy singer-songwriter from New Jersey named Bruce Springsteen. While it's fair to say that Clive's golden touch never quite worked its magic for Elf, the meeting was the catalyst for the completely unexpected events that would soon lead to the next phase of my musical journey.

The beginnings were certainly auspicious. In October 1971, Deep Purple was just beginning a US tour when singer Ian Gillan became ill with hepatitis, forcing its cancellation for three months. Bassist Roger Glover and drummer Ian Paice decided to stay on in New York for a few days before going home to England. Bruce handled the bookings for Purple at ATI, and so had a close relationship with the lads and asked them if they'd like to attend the audition of one of his bands with the potential of doing a production deal with Deep Purple's recently launched record label, Purple Records. That is, assuming Roger and Ian liked what they saw and heard. After all, they weren't exactly busy with the band off the road.

Bruce told us a few minutes before they arrived that two of our musical heroes would be there to judge us, as well as the imposing Clive Davis. No pressure, then. With nerves jangling and eyes fixed straight ahead, we ran through our best numbers. Before we knew it, hands were being vigorously shaken and smiles were wider than the sky. Roger was brimming with praise for our songs and performances and talked confidently about signing Elf to Purple's label in the UK, while Clive signed us on the spot to his Columbia offshoot, Epic, who would release Elf in America. Then we booked our first recording date for his label.

After years of busting my ass just trying to catch a break, refusing to be thwarted by car crashes, ego, and death, when the big deal finally came, it happened so quickly I don't know if I really felt fulfilled. If it had happened five years before I would have seen it as the dream coming true, but I was nearly thirty now, and instead of savoring the memories that got me there, I immediately looked towards the future and what we still had to do to succeed. The curse of the driven. I knew that being on a major label was only the start, that we still had a long way to go.

But, of course, I celebrated with the band all the way home. More than 250 miles of blizzard snow in a car with no heater and a van with bad brakes, but to us they had already been mentally transformed into a Rolls Royce and a Peterbilt. We arranged to meet at our local hangout, the Midway, the next evening, to really celebrate and brag to the guys in local bands who hadn't done what we just had. Gary had the bartender estimate how many bottles of champagne it would take to serve all the customers and had them lined up along the bar. Then he dropped and smashed each one as he walked the length of the place intoning a strange mantra, "easy street, easy street." All our troubles, washed away by bubbles flowing down Easy Street.

Arrangements were made to record the first Elf album in Atlanta, Georgia, at Studio One, which was actually in Doraville, a suburban hamlet northeast of Atlanta. Most of us had never flown before but we were so excited by what was to come that it was no bother at all. Poor fools! Little did we know our first flight would be one we would never forget.

The plane took off from Hancock Field in Syracuse and leisurely winged its way to JFK while we filled up on the free drinks they used to supply on cheap domestic flights in the good old days. We changed planes in New York, from the puddle jumper we arrived in to a shiny and powerful-looking jet. Four hours later we fastened our seatbelts and stubbed out our cigarettes as the plane readied to land in Atlanta. Looking out the windows, we could see the airport below, but the plane seemed to be going in circles around it for ages. Finally, the pilot came on the speaker system to explain why we hadn't landed yet. He said the landing gear wouldn't come down, and that we would have to land without it. Perfect, I thought. Another chance to dance with death. We were ordered to remove our shoes and position ourselves with head between legs, and while we prayed, the plane began its fitful approach. We came down on a bed of foam and skidded for what seemed like an eternity before finally the great metal bird came thudding to a halt. Nobody on board was hurt. The band was fine. It wasn't our time yet. We had an album to make.

We checked into our motel, got a rental car, and drove straight to the studio. It was pretty much how I expected it to be: a giant room to record in with a huge moving module only for the drums and a control room that looked as if it could power a starship. A producer-writer named Buddy Buie owned Studio One, which was home to what was fast becoming known as the Atlanta Sound, epitomized by bands like the Classics IV and, later that same year, the Atlanta Rhythm Section. The players in these bands were always hanging around the studio, bringing a very positive energy with them, making the place come alive.

Roger and Ian spent most of the first day in the studio getting the sounds of the instruments together, and late in the evening we were finally able to play and record a song the whole way through. We put it on tape and found it to be pretty good as it was. We had recorded the entire band playing and singing as if it were a gig, and it became the method we used to do almost the whole album.

On the weekends, we would head for Atlanta to taste the nightlife that Roger and Ian knew all about from the touring that Deep Purple had done in the area. The club of choice was Finocchio's, which featured live music and lots of live women, all of whom, as usual, needed to be with Mickey Lee.

We finished the album in a little over a month. Thirty-plus days of nirvana. From which came eight of the bluesiest, boogiest, most rocking and rolling tracks anyone had ever heard. Well, that's how it seemed to us at the time. There was "Sit Down Honey (Everything Will Be Alright)" and "Dixie Lee Junction," of course. Along with five other tracks that matched them in terms of upbeat, raw, and gritty rock a la Free, Faces, Humble Pie, and the rest. Plus one track that pointed to the possibility of something more from the band. A piano-led soul-baring epic Rock and Mickey had cooked up called "Never

More." This was our attempt to add credibility and depth to our existing repertoire, proof that beneath our carefree musical glad-rags Elf had real substance, including time changes, crescendos, and suitably "meaningful" lyrics penned by me: "Hell and fire burning higher / Now I can see the ever after...."

Okay, it wasn't exactly "Stairway to Heaven," but, as far as we were concerned, it showed we were on the right path. Armed with our masterpieces, we flew nervously back to New York and waited for whatever was supposed to happen next. We hadn't planned beyond the recording. Fortunately for us, however, Bruce had. Our first album, imaginatively titled *Elf*, would be released on Purple Records in Britain and Europe, and on Epic in the US. Happy and assured as we were to have Clive Davis in our corner, what really thrilled us was to be signed to Deep Purple's own record label. Roger and Ian had proudly taken the music they had produced for us back home and played it for Jon Lord, Ian Gillan, and Ritchie Blackmore, who all thought it worthy of signing. Amazing! Easy street for real!

The next order of business was to come up with some cover art for the record sleeve. More convinced than ever that our aim was true, Rock and I decided that we were best qualified to do the job. What we needed, we agreed, was a picture of—wait for it—an elf. Not just any elf, obviously. Certainly not the kind of elf that wore pointed shoes and hats and toiled at the cobbler's bench or was there merely to help Santa. My personal concept of the kind of elf we'd named the band after was the always-secretive creature that shunned civilization. The kind of elf that spelled danger. Not necessarily an evil elf, but an elf you might think twice about messing with.

When it was suggested that I actually dress up as this elf, I went with it. I was the frontman, after all. Who else was gonna do it? Rock and I went to a theatrical makeup shop in New York to begin my transformation into our Elf character. We bought a ton of facial putty for the nose and ears, and I got ready for the makeover. We constructed a long, pointed nose with ears to match and attached them to my existing parts. We did all this with great seriousness. When we were done, and I looked in the mirror, the gruesome image that gazed back at me was just what we wanted—a most fearsome-looking elf.

We loaded Rock's photo equipment into his car and set off to find a secluded wooded area (not too difficult in Cortland) to take the pictures. While still in the city, we were able to frighten the life out of anyone who pulled up next to us, proving once again that we had conjured up a monster. We realized that clothing was not an option for the creature. A plaid shirt and scuffed jeans simply didn't work, so off came my shirt and pants. I hunched over and glared menacingly into Rock's camera and he took the photo that would forever become our logo.

Now we waited, for the album sleeve to come through, and for the finished album to be pressed and delivered, all of it taking so much longer than we had the patience to handle. We pushed Bruce for answers: When the album is finally released, what happens then? Where do we tour? And how, on our own or opening for a bigger band? And if so, which band? When? What? How? But mainly, when? In the meantime, we continued playing our basic gigs. Round and round the same circuit we now knew backward.

Then, in July 1972, Deep Purple were playing in Providence, Rhode Island, which was only about 300 miles away from Cortland and, compared to some of our jaunts, relatively close. Roger Glover and Ian Paice invited us to the show to see them both again, and to meet the rest of the band. We met Jon Lord first, who turned out to be one of the most gracious men I've ever known. An awesome talent, and an even nicer human being. Ritchie Blackmore and Ian Gillan were going through their usual "I hate you" routine, so both were rather brusque and private.

Then came the show, and we were blown away. What a band Deep Purple was in its prime. Their latest album, *Machine Head*, was one of the biggest hits in America that year (the same album from which came the all-time classic "Smoke on the Water"), and the band was on fire. Great material, brilliant musicianship, full of improvisation and spontaneity, Purple in concert was all we imagined and more. This was what we wanted to be, and their performance gave us the boost we needed to be a bit more patient and wait for our chance to come.

Then, right out of the blue, it happened. *Elf* came out just a few weeks after that Purple show, and, along with it, thanks to Bruce, because we were on the band's label and it was in their interest to make it a success, we were booked to do some shows opening for Purple in the States. This was it: our opportunity to shine on the Big Stage. At last! Hold the front page! Elf was coming to a town near you!

We began with nine shows mostly on the East Coast, plus a handful in Florida, Georgia, and Virginia. These were three- or sometimes four-band bills, with Elf as openers, including half a dozen with Fleetwood Mac sandwiched between Purple and us. After that, Purple returned to the UK to tour but when they resumed the next leg of their US tour in November, Elf were there again to open for them: thirteen shows this time, including a couple in Canada.

Plus, and this really did feel special, opening for them at the Palace Theater in Waterbury. As we sat in our small dressing room before the show, I couldn't help but think back to the very first time I had gigged in Waterbury, at the old Sugar Shack, with Ronnie Dio and the Prophets. And, of course, that fateful night after our show at Guggie's, when Nicky lost his life in that awful car crash.

I put it all behind me, though, when we took to the stage. By now we had got the hang of what to do as the opening act for a superstar outfit like Deep Purple. We had prepared our set well in advance, which consisted entirely of our unproven new recordings, and polished them until they were second nature.

With Purple, we crisscrossed the US in our Pontiac station wagon with a new box for our gear on the roof. We had taken a friend, Ronnie Karesner, with us to road manage the trip, so we now had to pay for five instead of only four Elves. We somehow managed to finish the tour with little or no bother except for a stop in Dallas, in late November.

We very rarely stayed in a motel or hotel room, we just piled back into the Pontiac and told Karesner to put his foot down. This time, though, there was a day off after the show, so we decided to treat ourselves. We got one room and spent the night, rising early to begin the nine-hour drive to the next show in Kansas City.

Unknown to the rest of us, Gary had taken a pillow from the room for more comfort in the car. We had just finished loading our luggage into the car, but as Ronnie Karesner prepared to reverse it out of the parking spot, we were suddenly surrounded by police cars full of armed officers who promptly ordered us to vacate the automobile with our hands up! The motel manager had called them, suspecting us of theft, and lo and behold, up popped the pillow. Gary was arrested on the spot and taken to the local police station where he was booked as a pillow bandit. It cost us a $150 fine to get Gary released, and we didn't even get to keep the pillow.

Despite my years on the road as a singer in various lineups, playing all types of shows to all kinds of people, opening for Deep Purple on a major American tour was like going back to school again. Musically and performance-wise, we learned at the feet of masters, especially Ritchie Blackmore. His command of an audience and his amazing aura, coupled with his enormous ability on his trademark white Fender Stratocaster (a gift from Eric Clapton, he told us) were the standards by which we now gauged ourselves. With Ritchie and Purple guiding us, we were on our way.

After the Purple tour, we played some shows opening for Alice Cooper, another band having the best year of their lives with their million-selling *School's Out* album and hit single. Then we did a brief US tour opening for Uriah Heep, another British heavy rock band in the mold of Purple who had just had their first chart album in America.

The shows with Alice Cooper, in particular, were astounding. This was the original band known collectively as Alice Cooper, but Alice the frontman was already the star of the show. This was also our introduction to glam rock and a much more theatrical presentation for a rock show. Alice was hanged at one show we did with them, and then they upgraded it to an electrocution in another. It might sound tame to twenty-first-century rock audiences, but in 1972, this was the first time anyone had seen anything like that. It was the indelible memories of these shows that would later become the catalyst for some of the Dio productions of the '80s.

As a result of all these high-profile shows, and because we had an album out that we could point people to, Elf gained a good following in some areas of the US. Every time we played a place, our album would sell copies there. We could feel the momentum slowly building as the band just got better and better.

Our next big showcase was in Los Angeles at the famous Whisky a Go Go on Sunset Boulevard. Five shows, last week of December, including New Year's Eve, opening for the all-female band Fanny. It was a great spot to get: partly because the existence of an all-female rock band was virtually unheard of at the time, mainly because they were really good, and there was a really strong buzz about them which we hoped to capitalize on.

We couldn't afford to fly the band and its equipment to LA, so as usual, we drove the 3,000 miles that separated Cortland from LA. It took three days and nights. When we finally got to LA, we went straight into the hotel. It was a large high-rise on Sunset with a swimming pool on the roof called the Hyatt House. We discovered that the Hyatt was the place known by all the bands who stayed there as the Riot House, after the exploits of Led Zeppelin drummer John Bonham, who liked to toss TVs out the window when he wasn't riding his motorcycle down the corridor, and the Who's Keith Moon, who liked to stock his bathtub with piranha fish, when he wasn't trying to drive a Roll's Royce into the swimming pool. (Not so easy with the pool on the roof, but if anyone could have done it, Moony could.)

The Whisky was just down the Boulevard from the hotel, and we dutifully took our gear to the club to prepare for the first night's show. We carried our full complement of amps and got a little worried when we saw the tiny corner stage in the Whisky, but we squeezed all the cabinets in anyway and did a quick run-through. The owner of the club, the soon-to-be legendary Mario Maglieri, came bounding out of his office and told us that we were grossly over-amplified and that we should remove some of our Marshall stacks. We objected, but after some "discussion" agreed to each lose one.

We fired up and broke into another song, at which point Mario, hands now clamped over his ears, demanded that we lose more power. It was still too loud, he said with a serious face. We had come this far, we thought, let's just get through the first night then think about it. We reluctantly removed another cabinet, and once again began to play.

Again Mario objected. "You gotta lose another amp!"

This was too much for us. We were a power band! Not some easy-listening folk-rock group. We absolutely refused to take away another amp.

"Fuck off, Mario!" I told him. "We're going home..."

Mario looked at me with a furrowed brow then asked if I was Italian. When I told him I was, he laughed and said he understood now why I was such a hothead! Mario, it goes without saying, was also from the Old Country, born in Sepino, in the poor Italian south, nearly fifty years before. Mario was a tough guy, but he was also smart and funny. He told us to leave the gear up and play the show. This would be the start of a special relationship between Mario and I that would last for the rest of our lives.

When we finished, Mario suggested that we might like to try another place he owned a couple doors down, called the Rainbow Bar & Grill. The Rainbow would quickly become the numero uno rock hangout in LA. For any band from out of town, and many that actually lived in town, the Rainbow would become their LA home away from home. No one had a hometown club like the Rainbow. It would become a pivotal place in my life just a few years later. We'll get to that later.

We all sat there that first night in one of the club's red booths, spread out around one of their half-moon tables, drinking and bragging to anybody who would listen about our coming gigs at the Whisky, and inviting everybody to come and check out the best new rock band in America. (I think I mentioned we'd been drinking.) We dragged ourselves out when the joint closed at 2:00 a.m. and got a cab back to the two adjoining rooms we had at the Hyatt.

At about five in the morning, a very loud knocking at the door awakened us. We opened it groggy-eyed to find a bunch of cops with their guns pointed at us. They yelled at us to lie face down on the floor *now*, hands behind heads. They roughed us up a little, nothing too painful, just very threatening. They said we would be arrested and cuffed as soon as they found what they were looking for. What were they looking for? We sure as hell didn't know. Whatever it was, they never did find it—because, as we later found out, they had the wrong rooms! Welcome to Los Angeles.

Elf's first gig at the Whisky was horrible. Mario was right. We were too loud. We at least seemed to please some of the audience and took that away as a positive. The regulars at the Whisky were connoisseurs. Every great band in the world had played there, so we adapted the set, and the rest of the shows got better every night. So did our after-show activities at the Rainbow. The waitresses, all very pretty and friendly, seemed to have their own personal connections to the rock biz, and the only rule for the musicians seemed to be that there were no rules—ever.

We arrived in Cortland three days after leaving LA and settled back into our lives for a while. I was married to my first wife, Loretta, at this point, and I knew my constant absence must have been a trial for her. We lived next door to Rock and his girl, and we would hang out. Time slowed and suddenly Elf wasn't on his mind so much, it seemed to me. We didn't rehearse much anymore, and all talk of things to come was sidestepped.

Eventually I got Rock alone one-on-one and asked what the situation was. To my horror, he said he was leaving the band. That was it for me. The first person to share my dream, Nicky, was gone. The next, Rock, was now going. It flattened me. I was so overwhelmed I wasn't sure I was up to another challenge. Time to settle down, raise a family, enjoy a so-called normal life, maybe; I thought. Sure, why not? I was in my early thirties; I'd given it my best shot.

We had just bought our first house. It was small, but sparkling new. It had an unfinished basement and no garage, and for now I spent all my time making a family room and building a place for the car. Then what, though? The choices were pretty straightforward. Go to work at the steel mill, go back to school, live in hell forever.

I had been listening to some new music with a drummer and good friend, Mark Nauseef. Mark was an extremely bright young kid who'd had a taste of being a professional musician in the final line-up of the Velvet Underground. Lou Reed and all the other original members had long gone, but Mark joined the band for a final tour of the UK in 1972. Back in Cortland, Mark idolized Gary as a player and was amazed by his and Mickey Lee's antics whenever they got together. So much so that they moved into a tiny two-bedroom apartment together. It was the original train depot of the Erie-Lackawanna Railroad Line that ran through Cortland. What a dump! It was on top of a greasy spoon restaurant that catered to the railroad workers, and the smell of cheap frying oil permeated every pore of the rooms above. Doug Thaler had dubbed the flat "Buckingham Toilet." The name stuck and it became our new meeting place. Suffice it to say, one thing led to another, it was in the cards, the die was cast, and, just like that, I was back in the game.

I had decided, however, that I didn't want to play bass anymore. I was a singer now. I had proved myself, but I couldn't turn myself into a proper frontman if I had to keep holding onto a guitar. That meant finding another bass player. Fortunately, there was one we really liked playing in Mark's band. His name was Craig Gruber. Craig had great chops and was a much more modern player than I could ever be. There was one problem. Craig was very loyal to Mark's keyboard player, Dave "Bo" Bohash, and wouldn't leave without him.

Solution: let's join the two bands together!

Gary Driscoll and me.

──✛ EIGHT ✛──
· · · · · · ·

LA 59

The first objective for the revitalized Elf was finding a place to rehearse. Cortland was not geared for noisy things, so I contacted some relatives who lived in a tiny town six miles north of the city called East Homer. Almost everyone who lived there was either family or a friend, so volume was not a problem. We set up in the biggest area we could find, which happened to be an actively used barn. It was the middle of summer, and the heat and bugs made it unbearable at times, but we were a band, and that made it all right.

The second objective for the new Elf was to find a guitar player. Mark Nauseef's group only had Dave Bohash's Hammond B-3, Craig Gruber's bass, and Mark's drums. Bo suggested a player from Utica, about an hour's drive from Cortland, named Steve Edwards. Stevie was more of a Jeff Beck, *Wired*-era guitarist; he was into jazz-rock fusion and had the chops to pull it off. Musically, this was a foreign country to Gary, Mickey Lee, and me. Bo was into it and so was Mark, who joined us on percussion. But we now had a band with two totally different styles that we tried in vain to blend together. Suddenly

97

rehearsing at Buckingham Toilet took on new meaning for us. We stunk! I'd like to blame it on the odor, but it soon became evident that this was the wrong combination.

We kept at it diligently, though, until reality finally broke the spell when we were offered the opportunity to record another album for Purple Records. I knew that, come what may, we had to make this work, but that would only be the case if we reverted to the style that had won Elf the deal with Purple in the first place. Reluctantly, we said goodbye to Dave Bohash and pared down to more Elfish dimensions: Gary on drums, Mickey Lee on piano, Craig Gruber on bass, Steve Edwards on guitar, and Mark Nauseef playing percussion.

Musically, we suddenly recaptured our mojo. Personality-wise, though, we were a weird bunch. Gary and Mickey Lee were the kind of personalities that filled every room they walked—or fell—into. Craig was another funny, talented guy, except he hated everyone and everything. Craig was the guy who always seemed to get punched just because he was there. Stevie was thoughtful and introspective, and when asked once by our English publicist what he wanted from life, he mulled it over carefully before replying: "Uh...a rock star's life, I guess." Well, at least he had a goal.

Mark was a dynamo, on top of all kinds of music and filled with optimism about this band. A great drummer in his own right, he was happy to take the role of percussionist and defer to his mentor, Gary. We set on the road getting more and more comfortable with each other and looking forward to a new recording and hopefully a fresh start to our career.

We had already decided the album was to be called *Carolina County Ball*, after one of the new songs Mickey Lee and I had worked up. It had a great rolling rhythm driven by Mickey Lee's boogie piano and would eventually feature a New Orleans-style horn section on the chorus topped off by a perfect party-hearty guitar break from Stevie. The rest of the album would flow from there. We still retained a certain Faces-style swagger, but we were now developing our own musical identity.

A strong British influence with a very American heart, Mickey Lee and I now came up with some of our best songs, including "Rocking Chair Rock 'n' Roll Blues," our new come-on-in-the-water's-fine anthem; "L.A. 59," one of those traveling-band numbers that used to be called a train song, and which for some reason would actually become the title of the American release of the album. Plus a ballad I was very proud of, partly because we didn't write many ballads, but mainly because it was one of the most accomplished numbers Mickey Lee and I had ever come up with. When Roger Glover, who would be producing the album on his own this time, heard it, he was inspired to write a string arrangement for it. In fact, Roger was so inspired when he heard the demos that he invited us to England to record! Wow! Home of our heroes. A dream fulfilled. Easy Street, here we come again!

Roger booked us into a new residential studio called The Manor, in Shipton-on-Cherwell, near Oxford, owned by an up-and-coming English music biz entrepreneur named Richard Branson. Richard had used the money he'd made from opening his original Virgin record store, in 1971, to launch his own record label of the same name—and to buy the country estate in which he built The Manor. By the time Elf arrived there in January 1974, Branson and Virgin were on their way to their first major success with the debut Mike Oldfield album *Tubular Bells*—one of the first records made at The Manor.

Richard had his offices at the studio and was almost always there, working to build the business that would one day lead to an empire. To find ourselves not just in England for the first time, but in such exciting surrounds, gave us a tremendous feeling of right-place-right-time.

We lived at the Manor for a month, recording the songs Mickey Lee and I had mainly written in Cortland. While the vibe was great, the studio was weird, in that the control room was at your back, and so communication was difficult. The toilet was miles away, but there was a side door at the studio that led to a small fire escape where you could relieve yourself onto a target that someone had painted below.

I learned to drive on the "wrong" side of the road—right-hand drive in the UK—after "stealing" the equipment van one day from our minder, Colin Hart. Colin was a gem. He was from South Shields, a coastal town in the North East of England, and had a thick Geordie accent. He worked for the Deep Purple organization as part of HEC Enterprises, Purple's management firm. As he wasn't on the road with the band at the time, he got lumbered with taking care of these Americans who he only knew about from Roger. I had been pestering him to let me drive, but his constant refusals made me take matters into my own hands. I got hold of the keys one evening, jumped into the van, and drove off into the night. I assumed that because everything about driving in Britain was reversed, that the turn signals were as well. But every time I signaled and turned, I got a horn. Whoops! Left is left, and right is right. I drove the van home very slowly and never told anyone, least of all Colin, the story.

We spent the first few days in England hanging with Roger at his palatial home in Iver, a beautiful village in Buckinghamshire, tying up loose ends and being introduced to the now-infamous bootleg known as The Troggs Tapes. The Troggs were the legendary English band that had a hit all over the world in 1966 with "Wild Thing." The tapes were a fantastically funny real-life recording made of singer Reg Presley arguing in the studio with his band mates while trying to record a track titled—ironically—"Tranquility." Reg screaming: "Put a bit of fucking fairy dust on it!" It became so famous that John Belushi and Bill Murray later did a parody of it on *Saturday Night Live*.

Roger also played us another absolutely hilarious recording he had called *The Farting Contest*. Dating back to 1946, it purported to be a world title "fart-off" between reigning English champion, Lord Windsmear, and the challenger, Paul Boomer, an Australian who trained on a diet of cabbage. It may not sound like much on paper, but it still makes me laugh thinking about it again now all these years later. It was the beginning of my lifelong love of absurdist English humor. When *Monty Python's Flying Circus* first took off on American TV later that year, I was one of the first people to really dig it. When one of the big stars of that show, John Cleese, came out with his own show, *Fawlty Towers*, the following year, I was sold from the first minute. Somehow, that crazed, twisted British humor just chimed more with my own. But then, as I was discovering, I was becoming quite the anglophile. Working in England had also given me a taste for strong British ale and other things we simply didn't have much of in the US in that era but that proliferated all over the UK.

This seemed to be the way the band's career trajectory was now going too. We finished the album in a few weeks and sent Craig, Steve, and Gary home, while Mickey Lee and I went to stay with Roger at his big house in Buckinghamshire. Roger had left Deep Purple at the same time that Ian Gillan did. Liberated from having to be on the road with Purple all year round, he was free to stretch his own music wings and had just taken on the task of putting music to a children's book called *The Butterfly Ball and the Grasshopper's Feast*. It had originally been discussed as a solo album for Jon Lord produced by Roger, but with Jon still committed to Purple and Roger since ousted from the group, it was now Roger's baby.

When Roger asked if Mickey Lee and I would be part of it— co-writing with Roger and singing and performing on some of the tracks—we jumped at the chance. This was a golden opportunity to help create new music in a completely fresh context—and to repay Roger for everything he'd done for us. Rock operas were all the rage in that era—the Ken Russell-directed movie of *Tommy* by the Who had just hit the screens that year while the movie version of the stage musical *The Rocky Horror Picture Show* would also come out that same summer. Meanwhile everyone was releasing concept albums of various kinds, and live, the acts getting the most attention were the overtly theatrical ones like David Bowie, Genesis, and Alice Cooper. When Rick Wakeman released *Journey to the Centre of the Earth*, his concept album based on the 1864 Jules Verne sci-fi novel, he staged shows based around it in a London ice-skating rink!

When Roger outlined his plan to write a rock opera loosely based on the 1802 children's poem by William Roscoe, telling the story of a party for bugs and other small creatures, it felt like an inspired idea. There had been a 1973 *Butterfly Ball* picture book by Alan Aldridge, who had done some of the psychedelic illustrations for various books and album covers, including *The Beatles Illustrated Lyrics* book in 1969. With added text by the South African novelist William Plomer, the book expanded the original poem, focusing on the animals' preparations for the ball. This then turned into a short animated film based on Aldridge's illustrations, made in 1974. This was supposed to lead to a full-length animated film, but like a lot of great movie projects, it didn't pan out that way.

Undeterred, Roger simply turned what was to have been the soundtrack into a solo album. Roger was also writing with former Spencer Davis keyboardist-vocalist Eddie Hardin, and one of the tunes they wrote became my first Gold record and somewhat of a signature song for the project. It was called "Love Is All," based on the fictional song "Love's All You Need" mentioned in the book. (No prizes for guessing where the "inspiration" for that title came from, Beatles fans.)

According to the story, the frog sings the song. In the now-famous animation he also plays the bass. So I could relate. I performed two more "froggy" numbers, "Homeward," a dreamlike ballad I co-wrote with Mickey Lee and Roger, and a gorgeous pure pop number that Roger wrote called, "Sitting in a Dream." Roger, Mickey Lee, and I also co-wrote a wonderful bit of old English vaudeville called "Harlequin Hare," sung by another singer-songwriter friend of Roger's named Neil Lancaster.

The whole thing was fantastical and great fun to be involved with. Both Glenn Hughes and David Coverdale were also on the album, along with American soul singer Jimmy Helms and the great British singer-keyboardist-session player Tony Ashton, to name a few, including my three favorite girl singers: Barry St. John, Liza Strike, and Helen Chappelle, who also sang on *Carolina County Ball* and what would be our next album, *Trying to Burn the Sun*.

Mickey Lee and I did our parts, had a good time, then flew home and forgot about it—before suddenly we were back in the UK, opening for Deep Purple again. It made sense, seeing as the album, on Purple's label, was released there in April. Coming on top of the weeks spent in Oxfordshire recording, this was starting to feel almost like home. There were twenty-four shows, including five in Scotland, another place full of castles and mountains that I'd only read about before, plus a couple of shows in Holland, at the Concertgebouw in Amsterdam.

During the interval between going home and returning to the road, Gary decided it was the perfect time to get married. He got a second-floor apartment that he and his wife-to-be decorated. He had a big wedding, and we threw a great reception after the ceremony at our local bar. At about midnight, Gary's bride wanted to go home in preparation for a honeymoon trip to follow the next day. They left amid hugs and hurrahs, and we got back to the party and carried on.

About an hour later Gary turned up again, this time on his own. He said that he didn't want to miss the party, so he had waited until his newlywed bride fell asleep and climbed down a rope from his apartment. He then rolled the car down the road so she wouldn't be awakened by the noise and drove back to the saloon. We closed the place at 2:30 a.m. and went on to someone's house where we carried on until about five before we all finally crawled back to our homes.

Gary, of course, hadn't quite thought that far ahead, and was now faced with the arduous task of climbing back up the rope to his bedroom. Full of alcohol-fueled bravado, he clambered halfway up—then promptly fell back down, spraining his wrist and leaving himself sprawled alone on the ground on his wedding night. Forced to hobble to the front door and awaken his wife, he told her that we'd had an emergency band meeting that night, and he had gone down the rope in consideration of her getting a good night's sleep. How he managed to say all this with a straight face I don't know, but she bought it. What a great gal. Of course, Gary being Gary, things never did quite settle for him, and his marriage broke up after his mother-in-law arrived unannounced at his apartment one day and found him rolling around the floor with the Avon lady.

Fortunately for us, Gary's wrist healed properly in the remaining time we had off, so there were no worries about returning to tour.

And that really was a kind of honeymoon for us. After so many years spent touring the States, so much time working and living and now traveling all around Britain, to play in a wonderfully different city like Amsterdam really did open up my mind to new experiences and new ways of seeing things. The big news in Amsterdam, of course, was that cannabis was semi-legal and could be bought in coffee shops. Don't forget, at that time in many states in America, you could be busted and thrown in jail for possession of a single joint. What was this enlightened new land we had wandered into?

We only took guitars and piano pickups with us to Holland, so preparation was minimal. The flight to Amsterdam was uneventful, I'm happy to say. Our two previous shows had been at the Apollo in Glasgow, the roughest, toughest city in Scotland. It's also the city with one of the greatest, noisiest audiences in the world, and I loved every second. The people of Glasgow were unbelievable. The energy! The warmth! The offer of a "wee dram" everywhere we went or a "quick nip"—supposedly a shot of whisky, in reality, more like a long slug of Scotch! You will understand why then the after-show party after the second of the shows in Glasgow, meant everyone slept it off in heavenly peace on the flight to Amsterdam.

The tour was also full of more positive energy, the first by Purple since Roger Glover and Ian Gillan had been replaced by a complete unknown named David Coverdale and the fantastic vocalist-bassist from Trapeze, Glenn Hughes. Having our producer and, in theory, biggest supporter at Purple Records no longer actually in Deep Purple could have put us into an uncomfortable spot. But not having Ian Gillan around anymore made me very curious to see the new lineup. How would these new guys handle it?

When we were checking into the hotel, Coverdale and Hughes were in the lobby bar. They called us over and acquaintances were made. Great guys. I didn't know it then, but both David and Glenn would remain friends and colleagues for the rest of my life, both tremendous singers in their own right, of course, but great company also. We had a few drinks, swapped stories, and arranged to go out together later to the nearest shopping precinct to buy some of those "far out" hats and embroidered bellbottom jeans—what we called "European clothes."

On the taxi ride to the shops, we thought the record company had done a brilliant job of publicity for us because there were big ELF signs at so many different spots along the route. We thought, wow, they must really believe in us here! We later learned that ELF was the name of an oil company, and that the word *elf* meant eleven in German. A bit of a letdown, but at least we were one more than ten. Boom!

Our first stop was a shoe store. Holland being the historic home of wooden clogs—as most famously evidenced by my old mate Brian May from Queen—Gary rushed to the wooden shoe area of the store and bought some clogs. He wobbled around a little after trying them on, but soon seemed to find his sea legs. A few others bought some as well, and we paid and left the store in search of some cool stage clothes. We began to cross the street, and as Gary (have I mentioned Gary?) stepped off the curb, he fell from his clogs and sprained his ankle. The curse had struck again.

Our next show was the following day, and we knew Gary would never be able to play it. We took him to a doctor, who put an Ace elastic bandage on it and told him to stay off his feet. Gee, thanks, Doc. We called Bruce Payne in New York and told him what had happened, and his advice was to see if we could contact Mark Nauseef and hope that he was available. We did, he was, and we flew Mark out that night. We missed the first show but carried on after that with Mark until Gary's ankle healed.

From there—for once—everything just fell into place. The *Carolina County Ball* album did only modestly in Britain and Europe, but in opening for Purple, we had developed a fast-growing reputation as a great live band. When the album came out in the US in the summer—retitled, for some reason I've never been able to fathom to *L.A. 59*—it pretty much passed without comment, outside the growing circle of fans that had seen the band play.

Despite the lack of sales, the future for Elf seemed brighter than at any time before. We went down well opening for Purple. When *Butterfly Ball* came out on Purple Records at the end of 1974, it got a lot of attention in Britain and Europe. "Love Is All" actually went to Number 1 in France and the Netherlands, made the Top 10 in Australia, the Top 30 in the UK and, as mentioned, gave me my first Gold record. The animated version showed up on TV all over the world, from Britain where it still crops up today, to Australian and eventually American TV, when the album and single came out there a year later. None of which, frustratingly, had any noticeable effect on boosting the profile of Elf, but did, ironically, lead me quite abruptly to the next, entirely unexpected chapter in my own story.

Over the next year, in addition to our own club dates, Elf ended up doing around sixty major shows around the world opening for Deep Purple. The new Coverdale-Hughes-Blackmore frontline had completely rejuvenated that band. Their first album together, *Burn*, was a classic. Live they went in for long improvisational jams. They had the chops to do that. Their whole set including encores was only nine songs long, with just three of them from the pre-*Burn* years. These were the days when, if you didn't focus on your latest stuff, people considered you a sellout. They were inspiring to us, a band still trying to prove they had the potential to get to that level too.

Highlights: there were so many it was hard to keep up. After the transforming experience of recording and touring in the UK, we followed Purple into some of the biggest venues in America. Our first show was at the 80,000-capacity Orange Bowl, in Miami: Elf, followed by the J. Geils Band, followed by Deep Purple. How's that for a good night out in 1974?

Two nights later we opened at the 20,000-capacity Dillon stadium in Hartford, with Aerosmith replacing the J. Geils Band. Take a second to think about that. Strutting onto the stage, knowing you have to somehow leave an impression that will withstand the onslaught that follows—Aerosmith *and* Deep Purple. Then a couple of nights after that we opened, with the J. Geils boys back in tow, at the 78,000-capacity Arrowhead Stadium, in Kansas City. Followed by the 45,000-cap Houston Astrodome. We may not have sold many records in Elf yet, but we were now operating on another level. This was more like it!

We really lucked out with the travel arrangements on this tour. We were invited by Deep Purple to ride on their chartered Boeing 720 passenger jet, the Starship, from show to show. The interior had been converted into a huge living room replete with piano bar (actually an electric organ) and the first video cassette player we had ever seen, plus a library of new movies. The rear of the plane featured a small pillow-strewn room and a huge master suite with double bed and shower. They had painted the band's name on the sides of the aircraft in huge purple letters as they had for Led Zeppelin, who first used the Starship. We ate and drank like kings, usually arriving in the morning, to be offered champagne, shrimp cocktail, and the latest movie. This was the real big time, and if this didn't pique your appetite for success, you must be already dead.

The Astrodome in Houston was the standout night of the tour. No rock band of Purple's magnitude had ever performed there before, and we were awed by the structure. It was the first domed stadium large enough to accommodate a baseball and football team in a completely weather-proof environment. The audience was not allowed on the field because of the fragile AstroTurf covering it. They remained in plush seats with perfect views surrounding the empty inner area. They seemed miles away when we did our set, and it was a rock show with not a lot of audience involvement. Finally Purple went on, and Glenn immediately invited the audience to "come on down," and did they! They swarmed over the barriers and rushed onto the AstroTurf. The Astrodome management went crazy and threatened lawsuits. When the show was over, the band was charged $60,000 for damages. Ritchie loved it. You couldn't buy that kind of publicity, a statement we'd heard before and still believed might be true.

There was a second swing around the US with Purple at the end of the year, this time with the Electric Light Orchestra sandwiched between Purple and us. ELO, as they were known, were having their first hit single ("Can't Get It Out of My Head") and album (*Eldorado*) in America that year and were as different from what we were doing as could be imagined. Yet, I noticed, not that far from Purple at its most musically expansive. Indeed, Purple had made a conscious move in that direction with some of their new material, most especially the title track of the album, "Burn," with its neo-classical keyboards. I began to think about how we could move Elf in a more adventurous direction.

As the support act, we traveled as cheaply as possible. On a European tour, we traveled with Purple's crew on their tour bus. They instantly accepted us, being that most of us were as crazy as they were, with some obviously nuttier. We drank, smoked (anything we could get our hands on), played cards, and generally partied all night, every night.

Unlike the luxury buses of today's touring packages, there were no beds or toilets on these top-of-the-line tour coaches, only extremely uncomfortable seats. One of my perks, being smaller, was to always have a place to stretch out and sleep in the overhead racks. The first time I did that, the bus stopped at a rest area, and after eating, the coach tooled some miles down the road when they discovered I was "missing." They turned around and went back to the food stop to find me, but there was no Ronnie there. Cue: panic. When I woke up, climbed down from the overhead rack, and asked if there was any food to be had, they were not a happy bunch! Until later anyway, when we would sit around laughing our asses off recalling the stories.

It's almost impossible to sleep for long in that environment, even when you're bone tired, so in time-honored on-the-road style you resort to "help." In the decades that followed there would be dozens of sleep remedies available, but back in the '70s the choice was limited. Sleep on the Purple tour was provided by a drug I'd never heard of before, called Mandrax. They were like the Euro-version of the American Quaalude and were as available in those days as candy and twice as sweet. They didn't just put you to sleep, though. They put you into a whole other realm. My first experience of a "Mandy," as they were known, came at an ice cream stop in the Alps, which found me wearing an ice-cream cone on my forehead. I just couldn't find my mouth.

The drive through the mountains was awe-inspiring, especially whacked out as we all were after the Mandies and alcohol. We checked into the hotel and went straight to the bar. It was early afternoon, and a slightly more genteel clientele were enjoying a cocktail before their reservation in the very upscale hotel restaurant. One of our drinking companions was Ian "Fergie" Ferguson. Fergie was Ritchie Black-more's guitar tech and a larger-than-life character in his own right. I guess he had to be to work for a perfectionist like Ritchie. Example: the manager of the hotel was a bit full of himself but softened a bit when we explained we were with the Deep Purple party. The bar quickly filled up with our lot, and the game was on.

We were peckish, so one of the crew went into the kitchen and emerged wearing an apron and a chef's hat while wheeling out a tray with something that resembled chicken or beef or cheese sandwiches. Fergie had to relieve himself but couldn't be bothered to go to the men's room, so just peed at the bar. The manager saw this and went berserk. He insisted we leave, but Fergie charmed him for a while, and after a few drinks he was one of the boys. Until Fergie decided to repeat his performance and pissed all down the manager's leg. The Purple guys arrived at that very moment looking for beer. No such luck! The entire entourage was banned from the bar and restaurant, with us in the middle as the reason they were denied food and drinks.

The tour went well. We finished in Europe and moved onto London, Manchester, Newcastle, Birmingham....During an evening off in Coventry, the Purple guys were presented their backlog of Gold Albums by Warner Bros., who put on a large banquet with all the Deep Purple organization present. Everyone waited with bated breath to see if Ritchie would turn up for the festivities, but to no avail. He was a no-show, the man in black, moving in his mysterious ways. The party concluded at about eleven at night, and the Purple guys went home with their rewards, but the free alcohol had only warmed up the road crew. They (and us) continued to order drinks back at the hotel from the night porter until he shut us down.

When the night porter locked up the bar, we were left drooling after the forbidden drink. The temptation proved too much. Someone jimmied open a door—I'm not saying it was Gary, if that's what you're thinking, and even if what you are thinking might be right—and the now-freed bottles were passed around and hurriedly consumed. We finished what we had and retired exceedingly happy to our rooms, where we felt certain we would escape any blame for this thirst-driven crime.

We might have gotten away with it, too, but once back on our floor, a now-naked Gary decided that the fire extinguisher had been ignored far too long and promptly yanked it off the wall. Just at that moment a little old lady appeared in the hallway, saw Gary, then screamed and ran. Gary panicked, and as he went to return the extinguisher to the wall, he turned it upside down, and it went off. CO_2 began to foam everywhere, and Gary took off like a rocket to his room, still holding onto the extinguisher. He burst through the door, ran into his toilet, slipped, and the extinguisher fell into the basin and broke it clean in half. Now we had foam and a geyser of water quickly filling up his room. So we did what any real friends would do and ran to our rooms, bolting the doors behind us, leaving Gary to face his destiny. About half an hour later there was a pounding on the door and a shout from the other side.

"Police! Open the door!"

I did and was told to pack up my belongings and go to the lobby. I got packed, went down, and there were all the road crew and the rest of our band. We were being ejected—not just from the hotel, though, but from the city. The crew had pelted the police with pillows and rubbish from their rooms before going to the lobby, so there was no mercy shown now. They loaded us into our bus and actually escorted us to the city limits, then waited until we disappeared into the distance.

When we thought it safe, we returned to the city and tried to check into an alternate hotel, but they had all been warned of this rogue band of beer-stealing basin-bothering savages and cautioned not to give us rooms.

Now what? We had a gig that night, and nowhere to sleep off our hangovers. Someone suggested the local airport, so off we went. We parked the bus on an unused runway and stumbled off to collapse in an exhausted heap on the grass verge. Someone called the Deep Purple offices, and we received the bonus news that management were *not* happy, especially with us, and that one of them would be at the show that evening to fire us. That was it for sleep. What had we done now? There seemed to be no way out of this one. The crew thought it unfair to terminate us for a bit of "fun." Of course they did.

Thankfully, someone spotted a pub, the perfect spot, we decided, at which to console ourselves. (And the road crew.) We stayed there until it was time for the load-in at the show that night, by which time we had decided we were doomed. We hung out in our dressing room before the show, an eight-by-eight closet with two chairs and a dirty mirror hanging above a filthy broken sink.

What could we do to try and make things better, prove we were actually good guys?

So we busted up the place. Glass everywhere, shards of wood and chunks of porcelain decorated the room, actually brightened it up a bit, we thought, when in came Purple's manager John Coletta. He was *livid*. He told us we were stupid and fired, and that, worst of all, the press had picked up the story and blamed Deep Purple for it. As Coletta continued verbally laying into us, we heard a chuckle from the doorway, and standing there amid the rubble was a guitar-clad Ritchie. He told us that we should repeat our shenanigans at every hotel, and that you couldn't buy that kind of publicity. Wow, thanks, Ritchie—we think! Was he kidding? No, he meant it!

The whole situation was instantly transformed. John praised us for our good work and promised us more shows with Purple and his other bands. It was hilarious but at the same time...weird. *This was fame?*

I vowed never to let anything like this happen again. Fingers crossed; hope not to die.

NINE

RITCHIE BLACKMORE'S RAINBOW

t the end of the tour, we were put into a flat in Fulham, one of the smartest parts of London, to prepare for our third album. Jon Lord had lived in the ground-floor apartment and Ian Paice in the upper one until they both bought homes and moved away. We had the top floor and put an electric piano in the room where Mickey Lee and I could work.

We were very near Parsons Green Tube Station, so it was cheap and easy to get around town. There was also a great pub across the street. Every patron seemed to be a WWII veteran and still mightily pissed off at the Germans because they "bombed [their] chip shop." They were serious. But they had an out-of-tune piano to compliment the out-of-tune singers and helped us miss home a little bit less. We loved the idea of living and working in London, but as a band we had been away from home for most of a year. Luckily the beer was really cheap then, because we each only received £5 a week (around ten bucks US) to buy food and drink. Potatoes were the cheapest fare we could find, so we baked them, fried them, boiled them, sautéed them, and got really sick of them.

We saved most of our money on searching for something to smoke. We were always on the lookout for a supply. Having long hair and American accents helped, but London in the mid-'70s was not the easiest place to score good dope. Grass was what we knew in America, but it was very rare in London back then. It was all black hash and brown resin, mixed with a ton of tobacco.

Walking to the corner store one day we were approached by the driver of a massive '60s Cadillac who asked us if we wanted some grass. Far out! He wanted £10 for an envelope that appeared full, but we only had seven quid between us for the rest of the week. We asked if he would take what we had. Begged him. He finally said yes, so we emptied our pockets and rushed back to Harbledown Road where we lived.

When we got there, we lovingly fished out the rolling papers, and Stevie rolled what the Brits called a great big bomber, then lit it like a firework. We took our turns chugging on it—taking huge tokes—and waiting for the buzz to come on strong. After a few moments someone asked if anyone was getting a buzz yet. No one was, so we rolled up another king-size rocket and sparked it up. Magnet, one of Purple's road crew, had come by to see if we were doing okay, so we asked him what we were smoking. He smelled the contents of the envelope and declared it to be grass. We knew that, but why was it so weak?

"Because it's *grass*," he said, trying not to laugh. We still didn't get it. "...Freshly cut from someone's lawn."

Goddamn. The bumpkins had gotten burned again, only now we couldn't even afford a potato to share amongst us.

Mickey Lee and I put most of the material for the new album together in about a month, working from our little bedroom studio at the place in Fulham. Then we led the band into Kingsway Recorders, a studio owned by Ian Gillan, to put down the tracks. Roger Glover, who was producing again for us, had previously used the studio for various Purple mixes and felt really comfortable there. We recorded all of the basic tracks at Kingsway until we had to move out because the studio had another band coming in. Roger booked us into AIR Studios to finish the album. The first person we saw at AIR was the owner, George Martin. Yes, the Beatles' George Martin. We were awed, but he made us feel very comfortable and special.

Suffice to say, AIR was huge and state-of-the-art, with a lot of interesting people circulating. Our tape ops were the sons of two huge stars, Peter Sellers and Spike Milligan. Legendary Beatles engineer, Geoff Emerick, was also working there. It was in these creatively charged surrounds that we made the third Elf album, *Trying to Burn the Sun*.

For me, although it never really got the recognition or exposure it deserved, the third and, as it turned out, final Elf album was the best we did by some distance. By the mid-'70s, rock music as album art form was reaching its peak. Newer post-Beatles bands as diverse as Queen, Little Feat, ELO, Lynyrd Skynyrd, Genesis, and Eagles, to name just a few, were on their way to history-making greatness, while '60s survivors like the Stones, the Who, Zeppelin, Purple, and Black Sabbath were now at the top of their own musical mountains.

It was a time for pushing the envelope. Nothing was off-limits. Knowing this, Mickey Lee and I were at our most adventurous when writing. Where the first two Elf albums had focused on good-time rock 'n' roll, *Trying to Burn the Sun* lived up to its title, in that we were aiming high. Tracks like "Prentice Wood" demonstrated a whole new level of musicianship and songwriting ability, a little like the Allman Brothers at full tilt, while "When She Smiles" showed how accomplished we had become—somewhere between Zeppelin and the Stones, when they cooled out. Others like "Black Swampy Water" and "Good Time Music" kept the free-spiritedness of the band's earlier music, but with much more ease and confidence. Swagger with style.

It was the first time Elf went into the studio to do more than simply replicate our live show. Roger brought orchestral string arrangements in, arranged beautiful vocal harmonies, and encouraged us to absolutely go for it. Suddenly, on tracks like "Wonderworld" and

"Streetwalker," we had sophisticated musical drama and great performances. It was the beginning of something really special. We could feel it every time we listened back to the tracks. Maybe this would be our moment. The curse would finally be lifted.

But when it came out, I was gone—and so was the band.

It was while Mickey Lee and I were still in London making the *Butterfly Ball* album with Roger Glover that Fergie stopped by the studio one day. Purple was back in town and Fergie was staying at Ritchie's place. He asked if we wanted to go to a club one weekend with him and Ritchie, maybe have a jam. Of course we did. When? Where?

It was a small club called Winkers Farm, situated about halfway between Ritchie's home in the little country town of Camberley, and Kingsway Studios located in central London. Known to everyone almost inevitably as "Wankers," Winkers was on a real farm, in beautiful Buckinghamshire, and had been a stable, now converted into a club. It's still going today, I'm told. Only now it's full of reality TV stars. Back then, though, it had bands playing live on weekends.

Mickey Lee and I had a rental car and arranged to meet Ritchie and Fergie there. We were understandably nervous being around Ritchie for the first time in these circumstances. We were signed to Purple's label, had been touring with them all over the world, but we'd only had very brief on-the-road contact with Ritchie, certainly nothing informal like this. Fortunately, contrary to his standoffish reputation, Ritchie was a great guy to hang with. He loved to laugh and was always taking the piss out of someone.

We relaxed and soon the manager of the club, well known to Ritchie, came over to ask if he'd like to have a blow on stage. This was it. Fergie got Ritchie's guitars from the car, and we all jumped onto the stage together. He plugged into the amp that was there and immediately sounded great, even just tuning up. Someone suggested a blues tune, so we did "Stormy Monday," and though I'd performed it in clubs hundreds of times before, this was something else. We followed up with the Don Nix classic "Going Down," and again had a blast belting out together. Both these songs became our first choices whenever we

t age 5 months.

Age 3 with my Easter basket.

Boxing with Dad.

My famous "Gramma" who taught me the Maloik.

High school photo.

Backing in and out of our shared driveway had some bad memories: "Your father is going to kill you."

The Redcaps.

Recovering from the terrible accident that took the life of my best friend.

version of Elf: Steve Edwards, Mickey Lee Soule, Craig Gruber, me, Mark Nauseef, and Gary Driscoll.

ichie Blackmore's Rainbow. The first Rainbow album, basically Elf plus Richie. Gary Driscoll, me, itchie, Micky Lee Soule, and Craig Gruber.

Rainbow Rising. *Second lineup with Tony Carey, me, Ritchie, Cozy Powell, and Jimmy Bain, 1977.*

Long Live Rock 'n' Roll. *Third lineup with me, Bob Daisley, Ritchie, David Stone, and Cozy.*

Our wedding day, April 7th, 1978, New Canaan, Connecticut.

Mr. Udo flew all the way from Japan to attend.

Wendy and me at the airport.

Cozy locked the night porter in the bar.

A day off in Hawaii with Geezer, Gloria Butler, and Wendy.

Black Sabbath. Vinny, Geezer, me, and Tony.

n stage with Black Sabbath.

At home with my precious dogs, Buster and Niji.

t a charity concert with Lita Ford, Carlos Cavazo, Bruce Dickinson, Frankie Banali, and friends.

Dio band 1986. Craig Goldy, Vinny Appice, me, Jimmy Bain, and Claude Schnell.

With all my wonderful fans.

repeated the fun at other late-night places we found ourselves in over the next few years.

After that Mickey Lee and I went out almost every weekend with Ritchie to have a play. One night he asked me if I had ever heard a song called "Black Sheep of the Family" and was surprised to learn that it was a favorite of mine by a then little-known English progressive rock group called Quatermass (who, coincidentally, featured bassist-vocalist John Gustafson, who also featured on *Butterfly Ball*). In fact, "Black Sheep" had been recorded before then by the British singer Chris Farlowe, but I wasn't aware of that until later—after the significance of Ritchie's apparently random question had been revealed.

As I was to discover, Ritchie Blackmore enjoyed playing mind games. He was extremely good at them, too. He was also restless and always looking for ways to improve things. This would both work in my favor and, eventually, against me.

A few days after the night out at Winkers, I was contacted by the Deep Purple office and asked if I would be willing to sing "Black Sheep of the Family" for a recording of the track Ritchie wanted to do. Wow. I hadn't seen that coming. On the other hand, I suppose I had proved myself in his eyes with the job I had done with Roger on *Butterfly Ball*. Also the night jamming together at Winkers Farm. Still, this was something else.

They booked Kingsway for the session, where Ritchie was also using Matthew Fisher of Procol Harum fame on keyboards, another of my favorites. I thought the session went well. Ritchie seemed elated, but then everything went quiet and I didn't hear any more about it until several months later back on the road opening for Purple.

One of the last shows was in Minneapolis, followed by a couple days off before the final shows. We were back to traveling in our station wagon and at the hotel were all in two adjoining rooms that housed the band and our road crew of four. We arrived there in the afternoon, had a couple of cocktails, then went back to our rooms to freshen up for a night of revelry at the clubs in town. A few hours before we were to leave, the phone rang and, to my surprise, it was

Ritchie. I thought maybe he wanted to go out for a drink, which would have been great, as Ritchie was not known for socializing on tour with anybody he didn't already like. Instead, he asked if I would come to his hotel for a chat. Huh? Had the band or me done something wrong? Some on-the-road transgression Ritchie was about to punish me for? I grabbed a taxi to Deep Purple's hotel, wondering what the hell.

I made my way up to his suite and knocked on the door. A beautiful girl in a flimsy negligee greeted me. Inside, the drapes were drawn against the day, the room candlelit. Ritchie was seated at the edge of the light, gently strumming an acoustic guitar. He rose and greeted me with that wry chuckle that I would come to know so well. He got me a drink and we small-talked, until the reason for this get-together was finally revealed. Ritchie had decided he was going to release the version of "Black Sheep of the Family" we had recorded as a solo single. He had wanted Purple to record it, he told me, but the band had rejected the idea. They were on another path now, he said. The second album of the Coverdale-Hughes era, *Stormbringer*, which had just been released, was leaning more toward a rock-funk fusion, and Ritchie wasn't digging it at all. Most of all, I think he was affronted that the new boys had taken over Purple's musical direction. He decided he would record "Black Sheep" without Purple, partly because he was so stubborn, and partly just to piss Purple off, I think. He caught me off-guard, though, when he said he also needed a track for the B-side. He had an idea for a song, he said, that he was going to play me and if I liked it, maybe I could write a melody and lyrics for it. He played me the song and it was great, a big bombastic number that strutted and swaggered. The truth is, I was determined to like it just so that I could say I'd actually written a song with Ritchie Blackmore, then one of the most famous guitarists on the planet. I told him it was great and that I couldn't wait to begin working on it.

Ritchie nodded, then informed me he had a studio already booked for the following evening and wanted the Elf guys to play on it and me to sing it and finish it off with the lyrics I was going to write for him. No pressure, then. But that's the way I liked it. I was always up for a challenge. It brought out the best in me. I just prayed that would be the case this time.

I taxied back to my hotel, where the lads were all waiting, dying to know what Ritchie had wanted. I told them about the studio booking and they were ecstatic, even Steve, whose guitar would obviously not be needed. A bottle of bourbon was magically produced, and the party was on, while I retreated to a corner to write what I hoped would not prove to be my career obituary and get ready to sing for Ritchie tomorrow.

The introduction to the new tune was to be the traditional English folk song "Greensleeves," once thought to have been composed by King Henry VIII for his lover and future queen consort, Anne Boleyn. Now, it is better understood to be based on an old Elizabethan ballad. Whatever the case, I thought the time period was a perfect setting for the theme of the lyric I was to give it. I wrote about an evil feudal lord who had abducted a beautiful damsel, which had pissed off the local population to an extent that led them to revolt and seek final retribution.

This was the first time, though by no means the last, that I would write lyrics using this fantastical approach. Indeed, as the next few years sped by, I became well known for what the music press would sometimes chide as my "obsession" with writing about mythical figures, kings and queens, angels and demons, dungeons and dragons. For me, though, it really suited the kind of epically scaled rock music I loved to perform. It suited my voice, and it suited my imagination.

The following night at the studio I listened patiently as Ritchie and the band rehearsed then recorded the track. I decided that what I had put together lyrically would actually work. It wasn't myself I had to please, though. They finally finished recording late in the evening. Now it was my go. I was unusually nervous as I stepped up to the mic. Ritchie hadn't given any indication that I was doing anything more than a favor for him. But you don't ask someone to come and be the singer on your first solo single, help write and sing the B-side, then never follow up. What if it was a hit? Actually, I didn't even dare ask myself any of those things. "Love Is All" had been a hit, and it didn't really reflect any more starlight on me, it was all about Roger and the *Butterfly Ball*, and rightly so.

This growing musical relationship between Ritchie and me, from jamming at Winkers to singing "Black Sheep" for him, to this now, whatever this actually was, with all my friends in Elf as the backing band, I knew must mean something. I also knew that my entire future may just depend on the next thing I did in that moment.

Our engineer was the brilliant Martin Birch. He wasn't only the recording engineer for Deep Purple but also their out-front mixer on tour, and so Ritchie trusted him. I trudged into the studio and placed my hen scratching on the music stand. This was it, the ultimate trial of my skills. Martin played me the track to get a headphone balance and we began.

It was a great rousing track to sing over, but I thought my performance needed more work, so I asked for another try. I waited a moment, and when there was no response, I repeated my request. Silence. I couldn't see the faces in the control room, and in my panicked state, I thought they had all fled the studio in horror.

Just then a figure in black came striding into the studio and entered the vocal booth. Ritchie did his dark little chuckle and said, "That's the one." Amazing. I had done it! But then the perfectionist in me kicked in and I asked him to let me have another try. Ritchie nodded and walked out. I sang it four or five times more, until Ritchie once again said that he thought the first take was the one. Hey. Close enough. If the legendary Ritchie Blackmore was happy, then my work here was done.

We just needed a title for the song, but I had only written a story, and there was no obvious name for it. Ritchie suggested "Sixteenth Century Greensleeves," and that was it. Perfect. He put down an incredible one-take reference guitar solo and we were finished.

The final show of the Purple tour was in Baltimore a week before Christmas, 1974. Elf was scheduled to continue on to Europe with Purple for a few shows. By the time we reached Munich, the bad feeling between Ritchie and the rest of the Purple guys was all too apparent.

Jon Lord in particular was clearly very unhappy, while Ritchie kept his distance from him. Jon pulled me aside and told me Ritchie was leaving the band and that if he asked me to sing with him on his new project, to *absolutely not do it*, under any circumstances. Jon looked at me sternly, which he was very capable of doing, and warned that it would "end in tears," and that Elf had a great future, so rejecting Ritchie's advances was definitely the wisest choice to make.

I nodded appreciatively while paying no attention. I was too busy hiding my excitement. If Ritchie Blackmore wanted me to work with him, I was definitely *not* going to refuse an offer like that. Are you kidding? My dreams were all bound up in Elf, but after three albums that were decent but commercially unsuccessful, even after all the exposure we'd been given by Deep Purple, I knew it was only a matter of time before the game was up. I was going to be thirty-three soon—ancient in terms of still trying to make it in the music business.

When Ritchie took me to one side after the show that night and started talking about how he was now thinking past just doing a solo single and had an idea for a "more focused kind of band" that he had wanted to develop for the past few years, and that he believed I was the right singer and co-writer for this venture, it took all my strength not to jump for joy. Although Jon's words still rang in my ears, it was an offer I simply couldn't refuse.

The only thing that gave me pause was that I would be abandoning the guys in Elf. I knew this was a crossroads and felt that if I didn't take this step, I would live to regret it. But how could I leave those guys behind? I brought it up to Ritchie and to my immense relief he said he thought the whole band (minus Steve, sadly) would be perfect for what he had in mind. I didn't like the idea of saying goodbye to Steve, none of us did, but he understood there really was no way around that.

Jon with shaking head, David, Glenn, and Ian wished us all luck like the assured gentlemen they have always been. With blessings bestowed, we awaited the next adventure.

This was it. We were now officially on the corner of Cool School and Easy Street. It wouldn't last—nothing is that easy. But for the next couple of years I finally got to experience what life had to offer in a genuine big-time rock band.

The first order of business was to make an album. At this point, Ritchie didn't really have anything new written. He had two covers, "Black Sheep" and an absolutely insane version of "Still I'm Sad." The Yardbirds' original had chanting Gregorian monks on it. Our version had Ritchie Blackmore setting fire to the sky. But aside from "Sixteenth Century Greensleeves," that's all we had in the way of original material.

Ritchie had relocated to a beach house near Oxnard, a beautiful seaside town just west of LA. Gary and I flew down to stay there with Ritchie, where he and I began to write our first album. None of the other guys were involved in this part of the process. This was Ritchie Blackmore; he didn't need any help with the music, he just needed someone to write the lyrics and sing them.

Ritchie had some ideas he had recorded on his ReVox, so I spent most of my stay at his house in a little room with a guitar and tape recorder, while Ritchie, Gary, and one of the roadies, an English guy named Ian from Liverpool, hit the town. Ian was a "Scouser," as they call them in England, of the first magnitude: a great gift of the gab and fearless in any situation. He was originally a drummer, who had met Ritchie on the club circuit and eventually became his right- *and* left-hand man. Needless to say, he and Gary became instant mates and partied endlessly. I don't think the clubs of LA ever quite recovered!

The first song Ritchie and I wrote together from the ground up was "Catch the Rainbow." I think its best description is a "medieval blues." We had both agreed that we wanted a more classically based theme for most of the songs, and after "Sixteenth Century Greensleeves," here was another. The third song written in Oxnard was an unusual three quarter time tune titled "Self Portrait." I remember Ritchie later explaining to some wide-eyed music journalist how "Self Portrait" was actually a cross between Bach's "Jesu, Joy of Man's Desire" and Hendrix's "Manic Depression." The real crazy part was that that was exactly what it was. That's the headspace we were operating in.

Gary and I then flew home to help the rest of the band get ready to move to California. We were bringing quite a bit of clothing and small furnishings for our new abodes, and I wanted to take my car because nobody walks in LA, and our new homes were on the LA County/ Ventura County line. The crew and rest of the band were to be housed in two beachfront condos called Whaler's Village, while I had my own rooms at the Malibu Bay Club, another Oceanside condo complex.

My next door neighbor was Martin Birch. Jon Lord also had a place at the Bay Club. Purple had replaced Ritchie with the great Tommy Bolin and were also in LA, about to begin production on their first album with him. Then Mark Nauseef came out to stay with me, and so we had almost the entire Elf retinue there. The residents of the Malibu Bay Club were rather low key and private, but Whaler's Village was party central. We met the groundbreaking comedian Jonathan Winters, who had a place there to, as he put it, "escape the ball and chain." He was there on the weekends to paint—and to endlessly entertain us.

Ritchie took us into West Hollywood where he introduced us to the Rainbow Bar and Grill, the coolest club on Sunset Boulevard. I had been there on a previous trip to LA with Elf but hadn't witnessed the kind of red-carpet treatment Ritchie routinely received. Instead of threatening to throw me out, Mario, the owner, who I had previously had some run-ins with at the nearby Whisky a Go Go, which he also owned, sent over a bottle of champagne. I knew it was for Ritchie, not me, but I enjoyed bathing in the reflected glory for a moment, feeling my turn would surely come.

TEN

STARSTRUCK

y now the band had a name. Rainbow. Named after, yes, the Rainbow.

When it came to writing with Ritchie, the rules were simple: he wrote all the music. I wrote all the words and most of the melodies. The kind of songs I wrote with Ritchie for that first album all had a more Renaissance-style aspect to them. In Elf we had been a good-time band, only venturing beyond that on our last album. Now was the chance for me to really push myself. Ritchie and I had discussed it late into the night on many occasions; we wanted Rainbow to be a kind of summit musical meeting between heavy rock and heavy classical themes. What I wrote wasn't poetry, but it was written to say something more than "baby, I love you." It had to; the music Ritchie and I were now writing demanded it.

As a lifelong devourer of books, I attempted to bring some of my favorite themes to the lyrics. I was always a dreamer type of kid. I immersed myself into fantasy situations by reading science fiction and things that would let my imagination run somewhere. I think there's a tremendous kinship between science fiction and the mythological era, and I applied all of that to these new lyrics I was writing to go with Ritchie's music—which was vastly superior to anything he'd done in Deep Purple since their Gillan-Glover heyday. Unhindered by the demands of the younger, hipper Coverdale and Hughes to drive the music toward a more of-the-moment rock-funk fusion, Ritchie let loose. It was awe-inspiring working with him like that. It taught me so much.

We wrote and rehearsed until it was time to begin the recording. The studio booked was Musicland in Munich, where Purple had done a few albums and which Zeppelin, Queen, and the Stones all considered good enough to work in. It was located in the basement of the Arabella House Hotel, which was also where we stayed during the process. Ritchie loved everything German—even Babs, his wife, was German—and seemed to come alive in this Teutonic environment. Giorgio Moroder, who was honing the career of Donna Summer at the time, owned Musicland, but rock was still god then, especially in Germany.

When we weren't in the studio, we frequented two clubs in town: Tiffany's, which had a logo that looked eerily like "Ritchie," and the Sugar Shake. I met some wonderful people there who remain friends to this day. When whatever place we were last at closed, we'd simply move the party to the studio and carry on.

The festivities were fun, but we also worked as hard as we played. We hadn't written enough songs for the album, so we wrote as we recorded. Ritchie came in with a riff that I knew would be the cornerstone of all our efforts. It would be named "Man on the Silver Mountain," and I was right. Certainly because it had the same attitude as "Smoke on the Water," it immediately connected Ritchie's past with our future. We also recorded "Still I'm Sad," with Ritchie totally taking it to another realm.

The moving parts just seemed to magically write themselves. Many of the songs that would become cornerstones in my career were written then: "Man on the Silver Mountain," later chosen to open the album, was an instant classic. We knew it even as we were writing them. A number like "Catch the Rainbow" also had a certain Hendrix-like dream quality. But the opportunity it afforded me as a singer to really show what I could do, who I really was, to step up, was precious to me. Ritchie, of course, is magnificent, showing what a fantastic player he is but also what a great musical visionary.

We had plenty of good-time rock 'n' roll numbers we could have written in our sleep, but it was on songs like "Catch the Rainbow" and the other epic, the beautiful "Temple of the King," that Ritchie and I made our bones as songwriting partners. That's why I found it tough when the powers that be—management, record company, concert agents, and promoters—decided it would make more commercial sense to amend the name of the band to Ritchie Blackmore's Rainbow. That would also be the title of the album.

I understood the reasoning, obviously. But this was 1975 and the belief was that true rock artists didn't do anything for merely commercial reasons. I talked it over with Ritchie, and it was agreed that the group would be called Ritchie Blackmore and Ronnie James Dio's Rainbow. But when the first album came out, there it was: Ritchie Blackmore's Rainbow! Did this become a bone of contention between us? Well, seeing as I had co-written all the songs and sung them, the short answer would be yes. But watcha gonna do? Cry about it? Anyway, by then it was too late. We were off to the races.

A few minor adjustments still needed to be done back in LA and then we were finished. We all thought the album was a masterpiece, but Ritchie, rightfully so, because it was really his reputation on the line, couldn't be as positive as we unknowns were. Years later, while recording the first Dio album, *Holy Diver*, I felt the same trepidation, while the rest of the band hailed it as epic. Just as I would be when fronting my own band later, Ritchie was the one who really had his life on the line here. He was in no hurry to count any chickens before they'd hatched.

We spent the last few days before catching a flight back to California hanging out and having fun. The final evening was a blowout.

We went into town for a farewell to Tiffany's and the Sugar Shake and returned at five in the morning and went into the bowels of the Arabella to have a few more drinks in the studio. One of the road crew, who shall remain nameless but was acting as one of our minders while doing the album, discovered an open door in the basement and found some five-gallon containers of industrial detergent inside.

Now, the front of the hotel sported a large fountain that was on a timer that started it spouting at 8:00 a.m. This was too much temptation for the roadie. He lugged two containers up the stairs and poured them into the nearly empty pool of water. We awakened to a beautiful Munich day, happy and relaxed that we were going home. I opened my curtains to greet the day and gazed down upon the now non-existent fountain. Creeping up the side of the building were mounds of suds. It had spread out into the street and covered all the cars that had parked through the night. As we warily checked out of the hotel, we found the staff, including the manager, practically falling over with laughter. *Hey, welcome to the crazy world of big-time rock 'n' roll,* I thought. *It doesn't get much crazier than this!*

Oh, but it could—and did.

There were a couple of overdubs to be done before the album could be released. Ritchie, his road manager Colin Hart, Martin Birch, and I flew down to Jamaica. Ritchie couldn't record in the US at the time due to a tax scheme his accountants had arranged for all the Deep Purple guys, so we went to Dynamic Sounds in Kingston, owned by the ska legend Byron Lee. Dynamic Sounds was then one of the hippest places for major rock bands to record. Everyone from the Rolling Stones to Eric Clapton had made music there in the '70s. Ritchie said it would be a trip, and it certainly was, though not necessarily in the way I was hoping.

We were staying at a hotel in Ocho Rios, about sixty miles from Kingston, and had a rental car waiting at the airport—or so we thought. There was no reservation to be found, so we hired a taxi to take us to the Sans Souci Hotel. I was looking forward to this, having seen the brochure on the flight over. (No websites to check on your cell phone in those days. Hell—no cell phones!) The Sans Souci was a private beachfront luxury resort set on about thirty-five acres next to the Caribbean Sea. Five restaurants, six bars, all expenses covered. This was work? Forget about it. I couldn´ t wait to get there and swim up to the floating pool bar.

After a few miles bumping along in the taxi, though, we pulled up to a house in a crowded neighborhood with no sign of the sea anywhere. When we asked the driver where we were, he announced that this was his home and that he was going inside for his supper. We could wait in the car or outside on the street. We did both. Forty-five minutes later he emerged, and with a belch and a sigh he carried us on to our hotel. After a harrowing ride at high speeds over wooden bridges spanning deep canyons, we finally arrived at the Sans Souci. By which point all we were good for was hitting the sack.

The next morning, Colin, Martin, and I met for breakfast where we were told by the manager that there was someone from the government to see us and that we must immediately go to the lobby to speak with him. We found him and asked what he wanted, but he wouldn't tell us until Mr. Blackmore was present. That's when we said goodbye to breakfast. You didn't demand that Ritchie do anything, let alone get out of bed.

Colin called Ritchie, and he said he'd be right down. Then almost certainly went right back to sleep. Half an hour later the official requested Mr. Blackmore again, so Colin called him again, and Ritchie again said he was on his way. Then he went back to sleep. Another half-hour. Another request, from the increasingly irate government flunky. Another half-hour and now Mr. Government Official is getting royally pissed. Another half hour followed by the threat of arrest, and finally Ritchie turned up.

Mr. GO questioned Ritchie about the purpose of our visit. He examined our passports, then excused himself to make some phone calls. He returned and asked us if we knew that Queen Elizabeth and Prince Philip, plus all the prime ministers of the Commonwealth, were in Kingston that very day for an anniversary celebration. It seems that we had been mistaken for suspects in an assassination plot against the Queen. He explained this while a monumentally unimpressed Ritchie stood there glowering at him. He then made some mumbled apology and released us into the Jamaican sunshine.

That night we rented a car and checked out the local nightlife. We were bored within an hour, so we decided to head back to the hotel. On the way we spotted a funky-looking roadside bar and stopped for a nightcap. There we met a character, in the true sense of the word, who introduced himself as Johnny Cool Guy. Johnny offered to take us to "the best place in town." Having so far seen only the worst places in town, we gladly took him up on his offer, then jumped back in the car and followed Johnny in his car.

We veered off to a small side road that got smaller and smaller as it wound through the jungle. Yes, the jungle. By the time we had gone a few miles, we knew we'd never be able to find our way back alone, so we kept going. After what seemed an eternity we suddenly burst into a clearing, and there, improbably, was a big Victorian house lit up like a Christmas tree with neon "Welcome" signs in every imaginable language hanging in the windows.

Our car doors were wrenched open by ten or twelve barely-dressed young women who excitedly ushered us into the house and up to the bar. Johnny Cool Guy had delivered us to a jungle brothel that Martin dubbed "The Pink Oboe." We bought drinks for all the ladies and leaned back to toast our good fortune.

Suddenly, gunshots broke out, and amid the screams and shouts, we bolted for our car. Despite the chaos in the car park, Colin managed to navigate our way out to the primeval trail we had taken into the "Oboe." We followed another fleeing patron to the main road and finally found our way back to our hotel. We reeled into the lobby to collect our keys and were given a message that demanded an urgent call to our friend the Government Official.

Colin called him and was told we all had to head down to the lobby again the following morning to meet him. Jeez. What fresh hell was this? Down we all duly went in the morning, only to discover our friend standing there with two kids in tow. He was there for some autographs. No problem, anything to ensure our departure.

Ritchie Blackmore's Rainbow came out in August 1975 and was a hit right out of the gate. It made the Top 30 in America, the Top 10 in the UK, and showed up in charts across Europe. From a personal perspective, it was the biggest hit I'd only dreamt of ever having. Most delightful for Ritchie: It was a bigger hit than the first Purple album without him, *Come Taste the Band,* which came out a couple of months later.

There was, however, a cloud on the horizon. The first sign of trouble I got was during rehearsals for our first tour. I got a call from Ritchie one night, saying he had some concerns about Craig Gruber. He began to tell me about this other bassist he'd heard about who he thought might be better. His name was Jimmy Bain, he was in a band in London called Harlot, and did I have a problem with that? You bet I had a problem with that. Craig was my friend and a great player. In the end, though, there really wasn't much I could do except voice my support for Craig. Ritchie had already made up his mind. He was so convinced that he and I actually flew to London to see Jimmy play with his band at a then-famous little club in Soho called the Marquee.

Jimmy could certainly play, but what really endeared him to us was his company. Jimmy was a little guy from Scotland with a big-time personality, the original Good Time All The Time guy. When Ritchie and I met him, Jimmy was living in London at 11 Downing Street. Wait, wasn't that next door to the British Prime Minister at 10 Downing Street? Yes, it was. Jimmy's then-girlfriend was the daughter of the Chancellor of the Exchequer—the UK version of the US Treasury Secretary, only even more powerful. The first time I went to pick Jimmy up to come and have a jam at Ritchie's house, a proper Mary Poppins'-type butler opened the door.

"Hey, man, can Jimmy come out and play?"

"Certainly, sir. I shall fetch the master...."

Jimmy came stumbling out, and we went to the pub across the street to bathe ourselves in Stella Artois, the strong yellow lager they call "wife beater" in the UK. But when Jimmy strapped on his bass, he always delivered the goods, no matter how wasted he might be. We used to joke that Jimmy could play in his sleep. He was in.

About a week later, back at rehearsals in LA, another bomb was dropped. Ritchie was becoming dissatisfied with Gary's playing and wanted to make another change. I knew there would be no going back now. Ritchie had a great sense of what would be right for a live band, and that sixth sense told him that what we had so far just wouldn't cut it. I dreaded the task of breaking the bad news to Gary, but as always, he surprised me with his big-hearted reaction. He said that Ritchie was right, and that he only wished us both well, and could he stay in California with us for a while? Of course he could, and he did, until we finally found his replacement.

We had moved our rehearsal from Oxnard to Hollywood to be in a larger environment and to prepare for drum auditions. The old Columbia film studios on Gower and Sunset (known as Gower Gulch) had been abandoned and then reopened as Pirate Sound by former Purple sound engineer Robert Simon, nicknamed "Captain California." They had two massive sound stages. One was occupied by us for three months, while the other was a revolving door of bands, including Deep Purple, who were tightening up their new songs with Tommy Bolin.

We had gathered a list of prospective drummers and scheduled them for three days of auditions. Ritchie tested them all by launching into a superfast shuffle beat that lasted until he rejected them or until they passed out. After a futile search of LA band people, Ritchie got in touch with another guy then based in London, Cozy Powell.

Cozy had made his reputation with the Jeff Beck Group. Since then, he'd had a big solo hit single with "Dance with the Devil," a drum piece he'd come up with based on "Third Stone from the Sun" by Jimi Hendrix. He was also an in-demand session drummer for all sorts of British chart acts, including Julie Felix, Hot Chocolate, Donovan, and Suzi Quatro. Cozy could play. He was up there with the best of them at a time when great British drummers like Ginger Baker, Keith Moon,

John Bonham, Carl Palmer, Bill Ward, and Ian Paice had raised the bar to eye-watering levels—and he was just as over the top.

His plane didn't arrive into LA until late one night, but he wanted to get to the studio and have a go right away. He strode into the room, introduced himself, went to check out the rental kit we had for him, changed into his boxing boots—he always played wearing boxing boots, as though he was a fighter getting ready for a championship match—and announced that he was ready.

We began with the superfast shuffle, and after a few minutes of nothing happening but the beat, he stopped and said, "That's fucking enough of that, next!" Aside from how awesome he was for just the briefest of time, his no-crap attitude cemented it for us. All we had to do now was convince him to take the gig. Not as simple as we'd assumed.

Cozy was seriously involved in auto racing and had been advancing rapidly in Formula Ford in England. Once a musician, always a musician, though, and after some thought—and a trip with the guys to the Rainbow—he decided to come aboard.

Cozy and Jimmy moved into a house in the Hollywood Hills, and we started to rehearse our stage show. We had expanded Mickey Lee's piano-only role and outfitted him with a chopped-down Hammond B-3, a Minimoog, and an optical disc synthesizer called an Orchestron. It was full of string, bass, percussion, and woodwind sounds, which complemented the classical themes we sought to pursue.

When Ritchie wanted to have orchestral accompaniment on some a cappella guitar solos, he asked Mickey Lee which Bach or Beethoven pieces he knew. Now Mickey was intelligent and nobody's fool, but unless Jerry Lee Lewis had recorded them, the total number of classical pieces he knew was none. On the ride back to Malibu, we talked about Ritchie's request, and agreed that this was probably a good way for Mickey Lee to hand in his notice. He did give it a go, but it was completely removed from his musical personality. The exam came the next day, and he failed miserably. Down came the axe again. Except for my new Cortland road crew, I was now alone.

For a moment it felt like the roof had fallen in. I knew this wasn't Ritchie's problem. He knew what he wanted, and he wasn't going to compromise to get it. Not after everything he'd been through with Deep Purple. He'd earned the right. He saw Rainbow as headliners, he told me, not some new band starting from nothing. He wanted to start at the top and keep going. For that he needed a fantastic band, next-level players he knew could deliver in the grandest setting.

Ritchie asked me to break the news to Craig, Gary, and Mickey Lee that they wouldn't be joining us on tour, that it was, in fact, time to go our separate ways. Those were tough talks, but the guys were incredibly cool about it, totally understood that I had little other option but to take my chance. I'm happy to say we stayed friends and would, in fact, play together again in the future.

We turned up for our next rehearsal minus keyboards while yet more auditions were lined up. There were a couple of other bands rehearsing in rooms near us. Jimmy went for a walk one evening, just checking it out, and when he returned a short time later, he was full of excitement about a keyboard player he had just heard in some unknown band called Blessings. He suggested we give him a shot. I looked at Ritchie and could see by his face that we were both thinking the same thing: surely, this was too good to be true. Jimmy was certain, so Ritchie told him to go get this guy. Jimmy came back five minutes later with Tony Carey.

Tony was a native son of southern California, and he came with the stereotypical outgoing, over-sharing, some might say *loud* personality to go with it. Being loud and over-friendly were two characteristics that Ritchie found particularly annoying, but as soon as Tony started to play, Ritchie's attitude softened. Tony attacked the keyboards one moment, made them sigh the next. What sealed the deal was when Ritchie quizzed him on his knowledge of classical music and Tony reeled off a series of complicated orchestrations with ease. The Minimoog solos he did were awesome! Tony was in.

Finally, Ritchie and I were ready to set off on our quest for that fabled pot of gold.

Well, almost ready. I had one more thing to attend to. Something so beautiful it would transform my life forever.

Her name was Wendy.

ELEVEN

WENDY'S SONG

*I*t was at the Rainbow that something much more momentous occurred. It was where I met my future wife—and, later, manager—Wendy Gaxiola. Young, English, funny, smart, beautiful, blonde, Wendy was one of the supercool waitresses at the Rainbow. Ritchie introduced us, and I couldn't take my eyes off her. Ritchie explained that he'd known Wendy from the days back in England when she was Purple drummer Ian Paice's girlfriend.

We got talking, and later, after the club closed, I invited Wendy to come with us to a party up in the Hollywood Hills above the Rainbow. I began talking to her and didn't stop until we noticed it was getting daylight outside. It must have been around five o'clock so I said, "Do you want to go and have some breakfast?" She said, "Okay." So we all went down to Du-Pars diner on Sunset Strip and had breakfast with a whole bunch of people. Afterward, still doing my best Pepé Le Pew impersonation, I asked her: "Do you want to go see the sunrise in Malibu?" She said, "Well, that sounds like a good idea."

So began the greatest love affair of my life. Wendy would take a little longer to convince, but I knew right from the start; she was the one.

Wendy Dio: *I was working at the Rainbow Bar & Grill while I waited for my green card to come through. I had moved over here from England, and Ritchie came into the club one night with his first wife Babs. It was the first time I'd seen them both since England. Ritchie said he'd left Deep Purple and that he had a new band now called Rainbow, and wanted to introduce me to this new singer, Ronnie James Dio.*

I said, "Hello, how are you? Blah, blah, what's new?" Ritchie told me to go get a telephone book. Confused, I asked what for? Pointing at Ronnie, he said, "So he can sit on it." That was Ritchie making a joke. He had a very biting sense of humor, shall we say. Ronnie and I just laughed it off.

When the club closed at 2:00 a.m., they invited me to go with them to a party at their house. At the time they were renting a place up in the Hollywood Hills above the Rainbow. So I went with them and Ronnie spent the night following me around and talking to me, and I thought, well, he's a bit short for me. *But he continued talking to me and we had a nice conversation. Then around five in the morning we all went down to Du-Pars and had breakfast, and he said, "Do you want to go see the sunrise in Malibu?" I said, "Well, that sounds like a good idea." So we did.*

That was how it began between us. We started seeing each other and spending all our free time together, and I began to realize how much I loved being in his company. I had known enough big-time musicians to see that Ronnie was different. He was clearly very intelligent, would read a book in a day, mostly science fiction and magical mystical books, and he was very charming and fun company.

Ronnie and Ritchie had just finished writing songs for the first Rainbow album. (As the years passed, I became accustomed to the sight of Ronnie writing while watching sports on TV.) I saw Ronnie pretty much every day for about two weeks. He and the other guys were now in Malibu, staying in a luxury condo inside this gated community right on the ocean called the Malibu Bay Club. I knew they would be leaving soon to record the album in Munich, so we made the most of it.

A couple of days before they left for Germany, Ronnie said: "While I'm gone, if you want, you can use my car." I said, "No, that's okay, thanks." He was obviously looking for a way to keep in touch, but I didn't need a car to persuade me to do that. Anyway, he left and then about two days later he called and said, "Why don't you come on the road with me? Quit your job." I said, "Well, I can't quit my job, but I can fly over for a couple of weeks." I went to Munich to see Ronnie for a couple of weeks, and I never came back.

Ronnie was something else. He was a very different kind of person. I really fell in love with his intelligence, his brain, and his sense of fun. Ronnie had a lot of different sides to him. Over the years, I learned all the sides of him and though they were all very different, they were all one person. For example, he could be the sweetest person in the world. He absolutely loved animals. He loved sports. He loved reading and exploring ideas. And, of course, he loved music. But Ronnie was a perfectionist too, and you had to live up to his expectations. The house was always clean and tidy. His bandmates got used to him wanting everything perfect all the time.

Music was the most important thing in the world to him. After that, the most important people were his fans. Then maybe me, maybe the animals; I don't know where I came in, whether I was before the animals or after the animals, but his music was definitely his life. Creating music, playing music. He absolutely loved being on stage. That was the best part of being in a band for him, being on that stage.

Ronnie also had an amazing memory where he could meet people for the first time, talk to them for not very long, and they would maybe have a kid with them. He'd say hello to the kid, and a year later he'd see them again and remember their names and the kid's name. Ronnie always remembered everybody's name. His fans loved him for it.

He liked good manners. He had been well brought up in a very old-fashioned Italian family. His mother was an absolute sweetheart. His dad was very strict, in that old-school Italian way. So Ronnie was a real gentleman. He knew how to stand up for himself when he needed to. He would fight his battles to the finish. But he showed such courtesy to everyone he met. That's one of the things I really found appealing about him in the beginning.

Ronnie enjoyed people. He could talk to someone eight years old or eighty years old and everywhere in between. He was a good talker, but he was also a good listener. He knew how to bring people out of themselves. He had a great gift for always making a person feel important and warm and that they really meant something to him. He had a real knack of doing that, and they did mean something to him. It wasn't an act; he just really cared about people.

This was all happening before I ever saw Ronnie actually perform on stage. His first shows with Rainbow didn't begin until a few months after the first album had been released in the summer of 1975. They had begun with a show in Canada, at the Montreal Forum. It was a big arena, but I don't think they came anywhere near to filling it.

I remember being in New York with him in time for the next show, at the Beacon Theater. The Beacon is a regular-sized theater with a capacity of maybe three thousand and this time the place was pretty packed. I remember the arched Rainbow stage prop, this huge thing that stretched forty feet across the stage that was lit by over three thousand light bulbs but it didn't work very well. A lot of the times on tour it didn't work at all. I remember Ritchie getting really mad about it. It had cost an arm and a leg—actually, not an arm and a leg but arms and legs.

Mainly, I remember Ronnie and I sitting at a table in a restaurant somewhere after the show, and we were talking and talking and talking and then suddenly realized everybody else had gone, and they were trying to close up. We were already lovers, but we were also now becoming best friends.

My other main memory of those early years in Rainbow is how close Ritchie and I became. He would always want me to go with him to do press and radio interviews. He told Wendy it was because he knew I was a good speaker and that he was not. That's when I realized how shy Ritchie actually was. He often came across as being a real asshole, but we had a really good time together, mostly. He liked my sense of humor, which was always more British than American. We bounced off each other, not just musically but as friends. In fact, Ritchie and I were very, very close. I thought we would be forever.

David Coverdale once described Ritchie as "an interesting bunch of guys." I now found out what he meant. Ritchie was the most unpredictable, frustrating, though obviously talented, person I'd ever worked with. As a result, Ritchie and I had many amazing adventures. This was back in the days when fun was still fun and the only rule for being in a successful rock band was to always break the rules. That said, I'd had my bad-boy times stealing cars and chasing girls when I was a kid. I was now in my early thirties, and though I hadn't calmed down exactly, as anyone that ever encountered me at full blast could tell you, I was never into heavy drugs. I liked pot occasionally, but that was it. Mainly I liked strong English ale. As for girls, I was so in love with Wendy I wanted her with me on the road, in the studio, wherever I went. Groupies were simply no longer on my radar.

I liked having fun. Ritchie obviously felt the same. On the road, we had so much "fun" Wendy and I got used to never unpacking our suitcases, knowing we might be thrown out of whatever hotel we were in. It happened many times.

This was true of the other members of Rainbow that came in and out the band. Top of the list was Jimmy Bain. The more I got to know Jimmy, the more I just loved the guy. He was one of those who looked like he'd been born on a tour bus. The other guys were cool too.

Like all the best drummers, Cozy was wild. He wasn't into destroying hotel rooms like Moony and Bonzo, but he was the biggest prankster. One night in Trondheim, Norway, we left the hotel and asked what time the bar closed and were told it would be open until midnight. Perfect. But when we arrived back from the gig at 11:30 p.m. everything was locked up. We were not pleased. There was a folded crisscross iron gate that went across the bar with a small gap between the walls. Cozy, being very slim and in possession of a powerful thirst, slid through the gap and was handing bottles of booze back through the bars to us, which we were eagerly consuming.

The night porter heard the commotion and came out to see what was going on. He totally freaked when he saw Cozy inside the bar. He immediately got his keys, opened the bar, and went in to chase Cozy out, at which point Cozy slid out, locking the night porter in! We were all in stitches laughing. Wendy grabbed her camera and took a picture of him. The poor guy was clanging the bars, his face turning purple. We ran to hide in our rooms. Half an hour later the police arrived and threw us all out of the hotel.

Speaking of crazy drummers, I'll never forget the flight we took to London where I found myself sitting between Ritchie and Keith Moon. They spotted someone on the plane they decided was too posh, a straitlaced businessman, and Moonie decided to make his trip hell. He walked by him with a glass of wine and conveniently tripped and spilled his drink on the man's shirt. The gentleman complained and about an hour from Heathrow airport we were informed that Keith would be arrested upon arrival for his assault on the aforementioned passenger. Keith decided this would not do, so he retreated into the toilet, ripped his shirt from the front, then deliberately stumbled into the lap of the complainer, and a row broke out in the seat. Moonie claimed the business guy had grabbed him and torn his top! If he hadn't been such a brilliant drummer, he would have been an excellent actor. When we landed, sure enough, the police were waiting at the gate, but instead of taking Keith away, they arrested the victim!

Of course, the one you really had to watch out for was Ritchie himself. The first time Jimmy Bain came with me to Ritchie's house in London, he showed us into his private bar and said he would be back soon for a jam. In the meantime, we were to help ourselves to a drink. When Ritchie hadn't appeared after about thirty minutes, Jimmy and I took him up on his offer and dived into the drink. An hour later he returned, he and Jimmy broke out their instruments, and we began to play—when suddenly there was a massive thud from the upper floor. It was Babs, the beautiful blonde former go-go dancer from the Reeperbahn in Hamburg that Ritchie was then married to. Ritchie shook his head, excused himself, and we went back to the bar. When we saw Ritchie again, he was armed with a bottle of Scotch. He gave it to us and asked if we would wait in the car until he returned. Soon we heard crashing sounds coming from the house and looked up to see Ritchie's shadow in a top-floor window ducking lamps and other assorted missiles. A few minutes later he came rushing out the front door and told his driver, Fergie, to "Leg it!" Before we could get away, though, a pile of clothes and some of Ritchie's guitars flew out the bedroom window. Fergie expertly drove around them, and we fled into the night.

The only other American in the new lineup was Tony Carey. Tony was a great player but not as well versed in that scathing British humor that Ritchie reveled in. As a result, Ritchie picked on Tony more than most. He was always playing "pranks" on him. Tony didn't always see the funny side, which only made Ritchie pick on him more. The resulting lack of communication between the two would prove to be Tony's undoing. Musically, though, at that moment he fit right in.

Our first tour together as Ritchie Blackmore's Rainbow at the end of 1975 was confined to the States and amounted to barely more than a dozen shows. These were all theaters and auditoriums, holding a few thousand at the most. As we only had one album to draw from, the temptation was there to pad the set out with some of Deep Purple's greatest hits—"Smoke on the Water" would have been an obvious choice—but to Ritchie's credit he refused to go down that road. There would be times to come when we did dip into his Purple past, notably on "Mistreated," the show-stopping ballad from *Burn*, but by then it was by choice rather than necessity.

Instead, for this first tour, we included a couple of brand-new numbers that would go on to become classics for us: "Stargazer" and "A Light in the Black." Both would be included on our next album, where they would run to over eight minutes each. In those early shows, however, they could stretch almost into infinity. It was how I really began to understand why Ritchie had been so insistent that he needed different players in the band to perform live with. Depending on Ritchie's mood, "Catch the Rainbow" could run to nearly twenty minutes some nights; "Still I'm Sad," just three-minutes-plus on the album, now turned into an eleven-minute set-closer of monumental proportions.

You can't undertake that kind of intense musical journey without absolutely top-notch guys supporting you, adding, and building. Just as the guys in Deep Purple, all phenomenal players, had done for him previously. In Cozy, Jimmy, Tony, and me, Ritchie had assembled an amazing new band more than capable of being able to deliver on that level night after night after night.

I also began to develop as a frontman. I decided on a more personal approach to building my relationship with the audience. Rainbow offered a very different experience for the audience than the one I had grown used to in Elf. This was about more than just having a good time. When I stood on stage and sang now, I liked to imagine I was looking into the eyes of every single person in the audience, that I was singing specifically for them. Now when I introduced a song, I never shouted, I simply spoke to them as though we were having a private conversation.

Partly, this was because I've always hated frontmen who simply shout and leer at an audience, treating them as though they are one big blob. I've always thought that was so rude. Mainly, it was because I began to take what I did on that stage very seriously. I still liked to have fun up there, but I really did mean every word I sang or said. And I wanted people to know that.

As soon as that first tour was over, Ritchie had us back to writing and rehearsing new material, ready to go straight into the studio to make the next album. This was a very smart move. With the energy and excitement of the road still upon us, we were ready to explode into action. We were in Musicland in Munich with Martin Birch again, and most of the tracks were done in just one or two takes. The fact that we'd been playing most of the tracks live quickened the process. You can virtually hear the energy crackling on tracks like "Starstruck." At the same time, Ritchie wasn't averse to adding different textures only achievable in the studio, principally, on 'Stargazer', where we had the Munich Philharmonic Orchestra swelling the sound, making the whole thing soar.

There wasn't anything as spaced-out and warm as "Catch the Rainbow;" instead we had a fantastic live band really starting to flex its musical muscles. We called the album *Rising*—and that's how it felt to me: like a blistering new sun rising on an ancient horizon. It was a statement album that would set the course for everything Ritchie and I would achieve, musically, throughout the course of our careers, together and then apart. Ritchie indulged his gift for ambitious neo-classical rock. I continued my exploration of fantastical lyrical themes, all with hidden meanings, and things that related directly to my life.

I'd never explain what the lyrics meant to me. If you've read this far into the book you shouldn't need me to. At the same time, it's never as important as what each listener gets from the words, the music, the moment—the very real magic.

Not all of my lyrics continued in the fantasy realm. "Starstruck" was written about a real-life fan that was so crazy about Ritchie she would turn up everywhere. We would play Paris—she would be there. London, she would be there, at the airport. One time she even turned up at Ritchie's house, hiding in the bushes!

When *Rising* was released in May 1976, the reviews were uniformly amazing. People talked of *Rising* as almost a second coming of heavy metal and still do to this day. It became another chart hit in the UK and Europe, but also in Germany and Japan, places that would become very important to both Ritchie and myself as the years rolled by. The only place that *Rising* didn't do as well was in the US. It sold about the same as the first album; it just didn't light up the Top 40. This was perplexing to Ritchie, who was used to seeing his records in the American charts, and to me as the three-month tour we set out on in America that summer had been such a success. We still weren't big enough to headline arenas, but the dates we did in theaters and auditoriums went down a storm, an English expression I learned from Wendy.

The biggest kick I got that summer was when we arrived for our first big headline tour of Britain and Europe. We did ten shows around the UK, topped by two sold-out nights at the Hammersmith Odeon, the legendary London theater. It was also gratifying from a personal point of view that the tour was advertised simply as Rainbow, not Ritchie Blackmore's Rainbow, though they would continue to use the Blackmore's Rainbow sobriquet in other parts of the world whenever it suited some nervous promoter hoping to cash in on the Purple connection.

Things were going fantastically well. There was only one snag. After the final show of the UK tour at a packed City Hall in Newcastle, Ritchie took it upon himself to sack Tony Carey. I think the official reason given was that Ritchie felt Tony had overplayed on something that night. Or, that his playing overcomplicated things. Huh? I couldn't quite figure that one out. Everything about our live shows was meant to be freeform, progressive, no limits. Not for Tony, though. No warning; just sacked.

It left the few days off we had in London before beginning the European leg of the tour unnecessarily tense. Who would come in to replace Tony? Would we have enough time to rehearse with them? It seemed like a hell of a time to fire your keyboard player, especially one that did more than just provide a rhythm. Tony's role included orchestration and solos. Who would be able to step in and emulate that at the drop of a wizard's hat?

Turned out Ritchie must have been thinking the same because Tony was suddenly back in Rainbow as quickly as he'd been ousted. Nothing else was said as the next few weeks of the tour now took us to half a dozen countries around Europe, including ten shows in Germany where we were supported by a little-known band from Australia called AC/DC, whose singer, Bon Scott, I discovered on more than one very pleasant occasion enjoyed a glass of strong ale almost as much as I did.

It was great too that Wendy was with me. This was her first trip home to England since she'd left for LA three years before. Discovering different English cities and towns with my English wife brought an extra layer of understanding and enjoyment. Then in Germany, her ability to speak what Wendy called her "school German" also came in useful. It wasn't always easy for a strong independent woman like Wendy to find her role on tour with me, but she was a trouper. She made sure I was taken care of, fed me, and was there for me through the rough and the smooth. Being a good wife, which by her own admission was not something she'd particularly aspired to. She had always worked, fended for herself, tried to do things on her own.

Then came what for me was another life-changing experience when we set off to tour in Australia and Japan. I'd never been to either country so had no idea what to expect, except what Ritchie had told me, and that sounded almost too good to be true. That Australian rock crowds were like the ones in America—loud and boisterous and ready for anything! Japanese audiences were completely different than anywhere else in the world. Just as enthusiastic but very quiet while the band is actually playing. They liked to listen. Then if they liked what they heard, they'd go crazy at the end.

So it proved to be. We arrived in Australia in early November, just as their summer was beginning, and the reception we got was amazing. These were big shows too. The Hordern Pavilion in Sydney held over five thousand people and we did two shows there, plus four shows at the Festival Theatre in Adelaide, which held two thousand people. We did two shows in Melbourne and one each in Perth,

Brisbane, and Newcastle, not that we got to see much of these places. We had a day off in Sydney after the second show there, and it was like the circus had come to town. Everybody wanted to meet us or just hang out. The rest of the time we were on planes crisscrossing this huge country.

Our next stop was the one that really blew my mind, though—Tokyo, Japan. In 1976, being in Tokyo was like being on another planet, especially if you were a rock star. About eight hundred people showed up to meet us at the airport. When we got to the hotel there were fans all over the hotel. We felt like the Beatles!

This was one time when I didn't mind the connection between Deep Purple and Rainbow—namely Ritchie—being emphasized. The Japanese fans appreciated the history, but they had no hesitation embracing the new. Everyone I dealt with, from the fans to the critics and all the businesspeople, became a new friend of mine. I loved the emphasis on good manners at all times, showing mutual respect and honor. Jimmy Bain, definitely the lovable leader of the pack in these situations, and some of the other guys enjoyed the bathhouses, where the geisha girls were by the mid-'70s accustomed to welcoming visiting rock musicians.

I was more fascinated by the buildings—so futuristic—and the people—so clearly on another level than the rest of us. The culture, the food, the way they dug deep into music...touring Japan for the first time was a dreamlike experience. Then there were the actual shows. All headliners. All arenas. I was starting to feel like this was so much bigger and better than I'd imagined.

We began at a 10,000-capacity sports arena in Tokyo, then took off for two weeks playing some of the best shows we ever did in Osaka, Nagoya, Kyoto, and Fukuoka, before returning to Tokyo to end the tour with back-to-back shows to around 30,000 people at the fabled Budokan.

We had really taken the show to the next level now, too. We had the stage rainbow arcing across the stage, and this time it worked every time, and the show began each night with a tape recording of

Judy Garland giving the classic quote from *The Wizard of Oz*: "Toto, I have a feeling we're not in Kansas anymore. We must be over the rainbow!"

With the last word still echoing the band erupted into "Over the Rainbow," before moving like lightning into an insanely over-the-top new number Ritchie and I had come up with built around Cozy's relentless drums, called "Kill the King."

Fortunately, we recorded some of the shows, with Martin Birch there to ensure they were done professionally. I'm so glad we did. Of all the incredible shows we did in Rainbow, those are the ones I would want preserved, the ones that recall that band at its best, when it really was still a band.

Or as close to a real band as Ritchie Blackmore would ever get again.

TWELVE

KILL THE KING

itchie was a brilliant, genius-level guitar player, but he was very moody, to say the least. He always dressed in black and never smiled on stage unless he really couldn't help it. Sometimes he'd turn his back on the band and me. Sometimes he'd just get up and leave. One time he climbed out the dressing room window and left before we had a chance to even play. But I balanced that in my mind with the fact that I already knew *Rising* would be one of the best albums I'd ever sing on. It was such a shame how that lineup of Rainbow never got a chance to follow it up, but that's the way Ritchie liked to work. "Keep things fresh," he said.

By the time we got back home after the end of the '76 world tour, Tony Carey was gone, this time for good. I forget what reason was given to the press, but the fact is Ritchie and Tony got in a fight and Ritchie kicked him out. Tony knew Japan would be his last tour with us. We all did. At least we thought we did.

The one I hadn't seen coming and which really got to me was when Ritchie fired Jimmy Bain. I still don't know why exactly. Ritchie later complained in the press about certain members who were "taking quite a few drugs and consequently were falling asleep while they were playing because they'd been partying all night." I took that to be a swipe at Jimmy. There was no denying Jimmy liked to party, but he was renowned for his ability to take the '70s rock 'n' roll lifestyle to the limit, yet always be on the money the minute he walked on stage. So, that didn't quite ring true as the real reason why Ritchie got rid of him so abruptly.

Jimmy and I had become friends. We hung out in the studio and on the road. I wasn't in Jimmy's league when it came to having a good time all the time, as he would say, but I did wonder if it was that bond that had developed between us that had begun to get under Ritchie's skin. We were always laughing and joking. Maybe Ritchie thought we were sometimes laughing at him. Who knows? Maybe we were. But we laughed at ourselves even more.

Whatever the reason, I was sad to see Jimmy go. Ultimately, though, it was Ritchie's call. What really left a sour taste in my mouth was that Ritchie fired Jimmy a week before Christmas. I thought that was unnecessary, even for Ritchie.

As a result, the beginning of 1977 found me in a strange quandary. Rainbow seemed to be on a real high. Management and record company people were talking about how the next album was the one that was going to "put us over" in America. It certainly looked like that on paper, but the way Jimmy had been fired summarily, with zero input from me, had changed things for me. I was still as committed to making great music with Ritchie and Cozy and pushing the band as far as we could go, artistically, but a little light had gone out somewhere for me, I now realize. Some of the glow had rubbed off.

Instead of embarking on another big American tour, which had been the plan, the early months of '77 were spent auditioning replacements. There was a double live Rainbow album in the works, *On Stage*, drawn from some of the shows in Germany and Japan. That should have come out to coincide with the now-postponed US tour but was pushed back to July. At least it gave us a little time to find a new bassist and keyboardist and to come up with material for a new album, but it became much more of a slog than I imagined.

We tried out several high-profile keyboard players, including Mark Stein, who looked like a great fit. Mark had been in Vanilla Fudge, and Jon Lord had often remarked how much he admired Mark's playing. "He was a useful source of tricks on the Hammond," Jon said. Bizarrely, Mark had been playing in the Tommy Bolin Band before that. Tommy had only managed to make one album with Deep Purple before his drug habits sunk the band the year before. Since then, he'd put out a solo album, *Private Eyes*, which Mark was on. It got great reviews, but Tommy never got a chance to build on it, dying of a drug overdose in December while on tour with Jeff Beck. I did wonder where Ritchie's mind was going on this one. In the end, it hardly mattered. For whatever reason Ritchie decided Mark didn't fit the bill.

Next he invited Matthew Fisher to audition. I hadn't seen Matthew since the original session in London when we had recorded "Black Sheep of the Family." I loved Procol Harum so I figured Matthew might be the one. Wrong again. Then came Eddie Jobson, who knew about keyboards and synthesizers and also played an electric plexiglass violin. Eddie had been enjoying great success with Bryan Ferry and Roxy Music, but the band was now in some sort of long-term hiatus, and he needed a gig. Eddie would go on to play with Frank Zappa, Jethro Tull, and Yes, but he wasn't right for Ritchie.

Eventually, we settled on a Canadian named David Stone, who had been in a little-known progressive rock trio called Symphonic Slam. Ritchie heard a track by them on some FM radio station in LA and next thing, David's flown down to meet us. Ritchie and Cozy took him out to the Rainbow. I wasn't there that night. I was home with Wendy. I knew Ritchie was the only one who could decide.

After a prolonged series of auditions David joined the band, and we were to become friends. Not only was David a great player, he was trained in classical and jazz and knew how to create wonderful soundscapes. In the meantime, however, Ritchie had brought Tony

Carey back in so we could at least start recording the next album. So even though, technically, he'd now been fired twice from Rainbow, Tony ended up playing on three tracks, including what had already been decided would be the title track, "Long Live Rock 'n' Roll."

We were all in France by then, making the album, and Tony might even have kept his gig if it hadn't been for the fact that he just got on Ritchie's nerves. Tony was very boisterous, very American, and with Ritchie, you didn't really speak to him unless he spoke to you. He liked quietness and calm. It all came to a head finally because Tony kept calling home all the time. He had had enough of it all by then and was always on the phone to his people in LA. He kept talking about wanting to get home, so Ritchie granted his wish. After Tony left for the third and final time, Ritchie and I actually based a song on the situation that we called "L.A. Connection." Then David arrived in the studio and played keyboards on it.

We still didn't have a bass player, though. While we were holding auditions in LA, I suggested Craig Gruber, who I was still good friends with and who had done such an excellent job on the first Rainbow album. I thought Craig would be a shoo-in, but he only lasted a month before Ritchie showed him the door. Next came Mark Clarke, a technically gifted player most recently of Jon Hiseman's Colosseum, who made it as far as traveling to France with us. Once Mark started recording with us, though, Ritchie decided he didn't like the way Mark played bass—employing a finger-style as opposed to the traditional plectrum-style—and simply ran out of patience and sacked him.

Ritchie ended up playing most of the bass on the album, until, that is, he invited Bob Daisley to join us in the studio. Bob was a seasoned pro originally from Australia, who had played in acclaimed blues-rockers Chicken Shack amongst several other noteworthy outfits. His most recent band, Widowmaker, made up of former members of Love Affair, Mott the Hoople, and Hawkwind, had been promoted as a supergroup, but after little success they had broken up. Bob arrived in France just in time to play on three tracks, and to survive into the touring band.

The whole atmosphere surrounding the making of *Long Live Rock 'n' Roll* was strange. ELO was in Musicland studios working on a double album, *Out of the Blue*, so rather than wait for them to finish we went to France, to the Château d'Hérouville, near Pontoise, which we called Pantyhose. Built in the eighteenth century, the Château now housed a famous residential recording studio. Nicknamed the Honky Château after Elton John recorded his album of the same name there, it had since become home to a host of big-name artists, including T. Rex, Pink Floyd, Jethro Tull, David Bowie, and Bad Company, to name a few.

It was certainly picturesque and came with a long history. Frédéric Chopin was said to have conducted his illicit love affair with the writer George Sand there. The château had been the subject of a painting by Vincent van Gogh, who was buried in a nearby graveyard. When Bowie had returned to the studio to make his *Low* album, just a few months before we got there, he claimed to have felt a supernatural presence. Apparently, David took one look at the master bedroom and said, "I'm not sleeping in there!" He took the smaller bedroom next door. He said there was a darkness and coldness in the master bedroom.

Of course, Ritchie had that room when we stayed there, so I can't say if what David said was true, but Wendy and I nicknamed it the Château Horrorsville, and for good reason. For this is where Ritchie conducted some of his most infamous séances.

Ritchie was fond of playing elaborate pranks. People would come back to their hotel rooms and find the bed missing or the furniture completely destroyed. The bills from the hotels could be enormous, but Ritchie always covered them where he was responsible. Tony Carey was far from the first to be subjected to them, and definitely not the last. Ritchie was also fond of getting out the Ouija board and using it to try and contact the dead. To put it in perspective, in the '70s, this sort of thing was done all the time by rock musicians far from home and without much else to do once the sex and drugs had all gone.

Ritchie knew how to take things to a whole other level. He loved holding séances with a glass and his Ouija board, and being at the

Château found him in his element. Ritchie claimed that he looked in the mirror one time and saw Mozart or somebody looking back at him. You never knew with Ritchie whether he was bullshitting about stuff like that, but then weird stuff started happening to all of us.

At Ritchie's bidding, we had started having séances almost every night. It was uncanny how often it produced spooky results. Wendy and I would join in and try to figure out if someone was pushing the glass or cheating some other way. But there were too many times when something happened that it couldn't have been as simple as that. One night at the Château we conjured up Thor, the God of Thunder—I kid you not—and asked for a sign. Huge storms immediately cracked open the sky, which began to pour with rain, thunder, and lightning. We conjured up a lot of weird stuff at the Château. Then we would go to the studio the next day to record—and the tape would be wiped clean. This happened so many times. The twenty-four-track machine would actually turn itself on and off.

Finally, one night during yet another scary séance, Baal appeared on the scene. Baal is one of those all-powerful pre-Christian gods that shows up in varying forms in pretty much every religion. Not as some kindly old gentleman with a long white beard, but as a satanic prince of demons. He announced his presence in our company that night with the chilling declaration: "I am Baal. I create chaos. You will never leave here, so don't even try." Holy shit! We put the board away but then couldn't resist trying again later. This was without Ritchie in the room. Again there was Baal, only this time he asked, "Where is Blackmore? Oh, never mind, here he comes." The door opened and in came Ritchie! Ritchie sat down and we started again, and this time things got really bizarre. It was a round table and the glass went around the edge of the table by itself—we had all taken our fingers off it—and then smashed in the corner of the room! That was it. We all ran off and went to bed. The next morning Cozy said that someone had locked him in his room and that all the books had flown off the shelf. Then Wendy had a real fright when she was walking down the stairs the next day and someone pushed her in the back, and she fell down the stairs. When she looked behind, there was no one there.

We all got really scared after that and left the Ouija board alone. In fact, on that record it says, "No thanks to Baal."

During the day, on those occasions when the machines were working without "outside interference," and despite the uncertainty that hung over who would still be in Rainbow when the album was finally finished, we made some fantastic music. The title track, "Long Live Rock 'n' Roll," was a glorious anthem. One of Ritchie's catchiest riffs, the rest of the song seemed to write itself for me. It was the same feeling with "L.A. Connection," built around one of Ritchie's trademark ballsy riffs.

Then there was "Kill the King." Already a proven winner on tour, it was basically a case of capturing that lightning in the bottle of the studio. Because of the title, most people assumed the lyrics were another of my medieval themes, which, this time, they weren't. The song is actually about a chess match. I love chess—as a game, as a metaphor for life and death, as a wonderfully effective way of exercising your brain. And, in this case, as a great idea to base a song on!

The cornerstone track on the album, though, was "Gates of Babylon," another absolutely epic number that Ritchie and I had fashioned, featuring unusual chord structures with added orchestral heft courtesy of David Stone and the Bavarian String Ensemble conducted by Rainer Pietsch, who Ritchie had invited to fly in from Munich. Years later, Blackmore's biggest fan and guitar-star in his own right, Yngwie Malmsteen cited "Gates of Babylon" as a major high point in his own musical education.

There was also a song deeply personal to me, written purely and simply for the one I love: "Rainbow Eyes." I got the title because Wendy has the most incredibly beautiful eyes that appear to change color depending on her mood or the light in the room. Sometimes they are green, sometimes they are blue, and sometimes they are hazel. Ritchie had this tender guitar arrangement, to which we added some violins, a cello, viola, and flute. It became the surprisingly delicate closing track on the album. Both of our previous albums had ended on frantic rock guitar epics. This was very different. One thing about Ritchie, he was never afraid to do things differently, and I really wanted to say something about the love of my life, especially as she had now done me the greatest honor by agreeing to marry me.

Wendy Dio: *Ronnie and I got married in April 1978. It was the same day* Long Live Rock 'n' Roll *was released, and Ronnie was about to leave with Rainbow for another long world tour. By then we had all moved to Connecticut because there was no state income tax. Bruce Payne, who was their manager, lived and worked in New York, so it all made sense.*

We held the wedding at Waveny Castle in New Canaan, Connecticut, and Ritchie was one of the best men. Bob Daisley was a best man, along with a few of the road crew, such as Bruce Payne, Colin Hart, and Raymond D'Darrio. My friends came in from England and LA. We had guests flying in from all over the world, including Mr. Udo, the famous promoter from Japan. The next day we left for an incredible honeymoon on a cruise in the Mediterranean. The whole thing was really lovely.

It was after we got back from our honeymoon, and Ronnie went out on tour again, that things first started to get really bad. Those last months in Rainbow were very stressful for Ronnie, and he was traveling without me. I don't think he wanted me to suffer the atmosphere that was building behind the scenes.

I found us a wonderful house to live in while they were on the road. Ritchie was living in Darien, a beautiful town on what they call Connecticut's Gold Coast. It was ranked one of the top ten richest places in America. I found a place for Ronnie and me in New Canaan, also on the Gold Coast. It was a big house, five stories situated on five acres. It looked kind of like the Amityville Horror house, actually, and was kind of scary. It had a big carriage house as well. Bruce Payne's office rented it for us. We were told that the man who invented the cigarette machine, James Albert Bonsack, had originally owned the house. It was a wonderful place, but I was there a lot by myself.

I remember being very, very lonely at the time when I was there, and I remember getting a little spooked by it. We moved all our stuff there and then one night, after Ronnie had left for the tour and I was on my own, I remember hearing this weird noise: la-la boom, la-la boom, la-la boom, la-la boom. It sounded like it was coming from underneath the floorboards. I thought, Oh my God, there's aliens in the basement! When Ronnie came back, we were sitting there, and he started hearing it too. He was like, "What the hell is that?" I said: "It's aliens in the basement!" We went down together, and it was the oil heater making this noise.

When Ronnie was with me, we had a fun time there. We had a stable door at the back of the house, and I used to stand there with the top half of the door wide open. I'd put gloves on and feed all the wild creatures. They would all line up—raccoons, skunks, bear-cats, you name it. I'd feed them all.

It was a happy time when Ronnie was there, but it was a sad time when he was away because I was very lonely. I'd been uprooted from England and moved to California. I had made friends in California, and now suddenly I'm in Connecticut. I didn't have any friends. I didn't have anybody. Then I met an English girl in a supermarket. She was looking for what in England we call "jelly." In America, "jelly" is what in England is called "jam." She was trying to buy jelly and all they kept giving her was jam. I said, "Let me help. In America, jelly is called Jell-O."

We became friends, and once I had a friend, it was a lot nicer. In Connecticut, you don't go out to dinner as much as you do in California. You go to people's houses. We would go to people's houses and have fun.

When Ronnie was home, we would go to people's houses, have dinner, and play poker. Ronnie nearly always won! He was a very good poker player. He was good at poker, good at chess, and read books in a day. He had a great head for figures, for mathematics

*and science. It made him good at a lot of things. Rainbow's Scan-
dinavian promoter, Eric Thompson, used to play ping-pong with
Ronnie and always lose. They would make bets, as much as $500 a
game. Well, this poor bugger lost all the time because Ronnie was
really good at table tennis. Even Ritchie wouldn't play Ronnie at
poker or ping-pong.*

*Then Ritchie had the idea of throwing a broom over telephone
poles. And they would bet on that. What no one knew until too
late was that Ritchie was a world-class javelin thrower. He could
shoot these broom poles like rockets. Turns out, Ritchie had won
all kinds of things for javelin throwing.*

We were still finishing *Long Live Rock 'n' Roll* when *On Stage* came
out in July 1977. This was the era of great live double albums. Both
Kiss and the Rolling Stones released acclaimed live doubles later
that same year, and over the next year or so bands like Thin Lizzy and
UFO would also score high on the charts with live doubles. In the days
before the Internet, the only other way to hear your favorite band live
on record was through illegal bootlegs, most of which were third-rate
recordings sold for extortionate prices.

In the case of Kiss, and, before them, Humble Pie, their live double
albums had been the ones that broke open the US charts for them. I
think our record label was hoping that *On Stage* would do the same
for Rainbow. It got great reviews and became another Top 10 hit in
Britain and Europe, but it only reached No. 65 in the US.

Put a gun to my head and make me talk, I would probably point out
that, had we gone with our original plan, which was to tour America
extensively to coincide with *On Stage*, instead of breaking up the brilliant band that recorded that album, I'm pretty damn sure it would
have done a lot better in America. Instead, by the time we had a new
line-up rehearsed and ready to go, we were committed to a twenty-
five-date European tour, followed immediately by a seventeen-date
UK tour, followed immediately by a seventeen-date Japanese tour.
By that point, we were deep into 1978, and the run-up to the release

of *Long Live Rock 'n' Roll* in April, which heralded the big US tour we should have done the year before—sixty shows that stretched throughout the summer. Consequently, much of those months on the road are now something of a blur to me. However, there are certain things I'll never be able to forget, like the time in France when we grabbed Eric Thompson, took off all his clothes, and hung him from these wires above the stage. They had just had a production of Peter Pan in the theater and still had all the flying apparatus up. Poor Eric didn't know what hit him. The show started and he passed out! We found out later he passed out because he was straining to see if he could poop on Cozy's head. Wendy got a photo of that and it ended up on the front page of a magazine.

Another night from the *On Stage* tour we were in Vienna and Ritchie ended the night locked up in jail. We were playing this huge, beautiful old opera palace, the Stadthalle. There were about six thousand fans going nuts, but the police and security were beating them viciously every time they stood or made any movement at all. It was horrible. We could see these uniformed goons beating kids bloody with nightsticks. To add insult to injury, the venue manager, a real prick, decided to walk down in front of the stage and stand there with his arms folded, just leering at Ritchie, as if to say, this is my show, not yours, and I'll do whatever I want to your stupid fans. Ritchie just walked to the edge of the stage, still soloing, kicked him in the head with the heel of his cowboy boot, and sent the guy flying three feet in the air! Cue pandemonium. We finished the number and were forced to leave the stage. The crowd started going crazy, but not as crazy as these state cops. Suddenly, backstage, there were armed police everywhere with dogs, all of them looking to exact revenge on Ritchie. But Ox, one of our roadies, hid Ritchie in one of the large flight cases, which the crew were hurriedly trying to get loaded out. Ox sat on it to deflect attention, but the dogs sniffed him out. Still, Ox refused to get off the flight case. They literally had to drag him off. Then they yanked open the case and arrested Ritchie and Ox, and took them off to jail.

Ritchie spent the next forty-eight hours locked in a six-by-six stone dungeon in this five-hundred-year-old Viennese prison.

The rest of us went back to the hotel where they decided to keep the bar open all night for us. The following morning, we got a police escort out of Austria. They drove us right to the German border. Meanwhile, Ritchie was still in his cell. I thought maybe he'd never get out and that this would be the end of the band. It happened to be a day off, so we just carried on to the next hotel and waited for word on what to do next. Some people said he'd be in jail for a year. Others said he'd be out as soon as the lawyers paid off the corrupt police in enough cash. All I knew for sure was that the next show the following night was a really big gig at Munich's Olympiahalle, which was being broadcast live by the German TV station WDR.

Come the evening of the show, we managed to get the start time put back a couple of hours while we waited and prayed for Ritchie to show up. He still hadn't arrived by 11:00 p.m. so we started the show without him, padding things out with a blues shuffle, then a keyboard solo, then a bass solo, then a drum solo...I seem to recall ad-libbing my way through a half-assed version of "Lazy," the old Deep Purple hit. Then, just as the band and the audience were about to lose the will to live, word came from the wings: "He's here, he's here!" Next thing, you can hear his guitar being plugged in, and there he is, picking up his solo right where he left off two nights before. He looked terrible. I don't think they'd fed him or allowed him to even sleep, but here he was. First number he launched us into was "Kill the King." I don't think we ever played it better! Ritchie was on fire, and we played an amazing show.

The band was still very much an all-for-one-and-one-for-all gang at that point. Cut to nine months later and the 1978 American tour, and it was a different story. *Long Live Rock 'n' Roll* was another Top 10 hit in Britain, where the title track gave us our first Top 30 single. It also became our biggest seller yet in Germany and Scandinavia, but, in Japan, it didn't do as well as *Rising*. Most crucially, for Ritchie, it barely made the Hot 100 in the US, barely scraping to No. 89. This meant that a lot of the '78 US summer tour was done opening for REO Speedwagon. We also opened shows for Alice Cooper and Cheap Trick. I could live with that but Ritchie couldn't. He didn't tell me that, but that was my feeling. We did a number of headline shows but none in arenas. The whole tour seemed plagued with bad feeling.

At one show in Pittsburgh we only played for forty-five minutes before Ritchie walked off. The audience rioted when we didn't come back on. At another show someone threw one of those huge M-80 fireworks that exploded like a grenade just as we were coming on for an encore. Needless to say, there were no encores that night. Some nights Ritchie would turn his back on the band and me. Sometimes he'd just leave. One time he climbed out the dressing room window and left. No explanation. No apologies.

Another night in Atlanta somebody threw a bottle at the stage. It flew about twenty-five feet in the air and hit me smack in the head! It nearly knocked me out. Blood everywhere. I was taken backstage where an emergency doctor put stitches into my head. Word went out to the band, "They're sewing Ronnie up, keep playing then Ronnie will be back out." I probably should have gone to hospital, but I hated the idea of spoiling the show for the genuine fans. The band jammed until I staggered back on, my head in bandages, blood still running down the side of my head. I could hardly sing because I was told it would open the sutures. We did about three minutes more and then called it a night, at which point Ritchie got into a fistfight with REO Speedwagon's tour manager—on stage. Afterwards David Stone was so upset he threw a bottle of wine at the wall. It missed Ritchie by inches. Ritchie picked up a bottle of whiskey and smashed it against the opposite wall. After that it was pure frenzy, as the band proceeded to trash that dressing room. When the roadies heard the commotion, they ran in and joined in. They took the place apart!

The final night of the tour was a predictably horrible occasion too. We were headlining the Palladium in New York. The Palladium only held about three thousand people, but the place was packed, and it felt like a homecoming gig. It was a hot August night and AC/DC were opening. On paper, it should have been a glorious way to end the tour. Instead, we played just three numbers before the PA started going haywire. With apologies to everyone, we halted the show while the road crew did what they could to fix the problem. After ninety minutes they still hadn't managed to make it right, so I was forced to go out and personally apologize again to the audience—and offer to let them have their money back.

"We'll make it up to you next time, New York!" I announced consolingly.

Only there never was a next time.

—‡ THIRTEEN ‡—

· · · · · · · · · · · ·

CALLED BY THE TOLL
OF THE BELL

For years afterward, people would tell me how surprised they were when I left Rainbow in 1978. I would smile and say I was kind of surprised myself, but that was just a joke to disguise the frustration I felt. I loved being in Rainbow. I felt Ritchie and I had something special going between us, as songwriters and performers. And I will always acknowledge my debt to Ritchie, not just for the opportunity he gave me to work with him after he left Deep Purple, but for everything I learned from him—all the things to do and all the things not to do. By the time I made my decision to leave, I felt I was left with very little choice. He had already fired Bob Daisley and David Stone not long after that last US tour. You might say I jumped before I was pushed, but it wasn't that simple. Nothing ever was when it came to dealing with Ritchie Blackmore.

It was obvious things weren't working for Ritchie anymore. He wanted greater success for the band and felt the only way to make that happen was to alter the musical direction, to open things up and make the band more commercial. Mainly, I think he was frustrated that Rainbow hadn't made more of a mark in America. The records all did increasingly well in Britain and Europe, but in America it was a different story.

The biggest rock records in America in 1978 came from Boston, who had a No. 1 album with *Don't Look Back*, and Foreigner, whose *Double Vision* album got to No. 3. Both albums would eventually sell over seven million copies each in America. As far as Ritchie could tell, the only difference between those albums and *Long Live Rock 'n' Roll*, which barely scraped into the US Hot 100, was that they both had big Top 5 chart singles like "Don't Look Back" and "Hot Blooded" that were played to death on the radio that year. Rainbow never had anything played on American radio.

That's my theory anyway, born of the fact that in the leadup to working on new material for the next Rainbow album, Ritchie let it be known that he had grown dissatisfied with the writing and wanted to go more mainstream. The record label was in Ritchie's ear too. "To get to the next level you need to write more commercial songs. You need to write a hit single." Or so I was told. In fact, Ritchie had stopped speaking to me by this point. Instead, he had brought Roger Glover in as producer, and Roger now had the thankless task of becoming the go-between for Ritchie and me. It was Roger who had the odious task of letting me know that Ritchie wondered if I could "stop writing in such a fantasy-oriented way and write some love songs?"

My reply was no, I could not, though not expressed quite so politely. I had underestimated how serious Ritchie was about making Rainbow more commercial. Roger told me of Ritchie's idea to record a cover of "Will You Still Love Me" by Carole King. He thought it would make a great single. I thought he must have been joking. When I realized he wasn't, I knew I was in trouble. Of course, I had released my own version of the song back in the Ronnie and the Prophets days, but it was a flop then, and I was genuinely afraid it would not only be a flop now but would actually derail the band's career.

I went to see Ritchie and we ended up arguing about it. Ritchie was the kind of guy that the more you argued against something, the harder he dug in his heels. In the end, Rainbow never did turn "Will You Still Love Me" into a single, though they did perform it live when they headlined the first Monsters of Rock festival in England in 1980. Maybe Ritchie did remember my words. Instead, they brought in Russ Ballard, a proven hit-maker, who gifted them "Since You've Been Gone," which did, as Ritchie had planned, become a big hit single, though not in America where it died the same death as all their other singles.

I was long gone by then. Ritchie claimed he fired me. Maybe in his mind he did. My memory is that I left. I had to. I talked to Wendy about it and she agreed. We were sick of the whole situation by then.

That's when I discovered what life was really like over the Rainbow. We were left with no house, no car, and no job. During my time in Rainbow, management were in control of paying for the house and car rentals. On top of that I was paid $150 per week, which was to pay for food, gas, clothes, and anything else we needed. Wendy and I would blow through that pretty quick. We didn't give it too much thought. After all, I was the co-writer of all the songs on four hit Rainbow albums, there would surely be handsome royalties coming through to me soon enough. Wouldn't there?

Actually, there wouldn't be. It would be decades, in fact, before Wendy was finally able to get all the money I was owed. I was still very naïve at this time. I had even expected Bruce Payne to continue as my manager, but, of course, he was not interested—he had Ritchie and Rainbow. I was more hurt about Bruce not wanting to manage me than about parting ways with Ritchie. Bruce had been my manager since before Elf. Now I had no one. A musician is totally lost without a manager, so I told Wendy she had to manage me. She tried to talk me into other managers, but I said I would rather screw my manager than get screwed by them!

If it hadn't been for a modest inheritance received out of the blue from Wendy's grandmother who had just died, I don't know what we would have done. Fortunately, Wendy was a strong person. She'd made it to America on her own. A little setback like being made homeless overnight wasn't about to slow her down. With Wendy urging me on, we decided to pack everything up into an old station wagon we purchased second-hand and drive to Los Angeles, where Wendy had friends and I still had good contacts in the music business.

In LA, Wendy and I rented a house we couldn't afford and moved in some of our friends. At one point there must have been about a dozen people living there with us, musicians mostly, their girlfriends and wives, friends of friends, and other waifs and strays from the Strip.

I weighed up my options. I could try for a solo career. Why not? There were plenty of record labels that would sign a singer who had just come out of a hit band. I began working on material with Micky Soule, but neither of us had any money, and I wasn't sure how I felt about the prospect of working my way from the ground up again. I was also writing with Paul Gurvitz, the handsomely hairy bassist of the Baker Gurvitz Army. I was also jamming on the side with former Steely Dan and Doobie Brothers guitarist Jeff "Skunk" Baxter, whose own career was now at a crossroads. And I was talking on the phone with Bob Daisley and David Stone, just trying to keep the musical gateways open, hoping something would come through that looked like it had something going for it. I wasn't making any money, but at least I was having fun again. I realized that last year in Rainbow hadn't been much fun at all.

Wendy, meanwhile, had struck up a friendship with Sharon Arden, soon to become Sharon Osbourne. Sharon was working for her father, Don Arden, one of the most fearsome managers in the music business. In the UK, Don was known as Mr. Big. Don had mob connections he liked to boast of, liked it to be known he carried a gun, and had various expressions he liked to employ such as, "Legs do break." Especially so, the implication was, if you were ever foolish enough to cross Don.

Don made his money managing artists as diverse as Little Richard, Gene Vincent, the Animals, the Small Faces, ELO, and now Black Sabbath, to name just a few. He was so rich he lived in a vast

Beverly Hills mansion once owned by Howard Hughes. Living with Don at the mansion was Sharon. It was through Wendy's connection with Sharon that I got invited over to meet the Sabbath guys. It was all very nice and polite, and when we left, I thought no more of it. They were getting ready to make their next album with Ozzy and I was still thinking about my own next move.

Then fate took a hand in things. I was at the Rainbow one night when Sabbath's tall brooding guitarist Tony Iommi walked in. I liked Tony right away. I knew he was the musical leader of Sabbath, the mastermind behind some of the most classic guitar riffs in the history of rock. We got to talking and it turned out that we were both contemplating solo albums. Tony confided that the band had just kicked Ozzy out. Ozzy has been the first to admit that he was his own worst enemy in those days, at a time when his drinking and drugging were completely out of control. He was hardly the only rock star to suffer that fate. Tony explained that the band's bassist and usual lyricist Terry "Geezer" Butler was also going through some family issues. Hence Tony's inclination to consider some sort of solo project.

I was all about experimenting with ideas at that point and suggested a possible collaboration. Maybe. One day. Maybe not. No biggie. Next thing I knew I was riding in the back of Tony's limo to a studio in LA where Tony had this "idea for a song" he wanted to play me but that he was having trouble finishing without a vocalist and some lyrics. When he pressed play on the console, I could not believe my ears! This was no off-the-cuff idea that still needed a ton of work. This was a fully-fledged Sabbath behemoth!

It started moody and glowing, nimble acoustic guitars enhanced by magic ribbons of electric guitar. Then, suddenly, after about forty seconds, there it was coming out of the speakers like forked lightning, the ultimate in monstrous riffs. No other guitarist in rock history could have come up with anything like it. Heavy, pure, yet shining like a beacon. Before the song was halfway through, before Tony could even ask me for my thoughts, I was scribbling down the words that came to me immediately.

"In the misty morning, on the edge of time, we've lost the rising sun, a final sign...."

Then I was up singing them into the mic, Tony rolling the tape, a huge smile on his chiseled face. It was to be the first thing Tony and I ever wrote together—and it was to be one of the very best. We called it "Children of the Sea," and the first time we played the demo back in the early hours of the following morning we both knew. This is what we were going to do next, come what may.

At first the talk was of me working with Tony on his solo album. That notion was quickly dispelled as we came up with more and more amazing songs together. With Ozzy definitely out and Geezer starting to come back from his family crisis, Tony and Bill took the next logical step and invited me to join Black Sabbath. The truth is he had never wanted to end Sabbath. He just couldn't see how they could continue without Ozzy.

I admit, at first, I shied away from the prospect. I was desperate to do my own thing again after the years working under Ritchie Blackmore's rule. I was also unsure how on earth I was supposed to replace Ozzy Osbourne in Black Sabbath. Unlike in years to come, when groups like Van Halen, Bad Company, Iron Maiden, and even Queen could bring in a new frontman with impunity, in the late '70s, the idea of a superstar group like Sabbath replacing their frontman was considered unthinkable. Led Zeppelin without Robert Plant, the Rolling Stones without Mick Jagger? Sacrilege.

The fact that I was already well known to the rock audience as the singer of Rainbow was a double-edged sword, as I saw it. I could end up alienating both Sabbath and Rainbow fans. On the other hand, as Tony saw it, bringing in a new singer no one had ever heard of before was a much bigger risk. Tony told me he was sure I'd be able to pull it off. Well, vocally, for sure. Ozzy was a great frontman, but a great singer? Not so much. But Ozzy *was* Sabbath as far as their legions of fans worldwide were concerned. How would they take to the American guy from Rainbow, no matter how well I could sing?

Someone who definitely did not think I was up to the job was Don Arden, who went insane when he discovered what Tony had been up to, threatening all sorts of retribution. Don knew deep down, however, that the situation with Ozzy was no longer sustainable. It had also been years since that line-up had had a hit record in the States. At one point he even suggested that I write with Tony and sing on the album, but that they take Ozzy out on tour.

When Tony told Don where he could shove that stupid idea, that was the end of Sabbath as far as Don was concerned. He canceled the lease on the house he was renting for them and sold their management contract to a guy named Sandy Pearlman, then the manager of Blue Öyster Cult, one of the many American bands in the '70s to be directly influenced by primetime Sabbath. He then told Sharon to start taking care of Ozzy as a solo artist: the beginning of a long and incessantly winding road that deserves a book of its own.

In fairness to Don, though, I still wasn't fully convinced either. What tilted my hand in the end was the sheer quality of the songs Tony and I had been writing. That plus the fact that Tony assured me this would not be like my situation in Rainbow, where Ritchie was the boss and that was that. If I joined him in Sabbath it would be as an equal partner with equal say, musically and business-wise.

The real clincher though was when Wendy got hold of me and told me straight: "Ronnie, we've got less than eight hundred bucks in the bank, we've got to do something!"

Wendy was right, of course. She always was. I phoned Tony: "Okay, man, I'm in. When do we start?"

Wendy Dio: *We rented this small house in Encino. It only had two bedrooms, and there were maybe ten people living there, plus our two dogs and a cat. But it had this huge swimming pool in the backyard and the weather was so good we mainly lived out there.*

Financially, it was tough until Ronnie got the gig in Sabbath. Oh God, we were so happy! He got $800 a week, up from $150 in Rainbow. And this time he made sure he was an equal member, *sharing in everything—songwriting, record sales, tour income—or else he wouldn't have gone in.*

But Ronnie almost blew it before he'd even got started!

It was just before he went to Miami to start working on his first Sabbath album. He had gone to the Rainbow on Sunset with Mark Nauseef, his old friend from Cortland. I had gone there to meet him, and he was a long time coming in. There was a lot of commotion and I'm like, what's going on? Then someone said I should come outside; Ronnie was in trouble. I rushed out and there was Ronnie sitting with Mark in the car, surrounded by cops!

It turned out Mark had been to the dentist that day and been given a prescription for cocaine, this pure pharmaceutical stuff you could only get from doctors. Ronnie never did any hard drugs. He smoked pot. That was it. When Mark said to him, "Here, you should try this coke I've got," Ronnie was like, "No, no." But Mark was like, "Go on, take it, try it." So Ronnie bent his head down and had a little sniff and as he did, wow! There was a police car and cops, and the next thing Ronnie and Mark are being arrested.

By the time I came outside, Ronnie was sitting handcuffed in the back of this police car. Mark had a doctor's prescription for it so they let him go, but Ronnie was thrown into this police car right outside the Rainbow. The window on his side was down and I ran over and let him have it. I'd been through hell and high water with Ronnie and stuck by him through thick and thin. Just as it seemed our worries were over, there's this?

I started screaming at him. "You just got a job in Black Sabbath and you fucking ruined it! You fucking stupid asshole! You fucking fuck!" This cop who saw what was happening came over and said, "I'm going to send him home with you. I think you're going to give him far worse than what we're going to do to him." With that, they released him. And, yes, I did do worse to him! He never again touched coke or anything else, except maybe a little pot now and then.

We named the album *Heaven and Hell* after one of the very best new songs Tony and I came up with together. We recorded it in Miami, at the Bee Gees' studio Criteria. We rented the house and the studio, and Tony and Bill came down. Unconvinced by Tony's insistence on sacking Ozzy, and going through a divorce from his first wife, Geezer didn't come down until later in the sessions. For a while, I played some of the bass parts. I also suggested we bring in Craig Gruber, at one point, but the gig was always Geezer's if he still wanted it, and when he finally joined us it was better for everyone.

Another suggestion I made, which worked out spectacularly well, was hiring Martin Birch to produce the album. Ritchie had dropped Martin from the Rainbow team. In Martin's case, it was hard not to deduce that his recent involvement as producer on David Coverdale's first Whitesnake records might have had something to do with Ritchie's decision. Whatever the reason, I was delighted that we were to be reunited to work on our first Black Sabbath album together. The band hadn't worked with an outside producer for many years, and I felt it would help bring the sound up to date working with someone of Martin's caliber.

Every day we used to go into the studio at six o'clock at night and work and play until six the next morning. The house was gorgeous, right on the ocean. We had Bill's drums set up in the big hallway. After finding our groove immediately with "Children of the Sea," Tony and I went on a roll. Next up was a fantastic rocker called "Neon Knights," which Tony described as "our hookiest track since 'Paranoid.'" The minute we wrote it we knew that was the one to open the album with.

Then there was the title track, "Heaven and Hell." Again, this was something Tony and I got immediately excited about. Unlike Ritchie, who now wanted to run a mile from the kind of epic tales I wished to tell, Tony fully embraced every lyrical idea I came up with. This went beyond the "medieval" metal of my Rainbow days, though, and pushed toward something that, in the context of Black Sabbath, became monumental. When I sang, "The world is full of Kings and Queens / Who blind your eyes and steal your dreams," it worked on so many levels—epic rock classic meets contemporary acuity—that both the band and I were now reaching places we never had before.

Tony would tell me how overjoyed he was to finally be able to take Sabbath to the next level. Full of light and shade, tracks like "Heaven and Hell," he said, belonged in the same pantheon as Sabbath classics like "War Pigs" and "Iron Man," only now there was a real sense of melody involved. Then there were other, equally exciting moments, like "Die Young," another full-on rocker, but again, full of musical contrasts. There was even a ballad, something Sabbath had rarely managed before, in the closing track "Lonely Is the Word." It was musically multifaceted, full of highs and lows, and newfound confidence.

One night I took Wendy to celebrate at this famous restaurant called The Forge. It was a big fancy place, so Wendy got all dolled up and I put on a jacket and shined my shoes. I was feeling good and wanted to show Wendy a really good time. The minute we walked in we were treated like royalty. We were given our own private room, they popped open some vintage champagne bottles, and we had this spectacular dinner. I had no idea where this was all coming from. Could it be that when I'd made the reservation on the phone and given my name, they had somehow figured out that Ronnie Dio was the singer in the band that had just played at the big casino? It seemed unlikely, but what else it could be? I did start to secretly wonder how much all this extravagance was going to cost me, but when I finally asked the maître d' for the check, he just smiled and said: "That's on your Uncle Johnny."

My what? Oh, wait...shit! No! Uncle Johnny?

It turned out The Forge was a well-known hangout in those days for celebrities and organized crime figures. When I'd given them the name "Dio" on the phone they assumed I must be connected in some way to Johnny Dio. But that still didn't explain the reappearance in my life—albeit at a safe distance—of my "Uncle Johnny."

I explained the story to Wendy, and she couldn't stop laughing. I kept a straight face as we left, looking out of the corner of my eye trying to see if I could spot my famous "uncle." I thought the least I could do was thank him for being such a good sport all these years, but, if he was there, I couldn't see him. So I'll say it here instead— *molte grazie*, Uncle Johnny! *Grazie per il regalo.*

Once we'd finished in Miami, we left with Martin for Paris to mix and make plans for our first tour together. I still had my private concerns over how well Sabbath fans would accept the band with me and not Ozzy. What drove me on was that it was such a fantastic record, easily one of my favorite albums I'd ever made. Everybody was so excited when they heard it—management, the record label execs, journalists, radio people—that we knew we had done something special.

It wasn't until it was released in April 1980 that we knew just how special, though, when the fans went out in their millions to buy it. It wasn't just a hit all over the world: *Heaven and Hell* is now the biggest-selling Sabbath album ever.

I still had one final challenge to face, though—stepping into Ozzy's shoes to front the band live. How would the diehard Sabbath fans feel about that? Tony and the guys acted cool, reassuring me there would be no problem at all, but I knew in my bones that things are never quite that simple. I knew it wouldn't just be a case of whether I could sing the songs—that was the least of my worries. It would all come down to how relatable I was to the fans. Ozzy may not have been the greatest outright singer, but he was always seen by the fans as one of them. What could I do to show them I was the same, but in a way that was still true to me?

I finally found the key to unlocking that door when I was daydreaming in my hotel room one night, thinking back to my fearsome old Sicilian grandmother and that spooky hand sign she used to do to ward off evil spirits and freak out innocent American bystanders.

The Mano Cornuto! The Horned Hand! It was perfect! Ozzy was always associated in Sabbath with the flashing of the V-sign for peace. Raising my hand in the Maloik, as my grandmother called it, would be similar enough to that to echo Ozzy's famous peace sign, but different enough that it would clearly signal a new sheriff in town.

Would it work, though? There was only one place to find out—on stage with Sabbath.

The 1980 Heaven and Hell Tour began with half a dozen shows in West Germany. The venues were packed. The fans still clearly loved the band even without Ozzy standing on stage with them. Most of them were prepared to give me a chance to prove myself; you could tell from their good reactions, and when we came off stage most nights, I really felt like I was getting somewhere.

There were some, though, that felt let down by Ozzy's absence and bunches of people giving me the finger and shouting "Ozzy" at some of the early shows. I sucked it up. I was sure once they gave us a chance they would really get off on the new Sabbath. Fortunately, as soon as I started flashing the Horned Hands, the fans picked up on it and began flashing them back. Just a few dozen at first, but more each night as word of mouth spread—and the music press reviews began to mention it. Soon, I began to feel like I really belonged up there on the stage with Sabbath.

The crowning glory came when we hit London in May for four nights at the prestigious Hammersmith Odeon. This was our first big show in one of the music business capitals. All four nights had sold out. Everybody would be there: friends, family, bands—in this case, members of Led Zeppelin, Pink Floyd, Thin Lizzy, and others—plus critics, record company bigwigs, some of whom had flown in from America and Japan. This was make or break.

If I was nervous, I was too nervous to notice. That all went away the moment I stepped on stage and flashed what is now universally known in the rock and metal world as the "devil-horned salute." Four thousand gone-crazy fans flashed it back at me! I couldn't believe it! This signaled mass acceptance by the Sabbath fans on a grand scale. That show in London was the best of the tour so far. The second show was better. The third was even better than that, and by the fourth we were all flying so high I honestly thought we would never come down.

It wasn't just me. The whole band was revived. When I'd joined the band, Sabbath was a ghost ship. They hadn't had a Top 10 album in the UK for five years, hadn't sold a million records in America for seven years. *Heaven and Hell* reversed that. It made Sabbath important again. It showed that these guys were not a bunch of musical fools, which had been the general perception before I'd joined because of the last few disastrous years with Ozzy.

And it started heavy metal up a little bit again. That same year Iron Maiden and Def Leppard released their first albums, Motörhead released their breakthrough *Ace of Spades*, AC/DC released *Back in Black*, and Judas Priest released *British Steel*. After punk and new wave had taken over the business, briefly, in the late '70s, rock and metal were considered dead. Not any longer. 1980 heralded the start of a massive revival of interest in the form that would last through the decade, and Black Sabbath and *Heaven and Hell* were at the forefront of that. It's still the album I'm probably most proud of making.

Within a few years, my grandmother's cherished Maloik sign became a common sight at all metal concerts, a cultural signifier of something specific to that experience: brotherhood and rebellion, wrapped up in one beautifully executed piece of physical graffiti. The next time you see it, think of me.

—+ FOURTEEN +—
. . . .

WEST OF WONDER

If this lineup of Black Sabbath had been able to keep the good feeling we had going around the *Heaven and Hell* album and tour, we could have been the biggest band in the world. There were problems from the start. You don't get a band that's been around for as long and been so successful as Black Sabbath without picking up some scars along the way, stuff that had been there long before I teamed up with Tony. Stuff I couldn't really do anything about but that I was able to sweep aside as Sabbath took off again around the world.

The global success of *Heaven and Hell* went far beyond anything I'd ever experienced before. My life changed. My world changed. I suddenly knew who I really was, as a writer and musician, and as a singer and frontman. Most crucially, my offstage voice began to match my onstage voice. I was no longer the new guy, lucky to get his shot. I was a leader, an equal partner.

Writing with Tony had allowed me to move into much deeper, sometimes darker territory than with Rainbow. Tony was as excited by the new partnership as I was, maybe even more so. He was a fantastic music director, very commanding on stage and in the studio, but he did not enjoy the day-to-day hassles of being the band's chief decision-maker. He was relieved when I assumed the role of dealing with managers, record label people, promoters, merchandisers, video people, the media, the fans....

Tony and, to a lesser extent, Geezer had this notion that the band should remain somewhat aloof from the fans, that we shouldn't do too many interviews, and that it was better to cold-shoulder the media. I don't think they felt strongly about it; it was more like, after all these years, they had stopped bothering. This ran completely contrary to my own way of doing things, so, again, I took on the responsibility for doing all the press and radio interviews. It worked well that way, too. Tony genuinely was the strong and silent type. I genuinely was the guy that wanted to communicate with people. After every show, I made a point of standing at the stage door, or by the tour bus, signing autographs for hours. Nobody went home without an autograph. The boys on the bus would grow impatient and start moaning for me to stop and get on the bus so they could leave, but that had never been my way, and I especially wanted the Sabbath fans that I knew missed Ozzy to understand that the Sabbath legacy was in good hands.

Sabbath did attract some extreme reactions from their fans, though. One time a guy with a cloak and a dagger dropped onto the stage and tried to stab me. Tony told me the American fans had been like that their whole career. Another time, I realized Geezer had stopped playing. I looked around and he was out cold on the floor, blood pouring from his head. Somebody had thrown a bottle that hit him and knocked him out. He had to have thirteen stitches in his head.

When touring down south in the Bible Belt, we had all these people protesting and demonstrating at the shows—because I personally was a devil worshiper. Memphis, Atlanta, Fayetteville, the religious nuts were out with the pitchforks and torches. I went out and spoke to local press and radio, did everything I could to try and explain that I was not a Satanist, but it was a waste of time. I began to see why Tony had wearied of this stuff, but I really wanted this new

Sabbath to work, for everyone, and I was prepared to do whatever it took to make that happen.

It was a pretty spectacular ride, while it lasted.

Wendy Dio: *Ronnie was flying high because he felt like this was his band now. When Sabbath arrived for their first tour of Japan, Ronnie was treated like royalty because he had been there so many times before with Rainbow. With Sabbath, Ronnie felt more in control. Ronnie might have been small, but he knew just how to handle Tony and the other Brits around the band. British people had always surrounded Ronnie. Even in Elf he had some British road crew. He liked the way British musicians thought about music more than the flashy American kind. It was more melodic, and I think that's why later he wanted to have British players in his own band. It was almost like he'd been a Brit in another life.*

Ronnie and Tony had a fantastic relationship writing-wise, and the rest of the band playing-wise. They were musical geniuses, all of them. That was an incredible adventure, and those were happy times.

Tony was back on his throne. On stage he was the dark knight hurling thunderbolts. Off stage he would have covers draped across the windows in his hotel suite, black candles burning night and day. The roadies used to call Tony's room the Batcave. He would consume gallons of ice-cold orange juice and mountains of ice-cold "snow," but Tony was always on when it came time for the show. Bill was not.

On tour we had Geoff Nicholls on keyboards. He would play from behind a side stage curtain, or so far back by the drums you couldn't really see him. Geoff had played on *Heaven and Hell*, but he wasn't a member of the band. He was a friend of Tony's from the Birmingham days, and Geoff worshiped him. Often, while sitting in the hotel lobby waiting for Tony and Geoff to come down, I'd bet with one of the road managers on how much Geoff would be dressed like Tony. We would throw a couple of dollars down, then the elevator doors would open and out came Tony and out came Geoff—in exactly the same clothes.

Geezer was the only one I really became close to, forming a friendship that would last a lifetime. Terry, his real name, was an unexpectedly gentle soul. He came from a poor Irish Catholic family, and he didn't like to swear. Like me, he read books and was very creative. He could be a rascal, but he was a genuinely good guy.

Wendy Dio: *The road would get bumpy for a while later on between Ronnie and Geezer, but for that first year or so they became great friends. Tony lived in England but Terry lived in Los Angeles. He and his American wife Gloria had a place in Woodland Hills. Ronnie and I had bought a little two-bedroom house just a few miles from there, in Tarzana. The four of us would hang out together.*

Ronnie and Geezer's birthdays are very close; Ronnie's is the tenth of July, Geezer's the seventeenth of July. Gloria and I went out together and, with their money, bought the boys both Mercedes: 280 SLs. I bought one in red for Ronnie. Gloria bought Geezer a silver one. We hid the two cars at our place in Tarzana, with giant gift bows on them, and we had this big joint birthday party for them. Ronnie loved Indian food, as did Geezer, so I made curry for three hundred people. I made a vegetarian curry, a chicken curry, and a lamb curry, enough for everyone. Ronnie and I were so busy entertaining that at the end of the evening when we went to have something to eat, and by now we were both starving, there wasn't a bit left.

It was such a happy time while it lasted. Ronnie was on top of the world. He had a Dio number plate made for his car but after driving it around for two weeks he had to take it off. Everywhere he went people were honking their horns and giving him the Maloik sign.

The only really challenging situation arose with Bill Ward. I don't think Bill ever got over Ozzy being forced out of the band. He and Ozzy had been best mates in Sabbath. I knew how conflicted I felt when my best mate in Rainbow, Jimmy Bain, got pushed out, and Jimmy and I had only been in a band together for a couple of years. Bill and Ozzy had been friends since Sabbath had begun in the late '60s.

Unlike Rainbow, where people came and went, Ozzy was the first of the original lineup to leave Sabbath. Tony didn't care. He saw working with me as the best way to turn Sabbath into something bigger and better. Geezer had taken longer to make up his mind. He thought getting rid of Ozzy was a big gamble, but once Geezer saw how rejuvenated the band was and what an impact *Heaven and Hell* had made, he was fully into it. But it hit Bill badly. My impression, though, was that Bill had been suffering for a long time. He is the first one now to talk freely about the problems he was having with drugs and alcohol back then, but even that seemed to only hint at whatever was driving him down. He was still a fantastic drummer, one of a brilliant generation of English rock drummers that included Cozy Powell, John Bonham, Ian Paice, and Keith Moon. But now Bill was in trouble. You never knew which guy was going to show up, the mad guy or the sad guy. I honestly don't think I ever really met the happy guy.

We were rehearsing in this disused cinema in London when we first saw the video for the "Neon Knights" single. We sat in the stalls watching the playback on the big screen. It was a pretty straightforward performance video. Then Bill suddenly started screaming: "Oh, this beautiful! This is fucking beautiful!" Then he stood up and began ripping up the seats and throwing them around. As he finally stormed out of the room still yelling about how "fucking beautiful!" the video was, I sat there in astonishment. Tony and Geezer had clearly seen it all before, but I didn't quite know how to react. I later found out that Bill's beloved mother had died just days before, and Bill had been on a bender ever since. It seemed to me, though, that Bill had been on a bender for far longer than that. He was like an animal in pain.

These were still the days when rock musicians on drugs and in pain were to be found in any major band. As long as they could still do their gig. That was the attitude. So we soldiered on with Bill. Once we were on the road there was no escape anyway. Some nights Bill was amazing, and there were some days when he really worried me.

We had been playing almost every night for three months when we began our first American tour in July 1980. Having decided he couldn't handle flying to gigs anymore, not even on the band's private plane, Bill was traveling in a motor home with his brother and his wife and his kid and everything, which meant he never really left that drug bubble he was in, except to go on stage. It was a nightmare. For Bill most of all.

Sabbath was big in most parts of America, but it varied. We were huge in New York but less so in LA. We were a couple of weeks into a co-headline arena tour with Blue Öyster Cult—billed as the Black & Blue Tour—when we took off to appear at something called the Summer Blowout Festival, at the 90,000-capacity LA Memorial Coliseum. We were third on the bill behind Journey, who had supported Sabbath in 1977, and the headliners Cheap Trick, who I had toured with in Rainbow. The next day, appearing on the bill at the Day on the Green #2 festival in San Francisco, Journey were now the headliners, Sabbath was second, and Cheap Trick had dropped to third.

It was supposed to be a friendly backstage. Linda Blair, who'd been the teenage star of *The Exorcist*, came walking past us. She was going out with one of the guys from Molly Hatchet, who was also on the bill. Bill shouted something at her. It was one of those jokes no one laughed at. It didn't come out funny so much as crude and unnecessary.

That was the night Bill quit the band—"Forever!" It resulted in a week of canceled shows before Bill agreed to come back again. We managed another week of shows before Bill quit again. Only this time he forgot to tell us.

It was the night before we were due to headline at the McNichols Sports Arena in Denver. Talk about a showstopper. The McNichols was an 18,000-seater which had been sold out for weeks. After another week of canceled shows when Bill didn't come back this time, we were forced to find a new drummer. I suggested we reach out to Cozy Powell, who had just left Rainbow a few days before, but it was either too soon for Cozy or there was consternation about filling the spot in Sabbath with a second former Rainbow player.

Then Tony suggested a twenty-two-year-old New Yorker named Vinny Appice. Vinny was the younger brother of former Vanilla Fudge and Rod Stewart drummer Carmine Appice. He'd been in Rick Derringer's band and others, and Tony was a fan of an album by Vinny's own band, Axis. The idea was for Vinny to fill in for Bill until he was able to return, but the longer the tour went on, the more it became obvious Bill wasn't coming back. That's when Vinny became a permanent member.

One dream that did come true for me was when Sabbath headlined Madison Square Garden in October. I thought of those days twenty years and several lifetimes ago, when I would walk past the Garden, look up at whatever name was on the marquee, and fantasize about seeing my own name up there. I still didn't actually have my name up there, but my band did.

19,900 people showed up, and it was named the top grossing show in the US for that week according to *Billboard*. I finally got to sing at MSG. The show itself wasn't perfect. I remember having a row backstage with Sandy Pearlman, but that was all forgotten once I was on stage. It was a big moment for me.

It was great also to be in the band for their first ever tour of Japan. With Rainbow I'd gotten used to headlining to 15,000 at the Budokan. With Sabbath we did a string of smaller halls in Tokyo, Kyoto, and Osaka. Then we did a week of similar-sized shows in Sydney.

We fired Sandy not long after, and I assumed the management role until we could figure something out when the tour was over. It was around this time I got my reputation for throwing my weight around. It was true, I did become much more assertive. I needed to be. Sabbath was a ghost ship when I joined. They desperately needed a captain, and I was more than happy to take on that responsibility, before I realized just how deep some of the problems went and how unfixable some of them would prove to be.

Meanwhile, we had a second album to record. For the first one, Tony and I wrote in a controlled environment in a living room with little amplifiers. We approached the writing much differently for this one. We hired a studio, turned up as loud as possible, and smashed through it all. You could say it made for a different kind of attitude.

Geezer was now involved and almost inevitably it changed the chemistry Tony and I had enjoyed working alone. It became obvious that Geezer wanted to be involved again in the writing of the lyrics. Throughout the Ozzy era, although Ozzy came up with his own vocal melodies, Geezer almost always penned the lyrics. You only have to scan the lyrics of classics like "War Pigs" or "Children of the Grave" to appreciate how good Geezer is, but I had written all the lyrics on *Heaven and Hell*, and I had always written my own lyrics. I never needed a co-writer. I didn't need one now. Geezer and I were friends, but this is where I had come in with Tony and Sabbath: I brought the voice, the vocal melodies, and the words. This drove a wedge between us. We would eventually get past it, but for now it was a wound that steadfastly refused to fully heal.

Tony affected not to notice any change. He had known and worked with Geezer for his entire career; they obviously had a much deeper bond. That had not mattered when we first started writing together. And while we still worked well together, I felt Tony moving away from me—just a little at first then, later, a lot.

Tony's beef concerned a solo deal I had recently signed. After the success of *Heaven and Hell*, the band was able to renegotiate a better deal with our record companies, Warner Bros. in America and Polygram in Europe. The deal they came up with included the offer of a solo deal for me. It wasn't a big money deal and there was no discussion of trying to turn me into a solo star. It was a sweetheart deal that was supposed to give me the room to make my own album at some point in the future, somewhere between Sabbath commitments. My first thought was to make an album featuring me with all my friends, like Kerry Livgren from Kansas, the Elf guys, David Stone, Skunk Baxter, and other people I'd been jamming with before I met Tony. It was going be a fun album, one day. Tony didn't see it that way. I think he thought the offer of the album was divisive and he seemed pretty livid with me.

The first track we recorded was "The Mob Rules," which is what we eventually called the album. Tony and I had come up with one of our best rockers at John Lennon's former country estate, Tittenhurst Park, near Ascot: the famous white house in which they made and filmed the *Imagine* album. We were just jamming on ideas for a track we'd been invited to do for the soundtrack of a forthcoming animated movie, *Heavy Metal*, starring John Candy. The movie would bomb, but the track was hotter than a pistol.

We did the rest of the album at the Record Plant in LA. Martin was producing again and there was great energy to a lot of the music, but we couldn't quite escape the idea that this was the follow-up to *Heaven and Hell* and we had a lot to live up to. I admit "Turn Up the Night" was a subconscious attempt to create "Neon Knights" part two. "Voodoo" was conceived somewhat as this album's "Children of the Sea." The best track was "Sign of the Southern Cross," which for me was one of the best things we ever did, up there with "Heaven And Hell," maybe even higher.

When *Mob Rules* was released in November 1981 it didn't quite replicate the success of its predecessor, hitting Number 12 in Britain and again making the Top 30 in America. Reviews were more mixed. Those that liked it really liked it. Those that didn't get it just kind of shrugged. For me, it remains one of the best albums I've ever done.

Back on tour, Sabbath was as in demand as before. We did another Madison Square Garden show and we sold out the LA Arena and the LA Forum. We toured from November 1980 until August 1981, mostly in America. We were on a roll. By the end of it, however, I felt we were rolling in the wrong direction and might crash.

I was feeling increasingly alienated from Tony and Geezer. I liked to smoke pot occasionally and drink a beer, but I didn't do coke and had no time for hard drugs. Tony and I may have hit it off when we were jamming or writing together, but socially we were now poles apart.

Vinny was now my best pal. He was from Brooklyn. We were both New Yorkers. We liked a lot of the same foods. By the end of the tour,

Vinny and I would ride off in one car after a show, and Geezer and Tony would ride off in another.

Tony and I had begun to argue a lot and would end up screaming at each other. The level of mutual mistrust was out of control. In the summer of 1982, during a break in the tour, mixing began on what became *Live Evil*, a live double album, and things finally nosedived.

According to legend, a major rift was caused when Vinny and I allegedly snuck into the studio whenever Tony and Geezer weren't there, in order to bring the vocals and drums further up in the mix and push Tony's and Geezer's parts down. None of this is true. The very suggestion that I would do something like that is offensive. The truth is, Tony and Geezer had become night owls. We were booked to start work at the studio each day at 2:00 p.m., but Tony and Geezer might not show up until the evening. I don't like to waste time, so I would begin working. If anything, any meddling would have happened after I'd left the studio. Tony and Geezer would be in there alone together all night.

That's not the point. The real problem, as both Tony and Geezer would later insist in the press, was their shared fear that I was trying to take over the band. This could not have been further from the truth. Yes, I'd taken the reigns in all those areas where neither Tony nor Geezer cared to be involved—all the stuff that happens away from the studio—but when it came to the music, I was the same person Tony had been so delighted to hook up with in the first place.

Years later, after we had all moved on with our lives, we agreed the whole thing was the sort of tragedy that afflicted many rock bands. In the days when musicians still thought of drugs like cocaine as a "creative tool." Though again, it wasn't only down to the fact that Tony, in particular, had become temporarily snow-blind. It was the whole convoluted history of Sabbath's past, along with my own deep determination to never allow myself to be dictated to in the way I had towards the end of my time in Rainbow.

The end result was a live double album I had little to do with, and that I was disappointed by when I finally heard what they had done with it. Apart from my vocals, most of it was bolstered by studio overdubs. You could hardly hear the crowd. For me, it was a missed opportunity to leave a real marker of our time together as one of the all-time great live bands. Instead, by the time it was released in December 1982, I was gone from Sabbath. The last straw for me was when I learned that Tony had tried to impose a ban on me entering the studio. I tried speaking to Tony about it, but he hid from me. This was the same Tony I had sparked the second coming of Sabbath with just a couple of years before.

Geezer phoned me at Tony's instigation to say, "I don't think this is working out. We really want Tony to produce the album on his own." Code for: they didn't want me around anymore.

I said, "So if you don't want me involved with this album, are you saying it's over, then?"

Geezer said, "Well, er...yeah, I suppose so." They could never just tell you straight. It was all a device to force me out. As before with Ritchie and Rainbow, I was already halfway out the door by the time they called.

We could have been the best in the world, and if we couldn't quite achieve that, we could at least part as friends, even brothers. Instead, our personal relationships had degraded to the point where, adding insult to injury, they deliberately credited me on the *Live Evil* sleeve simply as Ronnie Dio. They knew I was particular about always using my full name. They did it just to be shitty.

FIFTEEN

A RAINBOW IN THE DARK

ou know that expression, "When one door closes, another opens?" At the start of 1983, I felt like that had happened to me—twice! I had the door slammed in my face first by Ritchie Blackmore then by Tony Iommi. This time I decided I'd make damn sure it never happened again by taking back the reigns of my own destiny and putting together my own band.

I began 1983 filled with both optimism for my new band and sadness for what had just happened with Sabbath. I wasn't happy with the way everything ended, but I felt proud of what I had achieved. I gave as much to Sabbath as Sabbath gave to me, probably more so.

Meanwhile, the solo deal I'd signed the year before gave me a head start. Even without that, though, I knew what I had to do. Instead of planning on a more leftfield kind of solo album, which had been the original idea, I switched all my time and energy into creating a band that could compete with the music I'd worked so hard to co-create in Rainbow and Sabbath—and then take it to the next level.

Vinny Appice left Sabbath and joined me in my big new adventure. This was a bold move for a kid in his twenties: stick with the arena-headlining world-famous band or take a chance in a whole new situation with me. I took Vinny for dinner at the Rainbow and laid it all out for him. He was like a little brother to me, and more than anyone else, had seen exactly how things had gone down in Sabbath. I would not have blamed him if he had chosen to stay where he was. Vinny said he wanted in and that was that. He started coming out to the little house in Tarzana (yes, it is named after Tarzan—Edgar Rice Burroughs wrote the original *Tarzan* novels there) and we would jam in a small wooden shack out back: Vinny on drums, me on bass, sitting on a stool, singing along. I already had "Holy Diver," which began as something I was thinking of bringing to Sabbath, and a couple of other riffs, like the one I turned into "Don't Talk to Strangers." We'd record them onto cassette, and some of it ended up on the first Dio album.

I'd chosen "Dio" as the name because I wanted to build a *band*, not a career as a solo singer. The label people originally wanted me to go out as Ronnie James Dio, but that didn't sound right to me. It ensured that I would always be labeled "ex-Black Sabbath singer Ronnie James Dio" or "Ronnie James Dio who used to be in Rainbow." I didn't want to be known for how I used to be. I wanted to be in a new band, one built in my own image, not someone else's, to show those Rainbow and Sabbath fans what I was truly capable of once I'd finally thrown off the creative shackles.

Wendy Dio: *It was just easier to call the band Dio. Also, with respect, it was Ronnie's name that was going to sell the album. The record company wasn't behind the idea at all. We had to do whatever it took to make it happen. If it worked, everybody would benefit, which is exactly what happened.*

Ronnie was a born leader. There was always a bit more tension in the room when Ronnie walked into the rehearsal room. He was definitely the boss. They got $500 a week for rehearsals when they first started the band. Then they were paid $700 a week when they *first went out on the road. Then it went up to $1,700 every week whether the band worked or not. Ronnie always looked after his band. When they went to Japan, Ronnie gave them each $5,000. I get mad these days when certain former members moan about how much they got paid. I have all the receipts and paperwork to prove how well Ronnie took care of them. Vivian to this day still picks up healthy royalty checks for the handful of songs he had a part in writing with Ronnie.*

First, though, there were practicalities to deal with. When I left Sabbath, I wasn't homeless and broke like I had been when I left Rainbow, but I was not yet a wealthy man. We would have to re-mortgage our house in Tarzana in order to fund Dio. I had my solo deal, but that's all I had. Wendy and I discussed it and agreed we could not sit back and expect the label to invest heavily in the new band. We would have to prove to them we were serious first by putting our own money into it. It was a big risk. It was expensive to put something on the road that could compete with what I'd been doing in Rainbow and Sabbath. I could not afford for Dio to look any less. Wendy knew that I had to start at the very top, not back at the bottom. I wasn't asking anybody's permission anymore. I was ready to go to war.

It was around then that Wendy officially became my manager, and, therefore, manager of Dio the band. Wendy had been taking care of the money side of things for me for years. When I first asked her to leave her life behind and come with me on tour with Rainbow, she told me, "I can't do that. I have to work because I like nice things, and I'm used to buying nice things and doing that." I said, "Well, you just take care of the money. I don't care about money at all." She learned the rest through our shared experiences over the previous ten years. She had never been shy at speaking up, even to Ritchie. Wendy knew her stuff.

She'd already branched out into management with the band Rough Cutt, so stepping up to manage the band just seemed like the best idea—especially given that I was banking our whole financial future on it. From that moment on, Wendy became my voice away from the microphone. I ran the music. She ran the business. As my wife, Wendy always looked after me like a wolf mother protecting her pack. As a manager, she became an attack dog.

All we needed now was the rest of the band. We put feelers out in LA for a guitarist. One of the first we tried out was a twenty-five-year-old kid named Jakey Lou Williams, soon to become more famous, ironically, in Ozzy Osbourne's solo band as Jake E. Lee. He'd been in Rough Cutt, who Wendy had recently begun managing. Jake was clearly talented, and we jammed for a while, but I just wasn't sure. He was not an easy person to get to know. Also, I had already decided I wanted to make the band more international, not just an American band. For me it was that combo in Rainbow and Sabbath that really worked the magic. Jake was a flashy guitarist. British guitarists tended to be more melodic. Wendy used to joke and say it was almost as if I'd been a Brit in another life.

Wendy felt sorry for poor Jake when I decided he wasn't right. Now he didn't have a gig. She ended up driving him to the audition for Ozzy. She'd told Sharon about him, and it worked out really well.

Now that I knew what I didn't want, I had a much clearer idea of what I did want: an American-British band. It was with this objective in mind that I flew with Vinny to London. We shared a room at the Royal Garden Hotel in Kensington. Vinny called us the Odd Couple, because I liked to read in bed at night before I went to sleep and he couldn't stand the light being on. It was winter and London seemed to be especially cold. We couldn't get the hotel room warm, so Vinny would be blowing the hairdryer to try and heat the room up. We laughed our way through it.

I had a couple of ports of call in mind. At the same time, with the British rock and metal scene blowing up right then, it seemed a good time to go out and catch a few gigs, see what was happening. Our first day, we bought a music paper and checked out the gig guide. That didn't turn out well. We went to one club to check out a guitar player, but it was a reggae band and the guy had dreadlocks. He was a good player but not really the music or the image I was looking for.

The next night we went out for dinner with Bob Daisley, grabbed a curry and some beers near Bob's flat in Westbourne Grove. I wanted to talk about the possibility of Bob joining as the bass player. Bob was more than just a bass player, as he'd proved when he joined Ozzy's band and co-wrote most of the material on Ozzy's first couple of solo albums. Since then, he'd left and joined Uriah Heep, but I'd heard he could be tempted into something a little more exciting. As chance would have it, Bob had just agreed to work with Ozzy again on his next solo album. Apart from a great curry, there wasn't much else to discuss with Bob.

Next, I turned my attention to the other great bass player I had first worked with in Rainbow: Jimmy Bain. After being fired from Rainbow, Jimmy had formed a great band called Wild Horses with former Thin Lizzy guitarist Brian Robertson. I'd actually gotten up and sung a couple of songs with them at a show in London a couple of years before, and it felt good being shoulder-to-shoulder in the middle of two such outgoing and exciting players. Although I wasn't thinking of Jimmy and Robbo specifically, the three-man frontline was definitely what I had in mind for my own band. By 1983, Wild Horses had run out of steam, and Jimmy had become an integral part of the team behind former Thin Lizzy frontman Phil Lynott, co-writing and playing on Phil's solo albums. Jimmy was just finishing up some final Wild Horses dates in Ireland, before going on the road with Lynott as his keyboard player, when I got him on the phone. I knew he was committed to Phil, I just thought Jimmy would know of any new guitar players on the scene.

The first one he mentioned to me was a young English firebrand named John Sykes. John had been the standout guy in a new wave of British heavy metal band called Tygers of Pan Tang. Later he would find American fame in Whitesnake, but right now he was being lined up for Thin Lizzy, who Lynott was planning on making one last album with.

The next name Jimmy came up with was a twenty-year-old unknown named Vivian Campbell from a Northern Irish band called Sweet Savage that had opened for Wild Horses. Although Jimmy admitted he'd never actually heard Vivian play, he said the buzz off the fans about this kid's playing was phenomenal. I decided I would check him out and asked Jimmy to arrange an introduction.

The next day Vivian flew over to London. I hired a rehearsal room and Jimmy brought Vivian down. I was surprised to see that Jimmy had also brought his bass with him. I assumed it was just to help out. We plugged in and played for about fifteen minutes, and it was good, really good.

Vivian didn't know much about Ozzy-era Sabbath, but he had completely memorized the *Heaven and Hell* album. It was obvious that he had also been a big fan of the original Rainbow. I let him run through his arsenal of flash guitar tricks before starting to push him for something more. He reverted to playing basic Chuck Berry rock 'n' roll guitar licks. That's when I really knew he might be the one. He was making stuff up, urged on by me, and it was really starting to cook. By the end of the session I had the band running through a version of "Holy Diver," and again it just took off. So we carried on and it really was like magic, all laughing and smiling. You just know instinctively when you've got the right bunch of guys together.

But what was Jimmy's deal? Wasn't he already in tight with Lynott and the Lizzy gang? I guess not. Jimmy didn't even wait to be asked to join. He just naturally assumed he was in after how well things had gone that first night with Vivian and Vinny. It reminded me of all the reasons why I loved him so much in Rainbow. He was a great bass player, who could also play keyboards, guitar, synthesizers, and he could write and sing. But most of all he was a real character. Devilish one minute, delightful the next, even a little dangerous, allied to a complete inability to take no for an answer.

I phoned Wendy with the news that somehow I had found the perfect combination: a half-American, half-British rock band that I knew I could mold into something truly unique and special. Wendy got to work and, within weeks, the new four-piece lineup of Dio was in LA, working at the Sound City duplex in Van Nuys: a courtyard with a rehearsal room on one side and a recording studio on the other. We already had "Holy Diver" and "Don't Talk to Strangers." The other seven tracks were all concocted at these sessions.

We used to go in there every night, playing and smoking a lot of pot. Friends would come down. It was a great atmosphere. The place let the band do what they wanted. The guys partied hard and did some damage to some walls, I believe, and a couple of vending machines. Then they opened up the pinball machine so you couldn't lose the ball. It was the most fun I'd had preparing for an album since the days of Elf. I remember jamming with the band as Jimmy lay on the stage on his back playing bass. Vivian had never seen anything like it. I told him, "Don't worry about it. That's the way he is."

Nobody in the band had a dime, so Wendy and I bankrolled everyone and everything. She put us all on $500 a week, which we could spend. Everything else—room, board, studio and equipment costs, food, transport—Wendy and I took care of. Vinny stayed at his own place in LA, but Viv and Jimmy had an Oakwood Garden apartment, a lovely big place for which I paid $1,760 a month so they had somewhere nice to live. All the big bands stayed there. Most nights they seemed to end up at the Rainbow, especially Jimmy, who quickly got to know everybody. Viv was certainly getting an in-at-the-deep-end education in the American music biz.

Wendy and I would also have dinner at the Rainbow, see all the crazies, hang out with the ones we liked, but only on a Saturday night. We'd dress up and make an entrance. Mario always gave us the center table, and the place would be buzzing around us. They treated us like royalty. Wendy had been one of the scene's original queens, and now she had returned as a VIP on her own terms. Wendy had earned her place at the table. And so had I.

Vinny and his beautiful French-Canadian wife, Justine, would often join us. Or we'd go 'round to their place for a barbecue. Me and Vinny were working hard, and when we weren't, we were very settled in our homes. Meanwhile, Jimmy and Viv were running rampant in all the usual LA hot spots. Somehow it all made for a genuine sense of expectation and excitement every night when we walked into that rehearsal room together. That was the real buzz, the buzz you only get from being in a band.

We didn't over-think things. In Rainbow and Sabbath, there had been this whole history behind the people I was trying to write with. You felt you had to make everything as perfect as possible. Here, though, we just jammed and allowed songs to emerge in their own time. We began with a concoction of parts from older songs that both Jimmy and Viv brought to the table, built around the two songs I had already written, and some thrown-together numbers we messed with.

One such piece was "Stand Up and Shout," which would open the album. It was a riff Jimmy had, but which Viv would always point out was similar to an old Sweet Savage riff he'd written. That riff was stolen from a Gary Moore riff, so it was six degrees of separation. Later, some critics suggested the riff to "Holy Diver" was not exactly a million miles away from Survivor's "Eye of the Tiger." I'd begun that song though when I was still in Sabbath. That anthemic marching beat has been the backbone of many a monumental musical moment. It's not the size, it's what you do with it. Survivor had a huge pop hit. I had a new heavy metal classic for the ages.

The album's other cornerstone track, "Rainbow in the Dark," was a truly collaborative event. Viv got the idea for the riff, he said, from a Sweet Savage song he'd written when he was sixteen, called "Lady Marion." Maybe so, but where we took it was completely new and different, so much so that "Rainbow in the Dark" became one of the new numbers that really forged Dio as a band. Vinny gave it his unique flavor, inverting the beat. As soon as they started playing, I started singing the melody on top of it. Then Jimmy went over to this little Yamaha and came up with the keyboard motif. That was it. We had the whole song done in ten minutes.

It was a similar story with "Straight Through the Heart." Jimmy had the riff left over from his Wild Horses days, and he and the boys started kicking it around. I came in with the vocal melody and lyrics, and we had the song. Same deal with another riff Jimmy had in his mind, which became "Shame on the Night," another real band composition, including my suggestion of a wolf howl at the intro.

Then there were happy accidents like "Invisible," where we had come up with a riff but hadn't done anything with it yet. The following night we smoked some particularly strong pot and our soundman put the tape in backwards. It started playing, and we all sat there laughing, going "You asshole!" Then I said, "Wait a minute, this sounds good!" The band wound up learning the riff backwards. It's the riff forwards then the same riff backward.

It was such a different way of working from what I'd grown accustomed to in Sabbath and Rainbow. Working out of Sound City, we recorded the first four songs and added some overdubs, then dragged all the gear back across the parking lot to where we had the rehearsal room. We would set up again and carry-on having fun, jamming, and seeing what we came up with. There was plenty of pot being smoked but no heavy drugs. It was just about creating a good atmosphere to work in. The boys would jam, and I would get up and sing. It was like the boys' club.

When we had four or five more songs, same thing, drag all the gear back across the parking lot and into the real studio to record. It started sounding really, really good, and eventually we had an album. One night, one of the techs said, "This is gonna go Platinum!" I couldn't afford to let myself think like that. I just hoped we would get out on the road with this and make it work. None of us really knew what would happen once the record hit the stores.

The end result, which I called *Holy Diver* after the first song I'd written for the album, was written and recorded in a little over a month and was one of the proudest moments of my career to that point. Rock, but not just noise. There were great songs on there and great playing too. And, I hope, some great singing. Coming at a time when hard rock and heavy metal were moving fast into a new era that would soon be dominated by MTV—launched the year before—and bands like Mötley Crüe, Def Leppard, and, right behind them, Metallica, for me *Holy Diver* harkened back to the classic '70s era of rock while at the same time embracing all the speed and poise of the '80s. This was a deliberate move on my part. I knew exactly what I wanted to do with Dio as a band and where I wanted it to go.

Wendy and I came up with the idea for the album sleeve: a devil drowning a priest. Or was it? We weren't deliberately trying to shock; I just wanted to make people wonder what the symbolism was about. This was a time in rock before social media and before CDs had replaced vinyl as the most popular format for albums, where meaningful cover art was an intrinsic part of the package. When we got the same kind of blowback from the religious fanatics in America that Sabbath had gotten, I would say, "How do you know what's actually supposed to be going on in that picture? How do you know that it's even a priest? Just because he's got priest's clothes on? What if he's the devil and the demon is the righteous one?" There was some trepidation from the label people that certain record stores in the south might not stock it, but then the stories started coming out in the news about the Catholic Church, with the priests who had been sexually abusing kids, so we thought, "Okay."

Released in May 1983, I was especially pleased to be able to get that first Dio album out there so quickly after leaving Sabbath. It was important to show that as far as I was concerned Dio was good to go. The best news of all, though, was how well the album was received by fans and critics alike. It got great reviews everywhere, and as the years went by *Holy Diver* became recognized—along with Rainbow's *Rising* and Sabbath's *Heaven and Hell*—as one of the greatest heavy metal albums ever made.

When the band did a signing session at Tower Records on Sunset Boulevard, where the album was made available for the first time at midnight, we were there until nearly five in morning. There were a couple thousand people there and, as always, I made sure me and the band signed every last autograph. No one was left out. All four of us sat at the table signing and signing and signing until we thought our hands would fall off.

Wendy Dio: *We knew Ronnie had a really good following of his own by then, but we never knew the album would do as well as it did. It was overnight almost! The record company couldn't believe it. They had not seen things going that way at all, which is why we did everything ourselves. We did our own marketing, promotion, everything. To be proved right so quickly, the elation was amazing. After all the things we'd gone through, the trials and tribulations, having no money, having nothing, and then all of a sudden it was all happening, was fantastic! Not "I told you so" because I never ever thought it was gonna get like that. More, "I showed you!" It really was great for Ronnie, unbelievable.*

At another record store signing in Santa Monica, there were so many people that they broke the window and charged through the store, which ended that. Once the band started touring, the shows kept getting bigger and bigger and bigger. Ronnie took it all in stride. He wasn't one to get overexcited or count any chickens, but I think when he saw all the kids coming into the signings and the shows and then the great reviews the band and the album were getting, he knew he'd really done it this time. He didn't read reviews. But I read the reviews, so I read the reviews to him. It was just an absolutely amazing time and great feelings everywhere and great people. It was a feeling that everything we'd worked so hard for, going all the way back to when he joined Rainbow in 1975, had finally paid off.

The first tour as Dio began in July, with a low-key show at a 3,000-capacity venue called The Concert Barn, in the Northern Californian town of Antioch. The album had been out a couple of months and the place was packed. It was a great night, a lot of fun—fun being a word I hadn't used about doing a show for a long time. I remember Jimmy falling off the stage during "Invisible"—he didn't miss a beat! Vivian's face was a picture.

Right after that we were booked as Special Guests on an Aerosmith tour. This was not the classic, cleaned-up lineup of Aerosmith that would make their big comeback a few years later. This was the Steven Tyler out-for-lunch period, and their performances were shambolic to say the least. I decided I couldn't take it anymore after Tyler led the band off stage after forty-five minutes at a show in Ventura, leaving seven thousand fans feeling shortchanged. We made our excuses and left the tour shortly after.

The best memory I have of those first few weeks came in August, in England, at the Castle Donington Monsters of Rock festival. As a "new" band we were the second act on that day, but from the moment we hit the thundering opening chords to "Stand Up and Shout" the whole place went crazy. Once again, *Holy Diver* had laid down a golden path for us to tread, but the warmth that came off in rolling waves from the mighty crowd when we performed older material like "Children of the Sea" and "Stargazer" pierced my heart.

I had decided early on that Dio shows should definitely include a handful of those numbers from my Rainbow and Sabbath days that I had not only co-written and sung, but that truly felt personal to me. Along with "Children" and "Stargazer," we blasted through "Heaven and Hell" and "Man on the Silver Mountain." What was so pleasing, though, was that new material like "Holy Diver" and "Rainbow in the Dark" went down equally well.

The reviews in the British music press were lavish. Like a homecoming! The most important mag for rock and metal back then was *Kerrang!* and they, above all, were incredibly supportive. In their end-of-year annual polls, *Holy Diver* was in the top five albums, and the UK tour we followed up with at the end of the year was voted one of the best. I'll never forget the thrill of walking on stage at the Hammersmith Odeon in London, scene of so many highlights from my Rainbow and Sabbath days, in November. It was the fifth—Guy Fawkes Day in the UK, which meant the entire night sky was filled with fireworks. It felt auspicious.

We returned to the USA with a renewed sense of purpose and set out on our headline tour with a wonderful new Seattle band named Queensrÿche opening for us. We started modestly in theaters, then almost immediately had to upgrade to arenas. Where there wasn't time to do that, we would add in afternoon performances, as we had to at the Civic Auditorium in Santa Monica after all five thousand tickets for the evening show sold out within days. The culmination came in December when we headlined to nearly ten thousand people at Long Beach Arena in LA.

While fortune certainly had its part to play in the band taking off so quickly, the main ingredients in our almost instant success were the desire, ruthless determination, and sheer bloody-mindedness of the team Wendy and I had forged together. The foundation was the band and the fantastic music we were making together, but what built that foundation into an impregnable castle was what Wendy did behind the scenes. For the American shows, Wendy sent an intern around in a station wagon, two weeks before every show, loaded with posters and tickets. They would go into all the radio stations in each city and town and say, "Here are tickets for the show. Come along as our guests." Then they'd go into the record stores, make sure the record was in the shops and give them posters to put up if they didn't already have them. They would get tickets for the shows as well. This was the old-school era of the music biz, and Wendy knew the value of personal contact. Each place we played, there would be a special guest room set aside so we could say hi and get to know all the local media and record store people. It was great because it also gave you first-hand knowledge of who these people were and how they liked to work. I made many good friends doing this that I stayed close to for years.

Wendy Dio: *Ronnie had always been a hard worker. He had always paid attention to every little detail. In Dio, he finally had the chance to do things exactly how he wanted to. Even when he was sick, he always managed to put on a show—for the people at the show and for everybody afterwards, particularly the fans. Ronnie* *had amazing energy. He used to call me the Energizer Bunny, but we were both like that. I think we generated it for each other. I pushed him and he pushed me, and we worked really well together. We fought like cats and dogs sometimes and had plenty of ups and downs. That's because we both really cared. We felt our lives were on the line, that we had to make this succeed or die trying.*

It could be quite funny sometimes. People in the band and crew learned very quickly that Ronnie and I would have heated fights, but if you dare say one word about me, you're going to get fired by Ronnie—and vice versa. There were people who learned after that, just walk on eggshells, get away from it, because they're having a fight. One time we were at the airport and I was counting out the per diem money. Ronnie was arguing with me: Why were we playing these smaller venues? Things were taking off and he was in a hurry to upgrade to arenas. I got so fed up I snapped: "Well, maybe if you were bigger, you'd play the bigger venues." He went absolutely berserk! I threw the money all over the floor and walked off. Later we would laugh at these things. But it kept it real. There was no pussyfooting around or resting on laurels.

I will always remember Christmas 1983, going into New Year '84, as one of the happiest times in my life. Dio had taken off like a rocket; *Holy Diver* had combed the Top 10 in the UK and was now on its way to going Platinum in America for over a million sales. And despite Wendy and I working so hard all the time, this was another level of closeness, happiness, and satisfaction we were enjoying.

For the first time ever, I had real money coming, which was a relief after re-mortgaging our house and putting every cent we had into Dio. But while it only felt right that Wendy and I should reap some of the rewards—not just for all the time and money invested in Dio but for all the years of getting to that place where we could finally do something like that on our own—I still put every spare dime into making the band bigger and better.

When we were at home in LA, we didn't go out a lot on the scene. We had done our ten thousand hours, as they say. Now we mostly stayed home and had people over, like Glenn Hughes and all our other friends. We always had people at the house. Plus, it was becoming hard for us to go out for dinner. I think it was partly the price you paid for the vast new exposure MTV gave artists.

I had made promotional videos in Sabbath and Rainbow, but they were just live show clips, because there were relatively few outlets for them. Now your videos had to be full-scale productions, or at least look like they were. For the first two Dio singles—"Holy Diver" and "Rainbow in the Dark"—we splurged on the first (sword-and-sorcery themed) and counted pennies on the second (me posing on a rooftop during a visit to London). The result was two Top 20 rock radio hits in the US. So maybe it was just that my face was becoming more familiar, or perhaps it was the way the whole LA rock scene seemed to accelerate out of control in the mid-'80s, but it became almost impossible for me to have a quiet night out in LA. Wendy used to get pissed off. We'd go out for dinner and then a fan would come over for an autograph, and I would be very nice, and Wendy would be fine. But then I would find myself talking to them and, as often happened when I spoke with fans, I'd find half an hour had gone by, while Wendy's still sitting waiting to eat her dinner. Sometimes I'd invite them to sit at the table and Wendy would get really annoyed about it afterward. Even I began to find it a little taxing when fans started popping up almost everywhere I went. I would go to Home Depot or somewhere and everybody would follow me around. I wasn't exactly dressed for the stage, either. At home I was a tee-and-sweats man. I'd find myself surrounded by fans and I admit it could feel just a little overwhelming sometimes. I can't imagine what it must be like for Elton John or someone like that, because it must be a hundred million times worse. Or better, depending which way you look at it.

The truth is I was now happier than I had ever been. I had a whole new life and career, fronting a band I considered friends, and a wonderful wife in Wendy. What more could I possibly ask for?

Well, let's see....

SIXTEEN

WE ROCK

They say success has many fathers, but failure is an orphan. After *Holy Diver*, I was about to find out how true that old saying was.

From nobody wanting to know, suddenly everyone at the record company had an opinion—on me as a singer, on the songs, on the band, on what we should do next. The reviews were through the roof, five stars here, five stars there, and I'd be a liar if I said it didn't feel fantastic. Of course it did. Wendy and I had staked everything on *Holy Diver*. Bet the farm, as the saying goes. Everything about it was the fulfillment of my vision, from the album cover artwork to the tour production. It was the ultimate self-expression, and it was a rush to finally be that free as an artist.

So, pull up a chair for a moment. Right here, I'm going to tell you a little bit about the way record companies work, because maybe you're a kid in a band checking out my story and dreaming about the day you sign your name on that dotted line and pick up your passport to fame and fortune at reception on the way out.

The clue is in the second word of the name: record COMPANY.

Here's another: music BUSINESS.

At major labels like Warner Bros. and Polygram, who I was signed to, you're signing up to a multi-million-dollar organization that exists purely to make money. At the top of the pyramid are the tiny percentage of acts that go Multi-Platinum each time out. They get the big marketing budgets and the red-carpet treatment, because they generate the biggest profits. Then you have the breakthrough acts. These guys have probably been signed by one of the company's star A&R men and they're gonna get the big push, because the truth is very few acts stay on the mountaintop forever and there is a constant need for new blood. Next come the mid-roster artists, acts that the critics rave over and that make your label look relevant and arty. They may sell hundreds of thousands rather than millions of records, but they bring you credibility and attract other cool artists to the label.

Now, if you're smart businesspeople—whatever anyone tells you, the people running record labels are usually very smart businesspeople, real sharks in suits some of them—you're gonna make a lot of money from a roster like that. Then the government and the IRS come along, and they want their share. You can either hand it over like a good citizen would, or you can say, "What the hell, we may as well take some of that money and sign a whole bunch of other acts, throw 'em all out there against the wall and see what sticks...." From the label's point of view, it's a free swing, right? And every now and again, one of those free swings connects and heads straight over the fences. If that sounds to you a little like something that happened to Dio and *Holy Diver*, well, you wouldn't be a million miles away. All of those hours and days that Wendy and I put in, the money we took from our own pockets to fill up with gas and hit up radio stations in every city, all of the months we spent getting every detail of the album and tour exactly how we wanted, that was like the part of the trick that the magician doesn't let the audience see.

In my case, the record company wheeler and dealers didn't see it while it was happening either. But now someone in a corner office at the Warner Bros. building is looking at the bottom line and it's, "Oh, okay, *Dio*....Debut record goes Gold in six months? Big buzz? Great press? Sell-out tour? Hey guys, we might have something here...." Now, we're no longer a free hit. The unexpected success of *Holy Diver* moved us up the ladder. Suddenly, we were being seen as major contenders. But if you've taken the trip this far with me, then you will know that I never did anything in music just for the money. Every choice I made was first and foremost an artistic one. If the art isn't right, if the music isn't happening, then I have never been afraid to call it quits and take the next big leap into the unknown. It happened with Rainbow, and it happened with Sabbath. I'm hard-headed that way because I know it's the only way to truly succeed, and if I don't succeed then at least I can still look at myself in the mirror each morning while I have a shave. Like the old cliché goes, if you've never been fashionable, you can never go out of fashion. Keep to your path and every now and again, the world walks alongside you.

By the mid-'80s, that was what was happening. Between them, Warner Bros. and Polygram had practically cornered the market in Platinum-selling rock acts: Mötley Crüe, Van Halen, the Scorpions, Def Leppard, AC/DC, Ratt, Bon Jovi, Twisted Sister, Billy Squier, Kiss, Dire Straits, ZZ Top—and Dio. In fact, all the labels with any sense were jumping on the rock and metal bandwagon. In 1984, as we began work on the second Dio album, Metallica were making waves with *Ride the Lightning*, Judas Priest released *Defenders of the Faith*, and a whole raft of new bands were marching over the horizon: Iron Maiden, Anthrax, W.A.S.P., Manowar, Motörhead, Hanoi Rocks, Queensrÿche, all making waves. Ritchie was back in Deep Purple in the reformed Mark II lineup. Jake E. Lee landed the gig in Ozzy's band and the "Bark at the Moon" video was all over MTV.

That's not to say that I personally loved all of that music or that I saw Dio as part of a movement of any kind. Call me arrogant if you like, but I didn't hear too many singers as good as Ronnie James Dio. I heard a lot that wanted to sound like me, which I took as a huge compliment, but the whole point of Dio is that it was never part of the crowd. However, the amazing buzz about *Holy Diver*, plus the US Top

100 filling up with metal bands, tripped the switch at Warner Bros. That was very much a double-edged sword, as I was about to discover.

As much as I was enjoying my new career as the leader of my own band, captain of the ship with no Ritchie or Tony beside me calling the shots, Wendy was spreading her wings wider as well.

Wendy Dio: *We drove each other on. I pushed Ronnie and he pushed me, and we worked really well together. But that energy could cut both ways. I'm an Aries and Ronnie was a Cancer. Aries works well with Cancer because Cancers can be stubborn and moody but they're very loyal. But when they clash—boy, look out!*

Sometimes, I would do something that Ronnie didn't like and he wouldn't even tell me what I'd done. I had to guess what it was. I'd rather he'd come out and tell you, "Hey, you fucked up," whatever. But the vast majority of the time we worked really, really well together, because our personalities were well matched. We're both very strong people, which is another reason why we both would knock heads some of the time. But, in the end, I never messed with his music. He never messed in my business. So, it worked really well.

I was always proud of Ronnie no matter what, and he was always proud of me. I think that's the most important thing. We would say terrible things to each other sometimes, in the heat of battle. But we were a family, and we'd kill for one another. Ronnie was intensely loyal to people that showed him that same loyalty.

Being my manager was never going to be easy, and it was going to be even more difficult if you happened to be my wife. A relationship like that is always going to be complex. It's not as simple as waking up together and then walking in two different directions when you leave the house, suddenly putting on the hats of artist and manager. I was on my third turn on the merry-go-round after Rainbow and Sabbath; Wendy was on her first as a big-time manager, and she had to learn fast.

Fortunately, she was as driven as me, and she understood what I wanted. With *Holy Diver*, I finally had that control. We both did.

Now we wanted to build something special, an organization in which everyone did their job and was respected for it, from the band members to the crew. Everything would be geared towards making the best records and putting on the best shows that we could.

At first, some of the crew were as green as Wendy. They learned together, became a team. Wendy and I always made sure to take them to dinner from time to time, to show our appreciation for their work. Our guiding principles in life were very much the same. I think that is what kept us together and on track. She knew that I'm a perfectionist and what I cared about was the music and the stage shows. I wasn't bothered about the cost, because it was about being the best that we could be. I'd heard Tony, and before him Ritchie, tell stories about all of the stuff they had been through with various managers, and I knew that would never happen to me with Wendy by my side. Coincidentally, or maybe not, Ozzy was experiencing huge success under his wife Sharon's management. Wendy was a quick study, too.

To the outside world we were a united front. She had my back. I had hers. But inevitably our relationship changed and had to grow, because our work life took a toll on our personal one. Wendy began to resent what she called 'wifely' things, mundane day-to-day stuff like picking up my socks from the floor and putting them in the washer. A few times we got to a point where one or the other of us was dissatisfied with our relationship, but we got over it. You have to work at it, and we did.

In the wake of *Holy Diver*'s success, things were changing quickly. As we prepared for the writing and recording of a new album, Wendy and I found the perfect new home. We had the house in Tarzana, but it was only a single-level place, nothing fancy. Now, with the royalties, song publishing and tour receipts coming in, and the advances on future projects looking rosy, we could put down some roots on the West Coast, five years after we had crossed the country with everything we owned in the back of a car.

We bought a wonderful new house in Encino; like Tarzana, an enclave in LA's San Fernando Valley, the beautiful, sprawling region behind the hills that hold the Hollywood sign. Encino lies in the shadow of the mountains. On a large lot shaded by trees, we found our castle, almost literally. The house was just three years old when we bought it, but it was built in the style of an English manor, with five bedrooms and five bathrooms, wood floors and paneled ceilings, even a turret. There were some more modern accoutrements too: a swimming pool in the grounds and a room I named "The Dungeon," which became my studio. We were soon filling it with the kind of things that make a house a home, at least if Ronnie James Dio lives in it.

On our trips to Europe, I loved to forage for antique furnishings from an age when craftsmen really cared about the work that they produced. The oldest piece was a wooden chest that dated back to 1510 and was said to have once had a home in Windsor Castle. There was two-hundred-year-old flooring from France, some Cathedral window frames that we put in the master bedroom which dated to 1790, and the *pièce de résistance*, at least as far as visitors to the house were concerned, a long wooden bar from a pub called the King's Arms in Essex. Our bar actually had an official opening, and there was only one man for the job—Mr. Jimmy Bain! Wendy bought me a pool table with gorgeous, intricately carved lion heads on the legs. There was a comfortable, book-lined library where I could sit and immerse myself in the kind of literature and research that I loved, firing my imagination with tales of the Middle Ages and medieval life. For the walls, we found coats of arms and other items of heraldry. I would even end up with my own suit of armor!

Meanwhile, Jimmy and Vinnie also bought beautiful new houses and Vivian bought a Ferrari.

The new house became the main venue for our social lives. Suddenly we had somewhere big enough to sprawl out and party in. I loved to cook and get behind the bar to play *mine host*. But I also had a rule to never get too settled in any one place because I understood the nature of the business we were in. I compared it to being out at sea. Sometimes the winds and the tides are in your favor, but you know that a storm could blow up at any moment, so it paid not to think too much about the long-term. For now, we had a wonderful home, a place where I could relax and write, and one that reflected my personality.

It also meant that despite our closeness, Wendy and I didn't have to be right on top of one another. I was proud of the steps she was taking as a manager, but another sticking point between us was the fact that she was managing other acts, most notably Rough Cutt. I made no bones about the fact that Dio needed to be number one with her, and we were. I was happy to help out where I could, too. I did some production work with Rough Cutt. As I mentioned, I had considered Jake E. Lee, their guitarist, for Dio before I found Vivian. Then the guys in the band told Wendy about this kid who'd driven out to LA and was living in his car—he'd spend his day going around guitar stores and suchlike, trying to get a gig. I could relate to that. His name was Craig Goldy. We found him a place to stay, gave him a little money, and he ended up as the replacement for Jake in Rough Cutt. I produced a song for them called "Try a Little Harder," which came out on a compilation album put out by the radio station KLOS and caused a bit of a buzz. Then Craig got another break when he joined Giuffria, the band put together by former Angel keyboard player Gregg Giuffria. They had just signed to MCA, and Craig got to play on their debut record.

Then things got a little more complex. Ted Templeman, the producer who was the in-house guy for Warner Bros and a heavy hitter because of his work with acts like Van Morrison, the Doobie Brothers, and Van Halen, got interested. Just as Warner Bros. were gearing up for Dio's second album, they were about to offer Rough Cutt a deal. And who is the name that the record company start to push at me as a producer for the next Dio record? Ted Templeman.

I understood they thought they were paying me a huge compliment by suggesting Templeman, but I was totally against the idea of Ted coming in. It was nothing personal. Ted was already super busy—over the next year or so he produced albums for Aerosmith, Eric Clapton, and David Lee Roth, which meant, ironically, that Rough Cutt ended up with another producer—and I was convinced that no one was better situated than me to get the best sound for Dio. *Holy Diver* had turned out pretty good, after all.

Too many cooks spoil the broth; that was my view. That's not how record companies think, though. Their mindset was: the first Dio album went Gold. The second Dio album can go Platinum if we make it sound a little more commercial and get it played on the radio. That was not my idea at all, as Ritchie Blackmore could have told them. For me, the better option was simply to double down and make another uncompromising Dio album.

After Templeman, other names got thrown around. There was talk about a single, and I hadn't yet written a word. You can probably understand why I might have gotten a little angry from time to time with all of this bubbling in the background.

I did have one change in mind, however. After he'd joined us on the road as an additional musician, I asked Claude Schnell to become a full-time member of the band. Like me, Claude was classically trained and had spent his early years in the cloistered world of lessons and recitals. He was a disciplined and precise player, and he brought something different to the band. He understood music in the same way that I did, and he was perfect for the concept I had in mind. Claude was also a real easy-going guy and fit right in.

One of the new numbers we had been working on as a band was called "Egypt (The Chains Are On)." It was a real epic that I was already thinking of as a great last-track finale to the album. That led to Wendy and I talking about an Egyptian theme for the stage show and our album artwork. In my head it was like those epic films of Hollywood's golden era, widescreen and Technicolor, with hundreds of extras and fantastical structures being raised from the sands, and, towering over it all, the demon that appeared on the cover of *Holy Diver*, who for some reason we had taken to calling Murray. We started to work up some cover concepts while lyrical ideas formed in my mind.

We won the argument over a producer, and to be fair to Warner Bros., they were prepared to back us. The idea of getting away to a residential studio rather than hanging around the same old streets in LA came up, and I liked the notion. Sticking around in the city the whole time could get very insular, and the bands all started to sound and look like clones of one another.

You couldn't get anything much different from LA than the place we chose. The Caribou Ranch was near a little town called Nederland in the Colorado Rockies. In 1972, a record producer named James Guercio had bought about four thousand acres of land with the idea of putting a studio into one of the abandoned ranch buildings on the property, a place where artists could create without worrying about record company executives "dropping by" to check on what was happening. You definitely couldn't just "drop by" Caribou. It was fabulously isolated; the studio itself housed in a beautifully restored wooden barn with a gabled roof and a stone chimney on one end. Beyond the wooded uplands, the Rockies stood guard. It was utterly majestic.

Caribou worked its magic, too. It got famous after Elton John named his 1974 album *Caribou* after it, and Chicago, the Beach Boys, and Joe Walsh had all recorded there with great success. It was a breathtaking place, peaceful but kind of like a Wild West town, a place that time forgot. We stayed in cottages dotted around the ranch, and after we'd spent a few hours gazing at the scenery, got down to it.

Throwing a band into a situation like that can go one of two ways. It can often be the making of a band—or it can sometimes be the breaking. Artistically, we were all united. I had the lyrics for what I felt were two classic rock songs in "The Last in Line" and "Egypt (The Chains Are On)." Viv had come up with the arpeggio intro for the title track, and we'd added the monster riff in a final rehearsal in LA. It always felt better to have the centerpiece of the album in place before recording began. With "The Last in Line," I knew we'd achieved that.

I'd also written "We Rock," a ferocious little song that would open the album. Jimmy and I had come up with a tune called "Mystery" that Wendy thought echoed some of our work in Rainbow, and much of the rest of the material came together in the same way that *Holy Diver* had; someone would have a riff or a lick or a melody and we would take it and build a song. Of the ten tracks on the finished record, half were credited to the four of us.

The sound was bigger, and by the time we left the ranch a few weeks later, I thought we had another killer record in the can: "The Last in Line," which would become the title for the album, and "Egypt..." had worked just as I'd hoped. Vinnie played some killer drums to open "We Rock," and Vivian was on fire. I knew having a player like him set us apart from all of the LA bands with their Eddie Van Halen-style soloing. The sleeve felt really epic, too, with Murray looming above a burning desert, the glowing sun beside him, and below, a kind of ruined city filled with people.

With the rise of MTV, a good video clip had become a major plank of the marketing, only this time instead of Wendy and I having to make the best of a very modest budget, Wendy negotiated a bigger budget and Warner Bros. stepped up to the plate—$200,000. We shot one video for "Mystery," which the record company wanted as the lead single, and another for "The Last in Line," which was where most of the cash went. We hired a movie director named Don Coscarelli, who'd made his name with a couple of films that were right up my alley, *Phantasm* and *The Beastmaster*. He was a great big guy, miles over six feet tall; he came from somewhere like Libya originally; and he was great. He really got what the band were about, and "The Last in Line," in particular, looked fantastic: the delivery boy who takes the nightmare elevator ride was played by Meeno Peluce, who had been in *The Amityville Horror*.

The Last in Line came out in July 1984, the week before my birthday actually, which was a pretty cool present. We got a stack of more great reviews, and the record started selling right away. We hit Number 4 in the UK, bumped amongst the Top 20 in the USA, and had our first big chart hit across Europe. I was delighted, and immensely proud, because, for me, it genuinely reflected the worth of the record we had made.

We had been over to Europe to play Pinkpop in the Netherlands, a big and well-established festival, just before the album's release, but the tour started in California, running all the way up the West coast before crossing the country. Opening for us as special guests on the first leg were Whitesnake, on what would be their last US tour before David made it really big with the 1987 album, *Whitesnake*. Another example of the swings-and-roundabouts nature of the music business, many was the night on that tour when I reflected back on the days when Elf would open for Deep Purple, fronted by David Coverdale.

When Whitesnake left the tour, Twisted Sister came aboard as another killer support act. You always needed your chops if you were going to follow Dee Snider on stage. He may not have been the greatest singer, but, as a wildcat frontman, he was in a league of his own. I loved the challenge of it, and night after night we more than rose to the occasion. The reaction was often ecstatic.

We did a couple of Monsters of Rock shows in Germany and kicked into Europe, this time with Queensrÿche opening. It was brilliant. British and European fans are among the most passionate anywhere, and I have always had a fantastic time touring cities like Newcastle, Glasgow, Liverpool, Aberdeen, Hammersmith, Amsterdam, Munich, Hamburg...the people that came to those shows filled my heart each night. This was why we did what we did, to be there in front of the fans playing the music we loved.

By the end of the year, *The Last in Line* had gone Gold in America and quickly passed *Holy Diver*'s out-of-the-box sales, eventually becoming the first Platinum Dio album in America, but those shows were worth more to me than all of that. We went back to America again after Europe, with Dokken in tow, except one show. When we rolled into LA to play the Inglewood Forum in front of 14,000 people, Rough Cutt opened up. Never let it be said I don't do anything for my wife!

The tour finished on January 27, 1985, at the Metropolitan Center in Bloomington, Minnesota. We had played more than 120 shows in seven months, which, however much of a road dog you are, is a lot of work, especially for a singer. Guitars and keyboards you simply plug in. Drums you hit. The human voice is a far more delicate instrument, especially when you're using it the way I use mine. Every show I always gave everything I had—anything less would be shortchanging the people who had waited a long time for us to come to their town. My classical training, knowing how to control my breathing and use my diaphragm for power, rather than just raking over the vocal cords, helped, but it's a little like being an athlete. You have to adapt your lifestyle if you want to perform at your peak. I was no longer the late-night partier of my earlier career. On the road, I now liked to look after myself. That meant no smoking. I probably still drank a little too much occasionally, but not enough to break my stride as a performer. The rest of the time I did everything I could to stay well. Once a virus strikes anyone in the band or crew, that's death for a singer, so I kept away from anyone who was coughing or sneezing.

I had always had a very strong mental attitude, but it helps to have a goal. As the leader of Dio I now had the biggest goal of all to aim for. *I'm going to be great every night; in fact, I'm going to be so good tonight, I'm going to reach that perfection. Tonight's the night!* As long as you have that goal every time, then your mind makes you work to try and achieve it.

I began this part of the story by saying that success has many fathers. Well, by the end of the chapter we had more success, but there was one part of the dynamic that was beginning to change: the band.

The first crack in the scenery occurred with Vivian. He had been forced to grow up pretty fast, as a professional musician and as a private person, and I always tried to be aware that he had not been around as long as Jimmy, Vinny, and me. As his confidence grew, Viv became a little headstrong, probably just as I was when I was in my early twenties. And maybe he had Jimmy's voice in his ear a little bit too. Jimmy was always slightly cut up about the band being named after me, and sometimes he would moan about the money or bitch about riffs and songwriting credits. Jimmy would say he had the riff for "Stand Up and Shout," Viv would say Sweet Savage had something similar and that he reworked it. Jimmy came up with the little keyboard part on "Rainbow in the Dark" and Viv had the riff, but that's all.

It doesn't make a song, and they were getting their writing credits. But you know what I say about success....

Wendy Dio: *It was always Ronnie's name that was gonna sell the band. And after Rainbow and Sabbath, Ronnie deserved to be the main man. As the future would prove, the only member that Dio couldn't do without was Ronnie.*

Vivian was later quoted in the press saying he made less money in Dio than the road crew, but he was making $1,700 a week whether he worked or he didn't. He managed to buy a Ferrari. When the band really took off, Jimmy and Vinny were able to buy houses. Unfortunately, Jimmy ended up losing his to the IRS. We spent so much money out of our own pockets and people, unless they've got their own band, don't understand how much money you have to lay down and what you have to put into it, blood, sweat, and tears, to make something successful.

And if Ronnie was unhappy, I'm the kind of person that says, "Ronnie's not happy, so we're going to change it." Ronnie didn't like change. He didn't like change at all, but he wouldn't have his back pushed up against the wall. Not anymore. I made sure of it.

It still makes me a little angry because Ronnie was fair to all of them. They wanted to be considered Ronnie's equal and get the same money as Ronnie. I'm sorry, but I said no to that. Ronnie got all the shit for it, but I'm the bad guy. Ronnie probably would have done it. As far as I was concerned, though, he had earned the right to do things his way. And he was making a great success of it. Everyone should have been happy.

Vivian later claimed that when we started out, I'd said to him that I would be bankrolling the band, but by the time we got to the third album, it would become more equal. After *The Last in Line*, I began hearing about it a little more often, but nothing is as simple as it sounds. We were all making good money, but the financial responsibility still lay with Wendy and me. I employed the road crew and all the other staff we needed. I paid for the recording studio and the stage production plus hotels, buses, trucks, crew, airfares, and everything else needed on a big tour. I made the decisions over what we should spend, because those decisions affected the artistic integrity of the band and how we did what we did. If I got that wrong, then there wasn't going to be any money to share.

I kept a lid on my feelings as far as Vivian was concerned, at least at first. If I imagined myself at twenty years of age on stage in front of 14,000 people, doing world tours, being awarded Gold and Platinum discs with my name on, I would have thought I was set for life, too. The reality was different, though. Viv would learn, just as I had.

Jimmy and Vinny did know better, but Jimmy still had a hair up his ass about the name business. He'd been around the block a few times, though, and Dio was now doing a whole lot better than Wild Horses. I don't think he liked the fact that his career was being managed by my wife, even though he'd seen us fighting often enough to know that she was far from a yes-woman.

SEVENTEEN

HUNGRY FOR HEAVEN

Wendy could tell I wasn't happy. She knew me inside out, and she realized what was wrong. It was ten years since I'd joined with Ritchie to make the first Rainbow record. In that decade, I'd made seven studio albums and two live records, been in three bands, played hundreds of shows, orbited the globe, and relocated from one side of the country to another. When I sit here and write that down now, I realize that is more than some people get to do in a lifetime. But, while it's happening to you, it goes by so fast you don't have the time to draw a breath.

It should have been a cause to raise a glass or three. I'd come a long way physically, spiritually, and artistically. I'd played alongside two of the greatest guitarists in the history of rock music and made landmark albums with them. I'd formed my own Platinum-selling band from nothing. How many people have achieved that? All of the millions that have given music their best shot and not had one taste of success, let alone done it three times.

The future should have been bright—dammit, it *was* bright—but as Wendy knew, my temperament is an artistic one, prone to storms and downpours that sometimes dropped out of the clear blue sky. In many ways I was married to my work. It wasn't something that I left behind me when I walked through the front door at night. I didn't like downtime. If I got any, I liked to watch sports on TV, listen to classical music, and read. Even then, my mind was restless, always thinking about what was next. Someone once told me that sharks have to keep swimming or they die. That's how I felt.

Inevitably, that would come across in the music. There was relentlessness to that, too. I had worked incessantly since forming Dio, and as soon as *The Last in Line* world tour was done, the cycle began again. The result would be the darkest and most brooding album I had made so far, as joyful and celebratory as anything I'd ever done in some parts and a million miles away in others.

I always had a vision of what the band was supposed to be all about: whatever you do, do it really, really well. If the images and sounds that were now coming to me were of a darker hue, if the band was beginning to lose some of the unity of vision and purpose that we'd had since we came together, then so be it. Make it dark and great. Nothing stands in my way.

That was my mood, anyhow. With everything that was going on and a long eight-month tour behind us, I decided that the new record should be made in LA. We booked some rehearsal space to jam and write, and before we started work, Vivian came to me to speak about money and credits. He said that he had understood that when the band started out I was using my own money to get everything up and running, but that when we'd made the first record, I'd apparently said that come album number three we would renegotiate. To me, this was really bad timing on his part. We had studio time booked and we needed to have the material ready for when we went in. The business could be sorted later, and I asked him to wait until the record was done.

Negotiating terms wasn't even my job. It was Wendy's, and she was damn good at it. Maybe that's why Viv came to me first. I think all of the bad parts of our relationship, which had been buried by the success we were having, now started to bubble to the surface. I was angry because I felt I had been fair to everyone. Let's talk straight right here: I valued Vivian's contributions enormously, but he was in the position he was in because of me. He was a twenty-year-old in a band no one had heard of when Ronnie James Dio came calling. Jimmy was the same: he had been kicked out of Rainbow, and Wild Horses were better known for their partying than their music. Vinny was my best friend in Black Sabbath and had opted to stick with me instead of staying with them. I didn't force anyone to do anything. Nobody had a gun held to their head, then or now. If they thought I was moody and stubborn, man, try working with Ritchie Blackmore. Try Tony Iommi if you think I'm a tough guy.

I know, because Viv told me, how much of a fan of mine he had been before we'd met. He'd listen to the *Heaven and Hell* album as a teenager driving around in his car. He said he hadn't been a Sabbath fan before that record came out. And obviously, he was nervous around me at the start of Dio, nervous about the whole situation he found himself in. I got it. In a way, I don't think Viv ever quite got over that. He always saw a version of me that he wanted to—the rock star, the boss figure, the leader that he had to please. He was intimidated.

As the result, the relationship between us didn't grow, and I'm not sure whose fault that was. Viv resented the fact, that, in his mind, he thought he should have had a bigger share now that we were three albums in. I had a different view. So did Wendy. Things festered.

Wendy Dio: *The thing that really gets me mad is when they say they were ripped off. They got all their writers' and publishing royalties, which they still get to this day. Let's put it this way, the band was called Dio. All these other people were relatively unknown.*

We wrote an album that was very dark, very Dio-esque, you might say, and I called it *Sacred Heart*, after one of my favorite tracks on it, another full-band composition. For me, the album was clearly a continuation of what I'd begun on *Holy Diver*. Indeed, I thought the title track was the equal of "Holy Diver" or "The Last in Line," as good as anything we'd done. The opening track, a thunderous epic called "King of Rock and Roll," was one of the best out-and-out rock songs we ever did, destined to become a highlight of the live show forever after, while "Rock 'n' Roll Children," which I wrote alone, is one of my favorite songs of any I've ever been involved with. "Hungry for Heaven" came from another opportunity our success had brought us, the offer to contribute to the soundtrack of a big Hollywood movie: *Vision Quest* (a.k.a. *Crazy for You* in the UK and Australia). It was a cool movie that starred Matthew Modine and featured Madonna as a bar singer performing "Crazy for You." Along with Journey, Foreigner, and Sammy Hagar, we were in some good company on that soundtrack.

As a result, we decided to cut a new version of "Hungry for Heaven" especially for *Sacred Heart*. We cut it at Rumbo Recorders in Canoga Park, only a short drive from Encino where Wendy and I now lived, up through Woodland Hills. Rumbo was a studio that had a great reputation on the West Coast. A lot of very fine albums had been made there. It was a lovely facility, but it couldn't replace what we didn't have. The vibes were still bad between Viv and I, our growing mistrust and mutual resentment simmering away like an evil potion on the fire. The relationship between singer and guitarist is key in any rock band, and when it's even slightly off, it doesn't work as well as it should.

As a musician, you're constantly trying to outgrow your own formula, stretch yourself in new and exciting ways. Along with the darker feel, the new album made more use of Claude's keyboard textures, but I would be lying to you if I said I was entirely happy with it. The feel was very different. There were a lot of people coming in to lay down their parts and then leaving, instead of hanging out as a band like we'd done on the first two albums. Then there was the record company, hungry for another hit at any cost.

I didn't realize how stressed I'd become, but on the day we finished and put the tapes in a box to go and be mastered, I came down with stomach pains and was taken straight to the hospital, where I had my appendix removed. It was as if my body was just holding out long enough to get the thing done before it cried out for a rest. I was in the hospital three days and, you know what? It was wonderful. I just lay there, slept, ate, watched TV, rested, and recovered with no one able to say a damn thing to me except to ask if I was okay. Wendy took the reins and got on with dealing with everything while I took my first real break in over ten years.

After, while I was recuperating at home, we worked on cover concepts, and a spectacular idea began to take shape. The album cover art was done by an artist called Robert Florczak and shows a pair of hands with long silver fingernails holding up a crystal ball, inside which is a dragon with a jeweled heart in its claws. In Latin around the outside, it says: "In the borders of dreams I found for you the Sacred Heart and the Golden Door."

The title song "Sacred Heart" was all about a quest. It was while I was contemplating those lyrics that I started to envision a stage show that incorporated the idea of a knight battling a dragon to fulfill his mission to recapture the sacred heart. I warmed to the idea because it worked on so many levels. For me, it was autobiographical, in the sense of the personal and professional battles I'd been through—was still going through, in fact. It was also just a great rollicking rock epic. One I thought could make a wonderful stage show for the next tour.

Back in the day at Disneyland, you used to be able to get what they called an E coupon. If you had the E coupon you could get onto more of the rides than the other ticketholders. I wanted the audience coming to a Dio show to feel like they had gotten hold of an E coupon because I decided I wanted the new show to be like going on one of those rides at Disneyland: pure fantasy. It was to be a show that would take you away from the cold outside world and leave you with memories that last forever, pure escapism into another world.

When I was well enough, we went up to San Francisco to see the dragon being made. When we got there, they'd only done the head. It was already kind of magnificent, by far the biggest stage prop we'd ever had, but there was something about it that didn't seem quite right. It looked more like a crocodile than a dragon. And then I figured out the problem. Its ears didn't move. As soon as they made one with ears that moved, that flickered forward and backward, it looked like a dragon. He was soon named Dean. For some reason the press started calling him Denzil, but to the band, once production rehearsals started, he was always Dean. He was twenty feet high, perched upon an eight-foot riser, and underneath his throat was a hidden door that I could pull open to reveal his sacred heart. We had lasers with bats flying around inside them and masses of pyro. Dean could breathe fire on command. All of the instrument risers were made to look like rocky cliffs, and Vinny and Claude were perched way above the stage in their eyries.

The dragon was the centerpiece, and it all came down to the guy that operated him, Steve Arch. Steve made that thing move around like he was genuinely alive. The idea was that during "Sacred Heart" I would grab a laser sword and battle the dragon until his chest opened to reveal the heart. Then Dean would breathe red-hot jets of flame above our heads. It was hugely ambitious, a show that had a lot of moving parts—no computer-generated tricks in those days—and the tour was planned as our biggest to date.

We kicked off in August 1985 with an appearance before 25,000 people at the Super Rock Festival in Tokyo. Three nights later, we began a six-month arena tour of the US. Dio was bigger and more popular than ever. *Sacred Heart* had been released in August, and immediately matched—then bettered—the chart performances of *The Last in Line*, quickly going Gold in America and again reaching Number 4 in the UK. It also became our biggest hit in Germany and the rest of Europe. Meanwhile, both "Rock 'n' Roll Children" and "Hungry for Heaven" became hits as well.

Despite all this, the album-tour campaign did not start auspiciously. Vivian came to me once again about the business end of things, so I told him to talk to Wendy. The stress at the start of a tour is high enough without that sort of pressure from the band. Every day you're worrying about your pre-sales; the crew are having to come to grips with rigging and putting up a new stage production; there is all of the press and hullaballoo around the album release. None of it was designed to lower my blood pressure, and when we got to Japan for the Super Rock Festival, I blew up.

Rough Cutt were to be the support act. Their debut album was in the can and due to come out midway through the tour. Tom Allom, best known for the work he'd done with Judas Priest, had produced it, and as their manager, Wendy had been heavily involved: she even had a couple of co-writing credits. I'd helped out too, co-writing the opening track, "Take Her," along with the band and Craig Goldy. (When the album came out, the sleeve artwork featured a knife cutting through a glowing red heart—hmmm, where had I seen something like that before?)

Once we got to Japan, Wendy had both bands in the same city but separate hotels. Given that it was the first show of the tour, she was extremely busy. That was fine. I felt I'd been really supportive of Wendy's career in the same way that she was of mine, but there has to be a line between the personal and professional. Dio were the headline act and needed to be her priority. It was a big festival with Sting and Foreigner on the bill, so we wouldn't have the full stage production with the dragon, but Andy Secher, the editor of *Hit Parader*, had flown out to see us. *Hit Parader* was an important magazine in the US at the time, one of the few American titles that celebrated hard rock and heavy metal, so I was anxious about putting on a great show, Dean or no Dean.

When I heard that Andy had missed our set because Wendy was busy with Rough Cutt, I exploded....

Wendy Dio: *We all rolled with it, especially Andy, but Ronnie was furious, totally furious with me! On that occasion, it was my fault. Somebody has to be yelled at, and this time it was me, and Ronnie really didn't care who saw him do it. The people that worked for us knew there would sometimes be lots of shouting and drama, as on all major rock tours, but that all would be forgiven thereafter. That's just how it worked between us. I understood the pressure Ronnie was under. He was the ringmaster, and it was on his shoulders all the time. He did his very best every day, and he didn't like it when others didn't do the same.*

The mid-'80s were a time of big hair and big records, big looks and big hits. If you bought a ticket to see an Iron Maiden, Judas Priest, or Ozzy Osbourne show, you got some bang for your buck. With *Sacred Heart*, we not only entered that realm, we captured the crown. The reviews were incredible, only matched by the audience reaction to the dragon. My aim to give the fans that E coupon to Disneyland and take them on a ride they would never forget worked. Years later, people still talked about that show. We were on bigger stages in large outdoor arenas—sheds as they're called in the business—so everything was on a grander scale. The first US and Canadian run was nearly ninety shows, but as it drew to a triumphant close, we were about to hit our first really serious bump in the road.

In my opinion, as I've said, Vivian no longer had the commitment to the band he had had in the early days. He was, and remains, an outstanding guitarist. At his best, I'd almost set him alongside Ritchie and Tony. Despite whatever disagreements we had, I never lost sight of how good he was as a musician. But as a person, he was no longer on the same page as the rest of us. That annoyed me immensely. When you've got four guys stretching and straining to do their very best and another clearly holding back, it makes for an unhappy camp. Viv came to me again about the money during the tour, and although he didn't say so, I had the feeling he was kind of speaking for the others, too.

Vivian was still a young guy and had no ties. He wasn't married, didn't have kids, a mortgage, or any of that stuff. He was still at the "have guitar, will travel" stage that I had enjoyed back in the day. I understood. I got it. He felt bulletproof. But what I'd also learned was that things in the music business have a natural lifespan. Nothing lasts forever, especially not creative relationships. I'd done three studio albums with Ritchie, two with Tony. They were great and then it was over. Both sides ended up being able to see why, and we didn't have that horrible experience of making mediocre follow-up albums just for the money.

I knew that the situation couldn't continue. The tour broke after the American leg in January of '86 and was due to pick up again in Europe at the start of April, after another round of promo. We all took some time out, and Vivian used the opportunity to fly home to Ireland to see his family. I met with Wendy to discuss the situation, as I'd promised Viv I would, and we came up with what we felt was a fair offer.

Wendy Dio: *This is another part of Ronnie's story that has been misrepresented in the press over the years, which I will now clear up. What happened is this: during the break between the US and European tours, out of the blue, Vivian had a lawyer call me. He said that what Vivian wanted was more money and a piece of the band. I can't remember how much more money he wanted as a salary, I think it might have been double the $1,700 he was getting, on top of which he wanted equity in the band, a cut of everything, not just the royalties he was due from the records, but everything else, too. This lawyer told me I had five days to make up my mind. If I refused, Vivian was not going to do the European tour.*

Ronnie and I being the way we were, we did not like anyone putting a gun to our heads. So, we decided, forget it. Ronnie was having problems with him anyway. When his lawyer called me again five days later I said, "We've already replaced him." That is the whole story.

Vivian felt he'd been fired, but I certainly didn't see it that way. He'd gotten his lawyer to present us with an ultimatum—either we complied, or he was leaving. We declined. He left. That doesn't sound like a firing to me. A part of me was sad that it ended how it did. Viv was and is a brilliant player, who had done exactly what I had asked, which was to bring that more European attack to the band, a sound that made Dio stand out amongst all the LA-type stuff that was coming along. But the pragmatist in me realized there was no going back. What we once had was lost, and once it's gone, it's gone...at least for a while.

As my old "uncle" Johnny Dio would have said, it was nothing personal, just business, although Vivian maybe took it a little personally. It *was* just business, kid: the music business.

There was one final project Viv was involved in before he left Dio, which made us both very proud. The whole Band Aid and Live Aid thing had hit me quite hard. The sight of people starving just for want of a helping hand touched me deeply, as it did millions of others, and I thought that the metal community deserved the chance to contribute in its own inimitable way.

After the Band Aid and USA for Africa singles, "Do They Know It's Christmas" and "We Are the World" came out, and as plans were underway for the Live Aid show—at Wembley Stadium in London, JFK Stadium in Philadelphia, and several other countries around the world—in the summer of 1985, Jimmy, Vivian, and I took part in a Radiothon fundraiser in LA. When Jimmy and Viv mentioned that it would be a great idea if a bunch of metal musicians could come up with a song of our own, I thought it was a great idea. Thus was born what we light-heartedly named the Hear 'n Aid project. This became a nine-track album with all proceeds going to African famine relief, featuring tracks from Dio, Motörhead, Kiss, Rush, the Scorpions, and even Jimi Hendrix.

Jimmy, Viv, and I wrote "Stars," which would be the single, and over the course of two days, eight singers and twelve guitarists made their way to A&M studios in LA to record the song. A&M was where "We Are the World" had been recorded, and as word spread around town, we soon had a stellar cast of our own. Davey and Adrian from Iron Maiden broke off from the World Slavery Tour to fly in. Rob Halford flew in. Neal Schon from Journey played a solo. We had various members of Quiet Riot, Twisted Sister, Queensrÿche, Dokken, Mötley Crüe, Blue Öyster Cult, Ted Nugent, and even a guest appearance from Spinal Tap. Frankie Banali and Vinny Appice played drums, Yngwie Malmsteen came by for a solo; the whole thing was a forty-eight-hour non-stop party that we filmed for a documentary, as well as the "Stars" video clip.

We had big plans for the single and accompanying album. There is no greater sense of purpose than doing something purely for the good of others. The only disappointment was that, in bringing everything together so quickly, it took a long time to get all of the permissions sorted, and the release was delayed until January of 1986, ironically just as Vivian was about to leave Dio.

None of which mattered in the end, as the records were unanimously well received all over the world; Bob Geldof got involved and came to the televised London reception; and the money raised was substantial, raising over £1 million in Europe within the first couple of weeks, and maybe double that in America.

On a personal note, you think you've seen it all, until one day you realize you are still learning, still capable of being amazed by human nature. The Hear 'n Aid sessions changed my mind about a lot of people. There were a bunch of guys in that room who have been castigated as rebels and characterized by their supposed egos and rock star lifestyles, but let me tell you this: For those two days (and nights) in the summer of 1985, they were the best people in the world. They left all of their egos at the door and just pitched in, like good neighbors, giving their time and talent freely. However much it eventually raised, if Hear 'n Aid saved or changed a single life, then, to me, it fully justified itself.

Meanwhile, Vivian's departure left some big shoes to fill, and we needed to fill them quickly. With the second leg of the tour almost upon us, I didn't have the time or the desire to start the audition process from scratch. I had a guy in mind, and it was someone I knew well and whose playing I respected. Some people were taken aback when Craig Goldy was announced as the new guitarist in Dio because they had only heard him playing in Giuffria, a band that had huge commercial success with their debut album, but that sounded a lot lighter and more radio-friendly than Dio did. Wendy and I had known Craig since he'd rocked up in LA with everything he owned in the back of his car. Craig was a serious guitar player.

It's a big job being the guitarist in Dio. I have very high standards, and Craig needed to play not just Viv's material but the Sabbath songs that I liked to keep in the set, plus the various Rainbow cornerstones I felt were mine. Vinny, Jimmy, and Claude had all been around the block a time or two as well, so it was no picnic fitting in beside them. Craig handled it all like a total pro.

Craig's first Dio gig could hardly have been more high profile. Before the European tour opened, we were booked to appear on *The Tube*, the most happening weekly music television show in the UK at the time. It went out live on a Friday evening from a studio in Newcastle and was presented by Bob Geldof's wife Paula Yates, who was a big star in her own right. The show embraced all genres of music, and all of the bands played for real, no miming or backing tapes, so you needed to pull it out of the bag, no second chances.

Talk about in at the deep end. Craig came through it with flying colors, not a note out of place, and after that there was no stopping us. I won't say that I felt better overnight, but the weight began to lift, and as the tour picked up again, my mood improved enormously. I began to see new possibilities, new light beginning to shine on the horizon. We toured right through Britain and Europe, including three sold-out shows at the Hammersmith Odeon in London, scene of so many early triumphs in my past. Then back to the US for another run, then back in Japan for seven sold-out shows in September, where to my absolute delight I headlined at the Budokan for the first time since my Rainbow days.

There were other great highlights—consecutive sold-out shows at the 12,000-capacity Forum in my adopted town of LA and the 11,000-capacity Cow Palace in San Francisco—before the one I had dreamed of all my life: headlining my own show at Madison Square Garden. I'd done it a couple of times with Sabbath, but this was the first time I got to put on my own show there, not living off the fumes of an already-giant band's reputation.

We pumped out the commemorative live album *Intermission* as a nice reminder of the tour and its success, and even recorded a great new song, "Time to Burn," a wonderful new Dio anthem co-written by the band with both Claude and Craig.

I did find myself having to bid adieu to one other hugely popular member of the touring band, though, and it was a big one. I had battled Dean the Dragon around 150 times on stage, night after night, and although (you guessed it) I always won, the big guy kept on coming back for more. Until, that is, the very final show in Japan. It was almost as if he knew his time to depart for his fiery Valhalla had come. After one last pyro blast from his glowing jaws, Dean kind of slumped over to one side—Vinny had to dive out of the way!—and that was it. The dragon truly had been slain.

Back in LA, Claude said he needed to talk. I knew that Vivian's departure would not be the end of things as far as the rest of the band were concerned, so I asked him over to the house for dinner. He told me that he'd been offered the chance to audition for Foreigner, and they had sent him a first-class plane ticket to New York, leaving the next day. Wendy and I let him know how sad we would be to see him go, but if that's what he wanted, then that's what he must do. He could go with our blessing.

Then I said to him, "Look, I know that we promised you a bunch of things that for whatever reason didn't happen, but I really want to make it right. There may be a keyboard solo on the next album, there will definitely be one on the next tour, I want to let you become the keyboard player you want to be."

Claude reminded me that I had offered something similar at the time of *Sacred Heart*, but as I explained, circumstances had changed since then. The stage design should have done a better job of incorporating his keyboards, and that was my fault. I took full responsibility and vowed we wouldn't make that mistake again. We talked on into the night about all kinds of stuff.

One thing we both agreed on was that LA was teeming with musicians. If you had a big gig like the one in Dio, you didn't give it up lightly, because however good you are, there is always someone out there ready to take your place. No one puts a gun to your head: In this business you always have a choice. Do or die. Sometimes you have to roll the dice.

It was funny, because as we were speaking, I realized that for Claude this could have been me talking with Ritchie or Tony, back in the days when I was still yearning to do my own thing in my own way. That is, if I had been able to have that type of conversation with those guys. I'd come a long way in ten years, and some of the lessons had been hard ones to learn. Ritchie and I had done fantastic work together, but when the time came and I walked out, he didn't blink an eye. He found Graham Bonnet, changed the sound of the band completely, and had a couple of hit records in Europe.

Tony, Geezer, and I had said farewell, and before I could blink, there was Ian Gillan fronting Black Sabbath. The world turned whether you wanted it to or not, and you had to learn how to turn with it. As we carried on talking into the wee hours, Claude decided not to get on the plane to New York, and I was very happy. We shook hands and parted that night truly excited about what the future held for the band.

If the last decade had taught me anything, it's not to make predictions. As the singer in Elf, I could never in my wildest fantasies have imagined what would happen to me, making music with some of the biggest rock artists in the world, cutting albums that would be talked about in the same way as the records I had played and bowed down to when I was growing up. Starting over from the back of a car when Wendy and I drove 3,000 miles down to LA and what so easily could have been the last chance saloon, putting a band together and building it from the ground up to world tours in giant arenas.... It sounds crazy, unreal even, but it's what happened.

Where do I go from here?

Well right now, having just finished another show, I'll be outside, signing autographs for the fans. Like singing on stage, writing your life in verse, or sitting remembering with Wendy, there is nowhere else I'd rather be.

PHOTO CREDITS

Interior

Page 4: Anna Padavona

Page 12: Anna Padavona

Page 62: Gary Driscoll

Page 76: David "Rock" Feinstein

Page 112: Richard Galbraith

Page 124: Richard Galbraith

Page 136: Wendy Dio

Page 150: Richard Galbraith

Page 166: Wendy Dio

Page 180: Richard Galbraith

Page 192: PG Brunelli

Page 208: Gene Kirkland

Page 224: Gene Kirkland

Page 240: Gene Kirkland

Photo Insert

Page 1: (all) Anna Padavona

Page 2: (all) Anna Padavona

Page 3: (bottom) Fin Costello via Getty Images

Page 4: (top) Fin Costello via Getty Images; (bottom) Brad Elterman via Getty Images

Page 5: (all) Wendy Dio

Page 6: (top) Wendy Dio; (bottom) John Harrell

Page 7: (top left) James Crowley; (top right) PG Brunelli; (bottom) Mark Weiss

Page 8: (both) PG Brunelli

All other photos from the Ronnie James Dio Estate.

ACKNOWLEDGMENTS

Diana DeVille, who typed up all Ronnie's notes.

Anthony Turner, who scanned all the photos.

Anna Padavona, R.I.P., who kept all the interviews,
photos and scrapbooks.

David "Rock" Feinstein,
Ronnie's cousin and my dear friend.

Paula Newman, Ute Kromrey, and Sharon Weisz.

And Jacob Hoye, who believed in this book in 2010,
and then again in 2020.

ABOUT THE AUTHORS

Ronnie James Dio was the most acclaimed heavy metal singer of his generation, and the only rock star to achieve multiplatinum success in not one, but three bands: Rainbow, Black Sabbath, and Dio. For Tenacious D's Jack Black, Dio was "the Pavarotti of heavy metal." For Metallica's Lars Ulrich, Dio was "one of the main reasons I made it onto the stage...." And for heavy metal fans all over the world, there were three words that summed him up: "Dio is God." He died in 2010.

Mick Wall is one of the world's best-known music journalists. His work has appeared in *Classic Rock, Mojo, The Times*, and a variety of other publications. His books include the international bestsellers *When Giants Walked the Earth: A Biography of Led Zeppelin* and *Two Riders Were Approaching: The Life & Death of Jimi Hendrix*. He has also presented and produced award-winning TV and radio documentaries. He lives in England.

Wendy Dio is the President and Owner of Niji Management. Over the past thirty years, she has been involved in many aspects of the music business, receiving awards from *Performance* and *Pollstar* for stage set design and concert video production, along with serving as executive producer on numerous Gold and Platinum albums. In 2010, she co-founded the Ronnie James Dio Stand Up and Shout Cancer Fund, which has raised over $2,000,000 for research, education, and early detection screenings.